CONTRACT
WARRIORS

FRED ROSEN

ALPHA

A member of Penguin Group (USA) Inc.

ALPHA BOOKS

Published by the Penguin Group

Penguin Group (USA) Inc., 375 Hudson Street, New York, New York 10014, U.S.A.

Penguin Group (Canada), 10 Alcorn Avenue, Toronto, Ontario, Canada M4V 3B2 (a division of Pearson Penguin Canada Inc.)

Penguin Books Ltd, 80 Strand, London WC2R 0RL, England

Penguin Ireland, 25 St Stephen's Green, Dublin 2, Ireland (a division of Penguin Books Ltd)

Penguin Group (Australia), 250 Camberwell Road, Camberwell, Victoria 3124, Australia (a division of Pearson Australia Group Pty Ltd)

Penguin Books India Pvt Ltd, 11 Community Centre, Panchsheel Park, New Delhi—110 017, India

Penguin Group (NZ), cnr Airborne and Rosedale Roads, Albany, Auckland 1310, New Zealand (a division of Pearson New Zealand Ltd)

Penguin Books (South Africa) (Pty) Ltd, 24 Sturdee Avenue, Rosebank, Johannesburg 2196, South Africa

Penguin Books Ltd, Registered Offices: 80 Strand, London WC2R 0RL, England

International Standard Book Number: 1-59257-302-9

Library of Congress Catalog Card Number: 2004115791

07 06 05   8 7 6 5 4 3 2 1

Interpretation of the printing code: The rightmost number of the first series of numbers is the year of the book's printing; the rightmost number of the second series of numbers is the number of the book's printing. For example, a printing code of 05-1 shows that the first printing occurred in 2005.

Printed in the United States of America

Note: This publication contains the opinions and ideas of its author. It is intended to provide helpful and informative material on the subject matter covered. It is sold with the understanding that the author and publisher are not engaged in rendering professional services in the book. If the reader requires personal assistance or advice, a competent professional should be consulted.

The author and publisher specifically disclaim any responsibility for any liability, loss, or risk, personal or otherwise, which is incurred as a consequence, directly or indirectly, of the use and application of any of the contents of this book.

Trademarks: All terms mentioned in this book that are known to be or are suspected of being trademarks or service marks have been appropriately capitalized. Alpha Books and Penguin Group (USA) Inc. cannot attest to the accuracy of this information. Use of a term in this book should not be regarded as affecting the validity of any trademark or service mark.

Most Alpha books are available at special quantity discounts for bulk purchases for sales promotions, premiums, fund-raising, or educational use. Special books, or book excerpts, can also be created to fit specific needs.

For details, write: Special Markets, Alpha Books, 375 Hudson Street, New York, NY 10014.

For my stepfather Edward who I love dearly

CONTENTS

Appendixes

INTRODUCTION

Until I began researching this book, I had no idea how much people hated the very idea of mercenaries—that is, in reality. In fiction and film, they are revered.

From Sir Walter Scott's *Ivanhoe* to Robert Stone's *The Dogs of War;* from Gary Cooper in *For Whom the Bell Tolls* to Arnold Schwarzenegger in *Predator,* the heroic image of the soldier of fortune or mercenary is a familiar one in Western culture.

As a culture, we have come to believe that mercenaries have an honor about them. Psychologists would say we are projecting this character trait to justify what is essentially a brutal practice: hiring someone else to do your own fighting and to kill (or even die) if necessary.

For more than 2,500 years, mercenaries have hired themselves out and made headlines in the process. It makes no difference whether the reporter is using papyrus, dye and quill, or a computer to write. Whenever mercenaries are involved in wars, the news organizations of the time will be there to cover it. Mercenaries just can't seem to stay out of the headlines.

In March 2004, 70 mercenaries made the front pages of newspapers worldwide when they attempted to overthrow Equatorial Guinea. They were captured in Zimbabwe before they could carry out their plan. Then late in the same month, four men identified as security contractors—a currently popular term for mercenaries—were ambushed in Fallujah, Iraq. Their bodies were hacked up and burned. The images of two of the burned bodies hanging from a bridge were transmitted worldwide.

For more than a decade, the U.S. government has been awarding contracts to private military companies (PMCs) to provide paramilitary personnel and expertise in war zones where American soldiers are, in the government's view, best put to other uses. Since the "end" of the aggressive military war in Iraq was declared in March 2003 by President George W. Bush, part of the president's overall strategy has been to use security "contractors" to take over from the U.S. military. The contractors are engaged in situations where security needs to be provided for civilians working on the rebuilding of the country's infrastructure.

The accepted use of mercenaries in Iraq is the latest leg in a 2,500-year odyssey that begins with Libyan mercenaries waging war for Egypt circa 500 B.C.E. In between are the mercenaries throughout history who helped to shape the modern world.

Acknowledgments

During a dark December night in a smoke-filled bar beneath Grand Central Station, I made the mistake of telling my long-time editor Paul Dinas an idea for a book that I didn't take seriously. Paul, of course, did. The last time that happened was with a book called *Lobster Boy*, which set me down a strange road of investigating homicides and writing about them.

This time, Paul sent me back along a timeline into the history of mercenaries and then forward, looking at the mercenary forces in Iraq. It has been a great journey. If this book is successful, it will be in no small measure due to Paul's lobbying for it.

I also want to thank my agent, Lori Perkins, who kept the machine oiled. Rachelle Gura-Green provided a wealth of research support, while Dr. Roger Green gave me perspective. And Stan Jacobs lent a steady ear and thoughts of his own. To all I am profoundly grateful.

CHAPTER 1

THE BUSINESS OF WAR

The U.S. occupation of Iraq was not more than a year old before Tim Spicer showed up in 2004.

In honor of his past service as a lieutenant colonel in an elite British fighting unit, Tim Spicer had been awarded the rank of OBE, Order of the British Empire. He also happened to be the world's most successful mercenary, and Iraq was too lucrative a market to pass up. After all, by the time the Americans handed civil government back to the Iraqis in June, 2004, the second largest fighting force in Iraq was composed of 50,000 mercenaries, a.k.a. "security contractors," in the employ of private military companies (PMCs). And Spicer had invented the modern PMC.

Like the men of his profession in the distant past, Spicer took the time to assess the situation, define goals, figure out what was needed to do the job, and then provide his client with an estimate to do the job and do it well. His client was the Coalition Provisional Authority (CPA). Headed by L. Paul Bremer and funded by the U.S. government, the CPA needed to name an overall commander of all the security troops in Iraq before the United States officially handed the country back to the Iraqis.

One of Paul Bremer's Blackwater USA security contractors stands in front of a monument built at site where a mass grave of Saddam Hussein's victims was discovered.

In his 1999 autobiography *An Unorthodox Soldier*, Spicer writes "There is a vast amount of First World military and professional experience out there which PMC's have the training and the experience to deploy and which governments should be eager to utilize. This work could be funded or commissioned by the UN or the intervening governments ... but the PMC would fit into the local command structure and work to a predetermined plan."

Five years later, in 2004, that prediction came through in spades when Spicer's own PMC, Aegis Defence Services, Ltd. won the contract for security on all major Iraqi government projects following the handover by the Americans to the provisional Iraqi government on June 20, 2004. By that time, Spicer was already hard at work on his three-year £280 million ($510 million) contract awarded by the Project Management Office of the CPA on May 25.

"I am pleased to confirm that we've been awarded a contract to assist the Project Management Office (PMO) in Iraq by the United States Department of Defense," said Spicer, from Aegis's Piccadilly offices. Having started Aegis in 2003, Spicer's "contract involves coordination of security support for reconstruction contractors and for the protection of PMO personnel."

The contract called for Aegis to provide 75 close protection teams of 8 men each for the companies that were keeping the oil and gas fields open and electricity and water supplies flowing. Further terms of the contract stated that it was for "security and justice," and included the implementation of security for prisoners and for the vetting of all local Iraqi employees. Even more important, Spicer would be coordinating the efforts of all the others PMCs in Iraq.

The fallout was almost immediate. You don't get to be the millennium's top merc without having a spotlight follow you around. First up was *The New York Times* op-ed piece on June 13, 2004:

Nation Builders and Low Bidders in Iraq

June 13, 2004

By P. W. SINGER (NYT) Op-Ed words

Late Edition—Final, Section A, Page 23, Column 2

From the abuses at Abu Ghurayb prison to the mutilation of American civilians at Fallujah, many of the worst moments of the Iraqi occupation have involved private military contractors "outsourced" by the Pentagon.

In his op-ed piece, Singer pointed out that Aegis, a boutique merc start-up, was not even on the U.S. State Department's list of recommended security companies, and yet it got the high-stakes contract. In fact, security companies in Iraq had been cooperating on an ad hoc basis since the beginning of 2004.

Throughout the summer and into the fall of 2004, at least one article a day appeared in the world press about Spicer's contract. Most noted his involvement with what has become known as the Sandline Affair, during which Spicer was accused of smuggling arms into a country under a UN weapons embargo. To make matters worse, Spicer's contract became an election-year issue in the United States among Irish Americans.

The Reverend Sean McManus, president of the Irish National Caucus, told the world press that the $293 million contract granted to Aegis Defence Service "has Irish blood on it" and was an "insult" to Irish Americans. "This could undo any credit you gained from Irish-Americans for your support of the Irish peace-process. U.S. dollars should not subsidize such a person as Lt. Col. Spicer. And long-suffering Iraq needs him no more than Northern Ireland needed him," McManus said in a letter to President George W. Bush.

Spicer commanded a Scots Guards unit in Belfast in 1992. Two soldiers under his command, Mark Wright and James Fisher, shot dead an unarmed 18-year-old Catholic, Peter McBride. A military tribunal found the two guardsmen guilty of murder, but Spicer allegedly helped them win early release. According to the Belfast-based Centre for Human Rights and Social Change, Spicer also resisted prosecution of his guardsmen and wanted to send them back on patrol immediately after the killing.

Whether the charges were true or not, McManus said awarding the contract to Spicer was a "terrible insult to the McBride family." He warned "This is going to be an election [year] issue" among Irish Americans.

Seizing on the issue, the British did the best reporting on the story and therein provided additional insight into how mercenaries are viewed by the world and how difficult it is in modern times for a country to publicly employ them. The *Weekly Telegraph* in Britain began its coverage this way:

US protest on Spicer's £160m Iraq contract

By David Rennie in Washington

(Filed: 10/08/2004)

Irish-American lobbyists, big business and "buy-American first" members of Congress have forged an unusual alliance to demand the scrapping of a £160 million Iraq security contract given to a firm run by Lt. Col. Tim Spicer, the British military contractor.

In this unusual alliance were DynCorp, a PMC that bid on the Iraq contract and failed; and Texas Republican Congressman Pete Sessions. In a letter to President Bush, Sessions challenged Aegis's experience as a start-up company that has "not demonstrated experience in security operations of the kind required in Iraq." But in Scotland, the home of Spicer's old regiment, the Scots Guards, the coverage was a bit more practical, like the archetypal Scots demeanor:

SOLDIERS OF FORTUNE

Aug. 5, 2004

Exclusive squaddies pick up £1k a day as security men in Iraq death zone

by John Ferguson

Scots squaddies are raking in fortunes by becoming private security men in Iraq. Former soldiers with the Royal Highland Fusiliers and other regiments are continuing to risk their lives by taking jobs as hired guns at as much as £1000 a day.

The story had a much more romanticized version of Spicer:

One of the world's most successful hired guns is former Scots guardsman Lieutenant Colonel Tim Spicer. The controversial soldier of fortune is said to travel around the world with his private army working for the highest bidder.

Spicer's acquisition of the contract was a big story in England, where he comes from, and in Africa, where he'd made his reputation. It was even big in Singapore, which had nothing to do with the Iraq War. But in the United States, most of its citizens did not know anything about the mercenary they were paying big bucks to take care of Iraqi security after the United States stopped policing the country. The American media didn't think Spicer's involvement was a big enough story to warrant any sound bites or ink.

Yet within the mercenary community, as early as February 2004, gossip began to swirl around Spicer that he might have some jobs available pretty soon. By late March 2004, the British armed forces began recruiting members of its Royal Signals regiment in Blandford Camp at Dorset for Aegis positions. The "open" positions were for radio technicians at a salary of $110,000 per annum, approximately three times more than jobs posted at the regimental resettlement offices. Also as part of the contract the enrollee was offered 100 days paid vacation per year.

Knowing that clerks form the administrative infrastructure of any army, Aegis also began recruiting for men to fill those jobs. By early April, jobs were posted at the Adjutant General's Corps in Worthy Down, Winchester, for clerks to maintain "clerical and administrative support for a headquarters-type environment similar to a military brigade/divisional headquarters with many of the same divisions of responsibility." The salaries offered for men with senior noncommissioned officer experience were $129,000. Junior noncoms would make a paltry $110,000.

Seven companies had actually bid for the Iraqi contract, including DynCorp, a Virginia-based company tasked with helping train and re-organize the Iraqi police forces. DynCorp also had contractors working in Afghanistan and Bosnia. The British PMC Erinys, one of the largest providers of private security in Iraq, also bid the contract and lost. Control Risks, another British PMC, had bid for the contract but was dis-qualified because one of the partners was under investigation for undis-closed reasons at the time the bids were evaluated.

With so much competition, how then did Spicer, with his boutique start-up, beat out such stiff competition? Part of the reason could be the growing resentment within Britain that the Americans got all the lucrative contracts in Iraq despite Prime Minister Tony Blair's loyal support of President George W. Bush and his "coalition of the willing." It could also be that the British really had a case. For example, the contract to rebuild the Iraqi infrastructure was awarded to Halliburton, an American company whose former CEO, Dick Cheney, was serving as U.S. vice president.

Whatever the reason, Spicer had the contract. Like a person running for high office who has angered a lot of people, Spicer's past was suddenly fodder for his critics. Peter Singer, author of *Corporate Warriors: The Rise of the Privatized Military Industry* and a fellow at the Brookings Institution, a liberal think tank in Washington, D.C., was quoted as saying "It's like a blast from the past, like I took a leap back into the time-machine to the late '90s ... To be honest, though, I am doubtful that the folks awarding the contract had any sense of Spicer's spicier history." Singer's witicism aside, like any good mercenary, "Spicer's history" is open to interpretation. His last big impact on the international scene was in 1998. Sandline, Spicer's previous mercenary-for-hire company, participated in an attempted put down of an insurrection in Sierra Leone. Despite operating with the sanction of the government, Spicer was later accused of violating a UN arms embargo against Sierra Leone; he had imported weapons for his mercenaries.

Sandline's involvement in the Sierra Leone project brought about various government investigations in Britain. It turned out that Sandline's contract violated the UN embargo on providing arms to either side in the military conflict. Spicer's defense was ignorance. He didn't know his involvement in Sierra Leone was in any way illegal. The British government subsequently decided to write new rules for British PMCs.

In 2000, Spicer left Sandline's offices in Chelsea to set up another company, Strategic Consulting International (SCI) in Knightsbridge. Spicer offered advice to governments and shipping companies on how to handle the threat of international terrorism to minimize their companies' potential losses. Changing the company's name to Trident Maritime, he moved offices again, this time to his current Piccadilly location in central London. And then he ran into a problem.

A British journalist discovered that the company's shareholdings and directorships were incorrectly registered and that no accounts had been filed. It was also discovered that a group of students at the University of Maryland had drawn up Trident's original business plan. In exchange for an agreement to allow them to make the plan public and submit it for a college competition, Spicer named them vice presidents of the company. Ironically, they lost, yet the plan has obviously yielded Aegis monetary success.

None of that should have made any difference. If anything Spicer should have scored points for using such qualified people to draw up his business plan. Instead, he was panned for it in the press. As for the problems with the company's proper registration of shareholders and directorships, it was simply an error; no charges were ever filed. But, again, the media picked up on the story and went to town on Spicer's problems.

The latter makes sense in a certain way because of the scorn Western culture reserves for mercenaries, who tend to be honored more as proud warriors in Eastern cultures. Americans in particular do not like to think of anyone fighting their battles except Americans, which belies the history of the United States over the past two centuries in which mercenaries regularly fought for U.S. Armed Forces.

Spicer, meanwhile, set out to cultivate a more respectable image than his forebears. He outbid other contractors for a prize: a contract from Lloyds of London to do a security audit of the Sri Lankan defense system. This was necessary because the Tamil Tiger rebel group practically destroyed Sri Lanka's international airport in July 2001. Spicer looked carefully at the security measures the Sri Lankans had taken since the airport devastation and told the government they had done well by their citizens.

After that, Spicer began marketing to the shipping industry, which was in desperate need of security expertise, and found his services in demand. In 2002, Spicer began his active involvement in the official war on terror when Per Christiansen, Norwegian shipping expert and director of Hudson Maritime, a company that markets emergency response support, called him. Based in New Jersey, Hudson had just won a contract from the Department of Homeland Security to review security at ports around the United States. Some of Christiansen's contacts in the London insurance business told him that Spicer should be considered for the job. Christiansen subsequently hired him to set up a joint venture.

Spicer brought with him a comrade in arms from the Falklands War, Mark Bullough. Bullough had gone into banking since leaving the service. Over the previous decade, in India, Hong Kong, Malaysia, and Singapore, Bullough had worked for Jardine Fleming, a Hong Kong-based investment bank. Bullough brought along a respected researcher from the banking business, Dominic Armstrong, who had worked for him at Jardine.

With the Hudson Trident venture proceeding, Spicer and Bullough established Aegis as a separate company in the same Piccadilly offices with the same phone numbers. Only Aegis's job was to provide private military support services. A fourth man, Jeffrey Day, joined them as chief financial officer.

Relying on his military contacts, Spicer then hired Maj. Gen. Jeremy Phipps, another ex-special forces soldier. Phipps was well known for leading a daring rescue of hostages at the Iranian embassy in London in 1980. Finally, realizing that a private military company headed by a man as controversial as Tim Spicer would naturally attract headlines, some of which would not be all that complimentary, Aegis brought on public relations consultant Sara Pearson. She had worked with Spicer on his Papua New Guinea and Sierra Leone contracts. Pearson's company, SPA Way, has high-end British retail and food stores as clients. She also has contracts with hair stylists and dental clinics.

When Spicer finally got the Coalition's contract, he became the military commander of 50,000 men. It was the largest mercenary army on the face of the earth since Hannibal's, more than two hundred years before Christ's birth. As for political astuteness, Spicer could rival his predecessor. Part of Aegis analyzes terrorist data and issues reports that governments pay for, thereby establishing a relationship with client governments.

On February 24, 2004, a letter from Sen. John J. Cowdery (R-Alaska), a co-chair of the Senate Transportation Committee, appeared in the *Juneau Empire* newspaper. In it, Senator Cowdery wrote:

> A recent report from Aegis Defense Services Ltd. on security in maritime transport brings starkly to light the wide range of opportunities for terrorists to utilize oceangoing vessels and containerized freight for delivering weapons or terrorists themselves. I've read the report, and it's sobering.

The mercenaries in Iraq were there legally and with the full sanction of the U.S. government. This was the natural progression of a process that had begun in the early 1990s when the world turned topsy-turvy and the Soviet Union fell. Suddenly, former KGB operatives were looking for a new job; the same for cops in the secret police forces of Iron Curtain countries that went democratic after the Berlin Wall fell.

In South Africa, Nelson Mandela not only got out of prison, he became president. That left South African Defense Force soldiers, many of them specialists in intelligence, interrogation, and counterinsurgency, out of work. Yet, with apartheid ended, communism defeated, and nuclear war between superpowers a thing of the past, just when it seemed that the world had become a whole lot better, it got a whole lot worse.

Spawned from dissatisfaction with Israel's very existence and the United States' sphere of influence, Middle Eastern terrorist groups flourished. Back in Africa, rebel movements crisscrossed a continent that continued to flow red with the blood of Africans who continued to fight over who would control what and for how much.

With so much roiling the world, with countries where the rule of law had broken down and the rule of the gun had taken over, there was a booming market for the mercenary trade. Unfortunately, good people are always difficult to find, no matter what the business. In his autobiography, Lieutenant Colonel Spicer addresses this point.

Spicer contends that British mercenary Michael "Mad Mike" Hoare's ill-fated invasion of the Seychelles in November 1981, which led to Mad Mike hijacking an Air India jet, "provided the basis for the popular concept of mercenary warfare: a bunch of thugs attempting to subvert the legally elected government and leaving chaos in their wake. The men who take part are, in the main, discontented former soldiers whose only trade is soldiering, and they will sell their services to the highest bidder."

Hoare's last escapade in the Seychelles left the impression in the Third World that "a few well-trained, white professional soldiers—though a large number of Congo and Angolan mercenaries were in fact black— could make a difference to the outcome of any Third World campaign."

The reputation of mercenaries, and with it the price to hire them, soared. Out-of-work soldiers and police officers from South Africa, Australia, South America, the United States, and Europe traveled to Africa and the Middle East serving as security contractors in various regional conflicts. Unfortunately, many were not the disciplined soldiers that professionals like Spicer respected, but thugs, pure and simple, who give the profession a bad name.

That is not good. Image sells the service.

CHAPTER 1: THE BUSINESS OF WAR

The emergence of PMCs in the 1990s as the primary means of selling mercenary services on the international market represents the biggest change in the profession since the Thracians began offering their services in the ancient world. A PMC offers a variety of packaged services, including but not limited to the following: military consultancy, support services, command control, training of indigenous troops, humanitarian support, support services to established law enforcement, operational support, post-conflict resolution, intelligence support, and logistics. These services can be grouped in any number of affordable packages.

The essential element that separates the PMC from the lone mercenary is that the PMC sees itself as a permanent structure. Long after any particular conflict is over, the PMC will continue to function as a permanent company with a permanent address. PMCs work out of established offices and maintain marketing, sales, administration, and accounting services on staff. The procurement section of the company hires the mercenaries needed from job to job based on a worldwide computer database kept of available soldiers and law enforcement personnel. PMCs sell "weaponry and systems within a wider package of training support and operational use."

The truly innovative pricing technique the PMCs use is to take a "piece of the action." Marketing themselves as a cost-effective solution to an international problem, PMCs accept a percentage of a country's natural resources (for example, oil, gas, or diamonds) as payment. Or if the client prefers, the PMC will take cash. Some combination of both is considered ideal.

At the beginning of the 1990s, there was no legislation banning mercenaries from engaging in conflicts. By 2004, many countries, including South Africa, had passed legislation barring its citizens from serving in a foreign mercenary force. But the United States had no such law. That explains why thousands of American mercenaries in the employ of the United States could operate in Iraq in 2004 with impunity.

The first PMC might have been the best: Executive Outcome (EO) was established in South Africa in 1989. A limited company registered with the South African Board of Trade, its success was attributable to a combination of corporate image and skilled mercenaries who were not afraid of operating within the new media, where wars were covered on live television as they occurred. So successful did the company become that by 1995 it had income of more than $50 million per annum.

From left, EO mercs Handsome Ndlovu, Steyn Marais, and Renier van Der Merwe pose next to a Russian-built MI-8 helicopter in the Angolan province of Lunda Sul, in late 1994. Reported missing several days after this photograph was taken, they were presumed killed in action by UNITA, the Angolan rebel movement.

Spicer attributes the company's success to its ability to insist on "corporate responsibility and accountability." By privatizing the mercenary function, EO believed it was making the mercenaries actions accountable. If they messed up, the parent company would suffer by not getting as many contracts. It was a service guaranteed to fail if it could not perform. But perform EO did.

Staffed primarily by former South African Defense Force (SADF) members or South African police, EO maintained an updated database with approximately 2,000 names of former military men. It was this very dependable military expertise that the company used in their sales pitch to prospective clients, usually a war ravaged African nation that couldn't combat some insurgent group on its own. Or perhaps it was the insurgent group revolting against an oppressive government. Either way, EO was sold on the basis of their highly trained personnel.

Its brochure said that EO offered "competitively-priced, high-quality services and products tailored to our client's requirements ... Executive Outcome provides tailor-made packages for government armed forces and stability and a stable business climate for investment."

That was what it was all about. The days of looting and plunder by mercenaries were over. They would be paid salaries instead, and the corporate hierarchy for the company would reap the profits. EO was the brainchild of Eeben Barlow.

Eeben Barlow is a mercenary mogul. A former member of South Africa's elite 32 Battalion Reconnaissance Wing, Barlow was born in Northern Rhodesia and moved to South Africa when he was a boy. Joining the SADF in 1974, by 1980 he had worked his way up the chain of command to become a member of 32 Battalion, known in South Africa as "the Fighting Legion." As a soldier in 32 Battalion, Barlow's unit was committed to assisting the rebel UNITA movement that, as EO's president, he would later help to bring down.

By 1989, Barlow had also served in SADF military intelligence. But apartheid, or rather the end of it, was about to cut his formal military career short. Before Nelson Mandela became South Africa's president, he insisted former South African President F. W. De Klerk dismantle the Special Forces units of the SADF. In addition, other SADF units that had been set up especially to enslave the black majority, including the Kovoet (Afrikaans for "crowbar") counterinsurgency unit and the Civil Cooperation Bureau, were ordered dismantled.

Faced with the prospect of unemployment simply because world politics had changed, Barlow did not want to abandon his profession. Instead, he got the idea to corporatize mercenary services, package them, and sell them to those countries and rebel movements that could afford to buy them. Barlow registered his company, Executive Outcome, with Corporate House in London. Based in Hampshire, UK, EO named Barlow and his wife as the majority shareholders, owning 70 percent of the company's capital.

Barlow's sleight of hand in basing his company in London took attention away from its South African origins and the company's other principal investors, Tony Buckingham and Simon Mann. Buckingham was an entrepreneur courageous enough or foolish enough, depending on your point of view, to invest in a mercenary start-up. Simon Mann came from an upper-class family and had joined the Scots Guards, before departing for the murky world of black ops.

Corporations doing business in unstable areas, particularly in the Third World, had seen their employees come under fire for doing as mundane a job as driving a truck. There was a clear need for a private military company that would lend out its soldiers and knowledge of munitions, communications, logistics, and all the things necessary to protect a client and, if necessary, conduct war to further those lawfully licensed commercial goals.

Many of the men Barlow would later employ in Executive Outcome had been with him in 32 Battalion. The unit was instrumental in holding off a Cold War invasion of Angola by a contingent of Soviet, Cuban, Eastern Bloc, and North Korean forces. It also did its part in maintaining and supporting apartheid. In a WorldNetDaily.Com article published in 1998, writer Anthony C. LoBaido quotes Willem Rattem, a former soldier of Rhodesia's Selous Scouts, and Barlow's mentor:

> It's kind of ironic that when Eeben fought for apartheid, the white race, anti-communism, and Christianity, he would end up without any money and was shoved out the door. Now he's fighting on the side of our enemies in Angola and on behalf of the interests of multinational corporations, he's become a wealthy man.

So as not to be misquoted, Rattem made sure to add "Eeben is a very capable soldier."

EO's first big splash in the international scene was its involvement from 1992 to 1994 in the Angola Civil War. To no avail, the UN had deployed soldiers there to keep the warring parties at bay. Civil war continued with casualties mounting. Spicer maintained that the UN's failure there was indicative of their failure in other conflicts they got involved in.

UN forces are impotent, Spicer maintains in his autobiography, because they are in the peacekeeping business when there is no peace to keep. Brought in during times of war, UN forces are not organized to provide concrete action to bring the combatants to the table. That's where a PMC such as EO in Angola comes in.

EO was hired by the Angolan government to recover an important oil refinery and operational base at Soyo that had been captured by the UNITA rebel force. EO was able to mount a small-scale military operation with state-of-the-art weaponry. In the hands of EO's well-trained mercenaries, those weapons were wielded so effectively the refinery was recaptured. In turn, that established EO's credentials with the Angolans. The Angolans picked up EO's "option."

EO was subsequently hired to provide the Angolan government with security advisors whose purpose was to protect military and industrial installations from enemy attack. Eventually EO mercenaries also went to the front lines and fought the rebels there as well. But EO's principal job was to train the Angolans.

EO committed 500 mercenaries to the field, whose job it was to train Angolan recruits, advise and direct intelligence missions (and sometimes to take part in the same), and to supply aircraft personnel to fly Angolan air force combat aircraft. Former Special Forces soldiers conducted commando operations into enemy lines. Other EO mercs trained the Angolans in air/assaults and night fighting.

By 1994, after the mercenaries from EO had been in the field for more than a year, rebel-controlled territory had fallen to 40 percent of the country from a high of 60 percent before EO got involved. The UNITA rebels sat down at the negotiating table and hammered out an agreement with the government that ended the rebellion. EO had succeeded in ending the conflict. This was due in no small measure to Barlow's soldiers. Each member of his army was specially trained in the use of a variety of handheld firearms, self-defense, and survival techniques.

At its height, EO boasted 500 military advisors and 3,000 trained soldiers on its payroll. But it was EO's ability to back up that training with armament that made the difference in battle. EO bought surplus Soviet-era

Mig fighter jets, Eastern Bloc and Puma helicopters, state-of-the-art firearms, tanks and artillery, anything that could give EO soldiers an edge in combat.

With Angola under its belt, the company was ready for its next big challenge, in Sierra Leone. Beginning indetermine 1991, the Sierra Leone government had been fighting a rebel force, the Revolutionary United Front (RUF). During this war, thousands of innocent people had been killed, and untold tens of thousands wounded and injured. Five million people were living in refugee camps. The UN didn't help, neither did other governments that were content to let the fighting and the killing continue. In an effort to stop the violence, the government hired EO.

EO made an "appreciation" or analysis of the situation in the country. They then deployed 160 mercenaries in the bush to retrain and reorganize the Sierra Leone Military Forces (RSLMF). In addition to basic military training, which went exceptionally well because the company had already done this in Angola, EO taught the RSLMF counterinsurgency tactics, including how to use intelligence units to determine the enemy's strength. It eventually became a rout when the EO-trained RSLMF drove the RUF guerillas from Freetown, the capital city, and the country's other population centers.

After a further series of defeats at the hands of the EO-trained RSLMF, the RUF was forced to the negotiating table. In November 1996, a peace agreement between the two parties was finally and successfully negotiated. As part of the agreement, Sierra Leone held its first free elections in 29 years. In 1996, the newly elected Sierra Leone president, Ahmed Tejan Kabbah, said that EO "did a positive job … protection by other means. We didn't consider them as mercenaries but as people bringing in some sanity." Spicer argues that the work of EO in Angola and Sierra Leone was the deciding factor in ending those conflicts. The company supplied the legitimate armed forces with the "means and skills to mount effective military operations in a way that had previously been lacking."

This is true as far as it goes. Spicer does not explain that the "legitimate armed forces" of the country were under the command of a dictatorship, that EO had contracted to supply their services to a dictatorship, and that the outcome, democracy, could hardly have been anticipated when EO first went in. But what ultimately made EO the PMC that all other merc start-ups will be judged against was its innovative idea of taking a piece of the action.

Until the 1990s, it was never standard for mercenaries to receive a percentage of a country's oil, mineral, or other rights. They basically worked for hire and, further back in history, whatever they could plunder. But EO was different. In mercenary operations that stretched from the African continent to Papua New Guinea, EO's payments were in the form of logging, mining, and oil rights in addition to hard cash and a percentage of a country's geologic deposits.

By making itself a major player on the international scene, EO changed the history of mercenaries. No longer could the roving Ronin expect regular employment. Mercenary services were now part of a corporate structure and hierarchy that would never again allow mavericks to be a part of it.

For example, after government forces under EO control regained control of the diamond-rich Kono district in Sierra Leone, EO got a piece of the country's diamond trade. Likewise in Angola, the country's oil- and diamond-producing regions were the first areas secured by the forces trained by EO. With control back in government hands, EO got a percentage of the mineral-rich action in those countries.

EO reportedly mined gold in Uganda, drilled boreholes in Ethiopia, and had a variety of interests in the other countries. Eeben Barlow's achievement was making mercenary work into a large-scale twenty-first-century business. Despite the fact that EO operated strictly legally, it also operated much more effectively in anonymity, which it enjoyed until the mid 1990s, by which time the international press caught on to its involvement as a major player on the international scene. Thus it made EO's activities subject to intense media scrutiny. As if that wasn't bad enough, South Africa's government then moved to effectively put EO and its ilk out of business.

South Africa's anti-mercenary law was passed in 1998, forcing EO to close its doors. As for EO's principals, Eeben Barlow retired to a beautiful home in suburban Pretoria. Tony Buckingham and Simon Mann continued in the contract security business.

CHAPTER 2

COLONEL TIM SPICER, OBE

Tim Spicer was born in Queen Elizabeth Hospital in London in 1952. His father, an officer in the British army during World War II, served in the Royal Indian Army Corps. His mother's first husband was a flyer named Frank Simon who died during the war. His mother honored her first husband by giving Tim the middle name of "Simon."

"My childhood fascination with matters military may have been a portent of things to come," Spicer writes in his autobiography. But as a young man, like many, Spicer floundered as he tried to figure out where he fit in the world. After a series of odd jobs, he finally settled on a military career which, of course, pleased his family. Using family contacts, Spicer got an interview with the commander of the Scots Guards, an elite British regiment, and after being passed over once was invited to join.

Britain's version of U.S. Army's Officer Candidate School is the six-month-long Standard Military Course of the Royal Military Academy Sandhurst, which leads to an officer's commission. Studying everything from military history to state-of-the-art tactics, Spicer was an outstanding student, winning the Sword of Honour. He then stayed on for another six months, studying the Regular Careers Course at Sandhurst, before finally joining the Scots Guards as an officer at Chelsea Barracks in London.

Besides its largely ceremonial, public duties of guarding Buckingham Palace, St. James's Palace, and the Tower of London, the Guards were a field unit that was deployed to Northern Island. That was one of the first times, if not the first time (Spicer is not specific), that he saw a man die under fire. The man he saw die was a British soldier killed by a bullet to the throat because he had not zipped his flak jacket far enough up his body to protect the tender tissue.

Spicer came away from the experience of Northern Ireland, where it was hard to say who was friend or foe, with a strong appreciation for the professional soldier's art of staying alive while finding a way to vanquish your enemy. Spicer was smart enough to know that something as basic as "cleaning your kit [uniforms and equipment]" could make the difference between staying alive and doing the job or being just another statistic in a war zone.

He subsequently served in the British army all over the world, seeing action during the Falkland Islands campaign and the American/British peacemaking in Bosnia during the 1990s. After Bosnia, Spicer was ready for new challenges. He left the military for a career in private banking. Despite his success with a London-based international firm, he yearned for the military life, which he sorely missed.

Tony Buckingham was an entrepreneur who, in 1993, represented an oil company that had drilling equipment seized by the UNITA rebels in Soyo, Angola, and he wanted that equipment back. Buckingham had contacted UNITA and asked its permission to return the equipment to its rightful owners. The rebels refused.

Spicer says that because Buckingham had to get the equipment back (because it was costing his client $20,000 a day in lease charges), he figured out a way to get the Angolan government to help. He suggested to them that they retake the town of Soyo because it was a major oil supplier/revenue producer. In the process of retaking the town, the oil company would get its equipment back. It was Buckingham who suggested to the Angolans that they hire Executive Outcome (EO) to do the job, which they subsequently did. Buckingham's client got its equipment back, and the government had its first victory over the rebels.

One week later, President de Santos of Angola summoned Buckingham by private jet to Angola. The EO operation had gone so well he wanted to negotiate a new deal with the company to train the Angolan army. Spicer's friend from the Scots Guard, Simon Mann, acting as Buckingham's go-between, wanted to determine whether Spicer would accept command of the Angolan training. Still in the service at the time, Spicer declined the offer.

By October 1995, Spicer had been in civilian life for two years and hated it. He had gone into banking and was unhappy with that career. When he looked around from private banking to see what else he could do, there was Simon Mann, once again looking for him. If the definition of luck is when preparedness meets opportunity, Tim Spicer was at that bountiful nexus.

Spicer's friend from the Guards, Simon Mann, called and said Buckingham wanted to meet him. Spicer had already thought long and hard about his two decades of military experience and where it could fit in the private sector. He had decided that he would only work for legitimate governments to help them solve conflicts within their countries. He saw this not as the activities of a team of mercenaries but rather the functioning of an organized, professional company that marketed military skills. What Spicer had done was to effectively reframe his ages-old occupation as mercenary and make it palatable to governments and multinational corporations to employ his services.

At their meeting, Buckingham asked Spicer whether he would like to set up what would be a first: a private military company operated along the ethical lines they had previously discussed. Like any good businessman, Spicer looked at what his market was and what defined it. He came up with three observations:

- First, since the Cold War ended, there was increasing conflict on the international stage.
- Second, the one remaining superpower, the United States, and the reduced superpower, Russia, were increasingly reluctant to get involved in world hotspots where they might get bogged down in a prolonged war.

- Third, there were insufficient police forces/training to handle indigenous problems.

Added to the difficulties of what had shaped up as a new world order was that everything was covered live, on cable and broadcast TV, 24 hours a day, 7 days a week, rain or shine, hurricane or earthquake, in every language. Such was the power of the image that the U.S. government severely limited news photographers' access during the Gulf War, lest Americans see graphic photos and video of the dead and lose their stomach for the fight. Such limitations were also imposed a decade later during the Iraq War. Even so, graphic still photos were uncovered of American soldiers' humiliating Iraqi prisoners at the Iraqi gulag, Abu Ghraib.

Spicer was a new kind of mercenary. He had military training and business acumen. He knew that graphic media coverage meant less public will to engage in a war. That opened up a market for a private military company, the kind that Spicer was going to create. Buckingham financed the venture, and Sandline International, Ltd. was created (with its main office in London). At first, it was just Spicer alone. Because of reputation and contacts, an opportunity came his way to help the elected government of Papua New Guinea (PNG).

The PNG defense minister, Matthias Ijape, contacted Spicer about obtaining some helicopters. Spicer, who was making it up as he went along, saw his fledgling company not as an arms dealer but as a company that would supply arms in the context of a greater military plan.

There was nothing illegal about the request provided international law was followed. To purchase arms, a country needs to be represented by a legitimate government that is not under a UN arms embargo.

With those two conditions were met, the rest is surprisingly simple. After the government in question has given the PMC its order, the PMC shops around to manufacturers, wholesalers, and arms dealers, trying to find the best price for the client. With the weaponry located and a price agreed on, end-user certificates need to be generated so that it's clear who is using the weaponry and for what. These certificates state that the weaponry in question is not going to a country under a UN or other sort of embargo. With certificates approved, the weaponry could be transported to the client as the monies were transferred electronically from the client's accounts into the PMC's accounts.

To make his PMC concept work, Spicer didn't want to operate in a vacuum. Sure, he could order the helicopters, but what were they going to be used for? What about pilots, maintenance crews, and spare parts? Did they need gun crews for protection? Without the answer to those questions, he did not believe he could service his client adequately.

Ijape told Spicer that the helicopters were needed for deployment in Bougainville, a part of the country close to the Solomon Islands in the South Pacific. After doing some research, Spicer saw what he might be getting into if he took Ijape on as a client.

PNG is an island nation located off Australia's north coast. It was an area where terrible battles were fought between the Japanese and the Allies during World War II. One of its islands is Bougainville, about 800 nautical miles from PNG's mainland. In 1989, a secessionist movement swept through Bougainville, and a guerrilla war broke out between the Bougainville Revolutionary Army (BRA) and the PNG Defence Force (PNGDF). During the course of this revolt, more than 10,000 people lost their lives, and thousands more were wounded. Adding to the cost was that Bougainville provided the government with more than 40 percent of its exports. The area's Panguna copper mine, which was particularly profitable, had ceased exports since the conflict began.

Spicer quickly realized that helicopters wouldn't solve the problem and flew to Australia with Tony Buckingham to meet with Ijape and other high-level members of the PNG government. During the meeting, Ijape revealed that despite his nation's close ties with nearby Australia, the Aussies, for their own reasons, wanted nothing to do with helping PNG put down the BRA. It was exactly as Spicer had predicted: a government that didn't want to get involved.

Colonel Spicer's prescription was to look at the problem using a fresh paradigm. How could they create a situation that brought the BRC to the negotiating table? Spicer and the PNG government agreed that Sandline would be paid $250,000 for a proposal on how to proceed.

A few weeks later, the first conclusion Spicer reached was that the PNG government needed to gather intelligence on the location, intentions, troop movements, and arms strength—whatever they could gather that would give them an edge over the rebels in combat. The way to do that was through electronic surveillance. The BRA was sophisticated enough to communicate through satellite phones, cell phones, and other modern communications devices. Many of the devices worked on radio frequencies. With the right kind of electronic surveillance, they could be monitored.

Spicer suggested to Ijape that air support for battle against the rebels could best be carried out with a KING Air fixed-wing aircraft, which could be used to conduct the surveillance more than adequately. He also recommended two helicopter gunships and two helicopter transports to move troops in and out of the jungle terrain quickly. Eventually Spicer had a more formal proposal that was ready to be presented to Gen. Jerry Singirok, the commander of the PNG armed forces. Singirok served at the pleasure of the prime minister, Sir Julius Chan, who, because of his Chinese heritage, was known as "the Chinaman."

Singirok sat for weeks on the proposal, during which time Spicer kept marketing his services to world governments. That was how he happened to meet Ahmed Tejan Kabbah, the president of Sierra Leone, a contact that would become very important to him later.

While in the Philippines during the summer of 1996, Spicer heard about the Kanga Beach massacre in PNG. It seemed that a large force of PNG soldiers had found themselves cornered on a beach with no place to turn. The BRA killed most of the government's soldiers. Still, Singirok did not call.

Spicer was discovering that in the mercenary business, a client accepted a proposal and awarded a contract only 10 percent of the time. Spicer went through further meetings with higher ups in the PNG government to convince them of the efficacy of his plan. He and Buckingham finally got a meeting with the PNG cabinet to present their proposal. Before they went in, they ran into General Singirok, who Spicer felt was not only obstructionist but royally pissed off that they had gone around him.

In a revised proposal that he presented to the PNG cabinet, Spicer advocated a special operations group trained as a "strike unit," to go in quickly and engage the BRA. The goal was not to defeat them militarily but to let their superior military presence be known. Spicer would bring in what he termed the "force multipliers," helicopters, to transport the special operations soldiers. The cabinet liked what it heard, and two days later Ijape called Spicer with the go-ahead. The price tag agreed to, Sandline's fee for bringing the rebels to the negotiating table, was $36 million.

Spicer's operational plan was to go into the jungle with the special ops unit, supported by the gunships, and engage the rebels, putting enough pressure on them to get them to the bargaining table. During the months of planning out the operation on site in PNG, Spicer became a friend and, he believes, confidant of the Chinaman.

Spicer advised the Chinaman that after the rebels sat down at the table, he should consider addressing the political and social issues that brought about the rebellion in the first place. Without realizing it, Spicer was alienating General Singirok, whose participation would be negligible with regard to such political and social concerns. And although Spicer's contract had been accepted by the PNG government, no money had yet changed hands.

Singirok then took center stage in January 1997, when he suddenly contacted Spicer. Spicer says that he requested that the M-17 helicopters be dropped from the plan, unless of course Spicer would consider adding two Bell helicopters, leased from a heavy-lift company in PNG, that the general would suggest. Spicer didn't feel the helicopters the general suggested would do the job; it took awhile for Spicer to get it sorted out. Finally, with elections in PNG pending in April 1997, $18 million was transferred from the PNG coffers into Sandline International's account. Spicer began assembling his mercenary force and arms shipments began arriving on the PNG mainland.

Up to that point, no one outside of PNG knew about the secret deal to hire Sandline. That is until Gary Hogan entered the mix. Hogan was the Australian assistant military attaché in Port Moresby, PNG. Hogan eyed one of the M-17 helicopters being unloaded at Port Moresby's Jackson Airport. It was Sandline's own private aircraft, and yet PNG officers were supervising the delivery. Hogan thought this was odd and reported his suspicions back to his Aussie bosses. An Australian newspaper soon broke the story of the secret deal between PNG and Sandline.

Sandline claimed that it had neither done anything wrong nor violated any laws. It had done business with a duly-elected democratic government that employed it to help with an internal struggle. And PNG was not on any international embargo list. However, the international publicity that resulted from the revelation made it seem that PNG had hired a group of trigger-happy mercs to take down an independence movement.

Fully aware he was combating the merc-as-thug image in the media, Spicer advised Prime Minister Chan to tell his side of the story quickly. In his autobiography, Spicer confesses that "I rather wish we had prepared some statement, as PNG were not really ready to handle the press and the story was poorly presented."

Australia put diplomatic pressure on Chan to abandon his plans with Sandline. Chan refused. Meanwhile, with the press reporting about the size and scope of the Sandline force, the rebels now knew what would oppose them. Despite losing the element of surprise, Spicer still believed that the rebels could be intimidated to the table.

On March 17, 1997, Spicer had a meeting with General Singirok. As he drove into Murray Barracks, where the general had his headquarters, Spicer felt something was amiss, but he couldn't put his finger on what it was. Spicer had previously been at a meeting with Chan and was running a little late; he had sent his adjutant on up ahead.

When he got to Singirok's office, Spicer was deliberately made to wait in the outer lobby and not treated with the respect due an officer. Assuming that the meeting was already going on in Singirok's office, he lost his patience, barged past an orderly, and found himself in Singirok's empty office. Perplexed, Spicer looked around. From a rear door in the office came PNG soldiers armed to the teeth with automatic weapons.

"You are under arrest," one said in English, "this is an officers' coup."

For the next week, Colonel Spicer and his mercenaries were held incommunicado by a junta led by General Singirok. Spicer was detained separately in a range of "accommodations," from the damp hold of a ship to the floorboards of cars used to transport him from location to location while the general worked out the details of the rest of Spicer's life, or so it seemed. Politically, it all depended on how Prime Minister Chan reacted, and Chan was none too pleased with the general's attempt to overthrow his government. Chan still maintained overall rule of the country, although the general controlled certain areas.

Spicer was a survival expert and looked for any opportunity to escape. He carried with him what he considered a standard survival kit for this type of situation—a knife, compass, and £4,000 in cash. The money was to pay for things needed or to bribe corruptible officials. During his seven days of captivity, his captors never discovered his survival kit.

While politics were taking place on the outside, on the inside Spicer was being roughed up every time he demanded to know what was going on. He had quickly put two and two together and realized who was behind his detainment. Spicer was eventually freed by his captors and handed over to civilian government authorities, who charged him with the illegal possession of a firearm!

It was absolutely ludicrous: He had imported about 50 tons of military hardware with the full knowledge of the elected PNG government, and he was being charged like this? Chan, unfortunately, could not protect him. The prime minister had been forced to resign in disgrace when the press exposed the secret Sandline deal. It made Chan look like a weak political hack who couldn't take care of his own country without the help of outsiders.

Eventually Sandline's lawyers got the charges against Spicer dropped; he was deported back to Britain. But Spicer was a new kind of mercenary, as good at business as battle. General Singirok may have betrayed him, but that didn't mean PNG didn't have to honor its contract with Sandline. That meant Sandline was due its money. Papua New Guinea owed Sandline International $18 million, plus $400,000 in expense money stolen, Spicer claimed, out of Sandline's safe in Port Moresby by the general's men.

Sandline lawyers sued the PNG government for the money and finally secured a judgment in Sandline's favor for the full amount in October 1998. Spicer had only been in the mercenary business less than a year and already he had redefined it: He was $18 million ahead without a shot being fired! Sandline was ready for its next job, in Sierra Leone.

Tim Spicer of Sandline International leaving Papua New Guinea. Spicer had been hired by the prime minister to put down an insurrection.

President Ahmed Tejan Kabbah of Sierra Leone, who had previously employed Executive Outcome to help with his nation's internal struggles, was overthrown in a military coup in 1997. Kabbah fled to Guinea. Sandline, being a modern PMC, had business interests in Sierra Leone, specifically security work. Through a subsidiary, Lifeguard, Sandline had the contract to guard various industries in the country, including a diamond mine, the Bumuma Dam, and an industrial plant.

As conditions in the country worsened with continued warfare, the U.S. Air Force came in to evacuate civilians. Sandline used its own helicopter to get people out from the up-country mining area. By May 1997, Spicer had contacted President Kabbah in Guinea and told him that if there was anything he could do to help his legally elected government, to let him know. Because of Sandline's participation, through Lifeguard, in what was happening in the country, the company regularly briefed the Western intelligence community.

In the summer of 1997, Sandline was hired by a Vancouver business-man, Miles Tenant (name changed), to propose ways in which Kabbah could retake power. It seemed that Tenant had a deal going with the government before the coup that allowed him various mineral concessions worth millions. He wanted Kabbah back in power so that he could see his deal done.

Spicer had a problem. His ethic was only to deal with a legitimate government. That was a nonnegotiable point. Also it was none of Sandline's business whether Tenant got his mineral concessions or not. Sandline could only go into Sierra Leone if Kabbah signed off as the legitimate representative of the legitimate Sierra Leone government. When Kabbah did, Sandline was free to act.

The company agreed to conduct a "commander's estimate" of what it would cost for Sandline to effectively drive the military junta out. Just as the operation was ready to take off, the story of Sandline's involvement in Sierra Leone broke in the Canadian press. That delayed further negotiations between the company and the country, until it was finally agreed that Tenant would fund the commander's estimate and some other work in return for being allowed to recoup his money through mineral concessions, which Kabbah granted.

The contract was signed. By January 19, 1998, Sandline already had 15 people and an M-17 helicopter in Sierra Leone. Then things started going wrong. Miles Tenant was picked up at Vancouver airport with a false passport. He had also neglected to make any payment to Sandline.

The Canadians put Tenant in jail. Kabbah, seeing Tenant's problems, began to lose faith and cancelled the contract with him. Sandline had gone into the hole for 35 tons of weapons, costing millions of dollars, that had already been imported into Sierra Leone under their banner. To make matters worse, Spicer's own government, the British, turned against him.

Some in the British government held the mercenary colonel in absolute disdain because of Sandline's involvement in Sierra Leone. He may have been in the right legally, but Spicer had positioned his company as an international player, and the rules were different at that level. Despite the fact that Spicer was helping the democratically elected government of PNG and as far as he could see had done nothing illegal, he was still meddling in international affairs (something best left to experts according to government thinking).

Spicer's own government threatened criminal charges. Once again, Sandline lawyers got the charges dropped. Despite the fact that Sandline never really showed what it could do in Sierra Leone and PNG, it had gone on to other assignments around the world that did not get the same kind of media attention. And people in the mercenary business knew of Sandline's successes.

On November 10, 2003, Col. Tim Spicer spoke at the Nixon Center, a nonpartisan think tank, in Washington, D.C. By that time, he was the most famous mercenary in the world. Spicer's speech as honored guest expert on antiterrorism at the Nixon Center shows how far mercenaries have come over the centuries.

CHAPTER 3

IRAQ—2004

In the April 19, 2004, edition of *The New York Times*, David Barstow wrote:

> Far more than in any other conflict in U.S. history, the Pentagon is relying on private security companies to perform crucial jobs once entrusted to the military. In addition to guarding innumerable reconstruction projects, private companies are being asked to provide security for the chief of the Coalition Provisional Authority, L. Paul Bremer, III, and other senior officials.
>
> The mercs were also hired to defend strategically important locations. These included 15 regional authority headquarters. They were also entrusted with security in the Green Zone in downtown Baghdad, an area thought to be in total U.S. control.

If nothing else, the American experience in Iraq has changed the idiom. It was in Iraq that the word "contractors" became a far more publicly acceptable synonym for what they really were—mercenaries. To the governments that hired them, the distinction was important. What Tim Spicer had wrought was a revolutionary way of packaging mercenary services by calling it something else. It was as effective a piece of flimflam as anything ever pitched by a carnival barker. But the marketing didn't stop there.

The company that employed the mercenary was not a war profiteer but a government contractor. It was an easier way to sell the idea to the military and the government, but especially the Department of Defense, which issued the contracts that employed the government contractors in the first place.

Between deployment in Iraq, Afghanistan, Korea, and Iraq, the U.S. military had been stretched to the limit: 350,000 soldiers deployed around the world by 2004. In Iraq alone, 135,000 soldiers were serving in 2004. It would later be revealed this was too low a number to win the peace. In total, it was estimated that out of the $18.6 billion the Bush administration allocated for Iraqi reconstruction, about 25 percent (or more than $4.5 billion) was allocated to pay government contractors who then supplied the U.S. government with mercenaries for deployment in Iraq.

Unlike Hannibal of Carthage, who blended his mercenaries with his native Carthaginians for maximum military effect during battle, the mercenaries in Iraq acted independently from the Coalition troops. The Coalition Provisional Authority made that a reality when it passed a resolution that mercenaries would not be subject to Iraqi law, nor would they be subject to American law, effectively making them impervious to prosecution. That would become particularly relevant when U.S. soldiers tortured prisoners at Abu Ghraib, the notorious Iraqi prison.

As for pay, Iraq was a goldmine for mercs. Pay averaged in the $1,500 to $2,000 a day range, for experienced white soldiers. In a bizarre form of racism, nonwhite merc—Africans, Fijians, South Americans—were paid about half as much. Of course, regardless of skin color, the more specialized the military experience, the more the client would have to pay to "rent" it. What they faced was not what was originally anticipated.

The initial justification for the U.S. invasion of Iraq offered by President Bush was that Saddam Hussein, the country's president, had developed weapons of mass destruction that he could deploy against the United States. The category "weapons of mass destruction," a.k.a. WMDs, encompasses what used to be known simply as nuclear, chemical, and biological weapons. But when the mercs got over there, they, along with everyone else, discovered that Hussein had been telling the truth: He had previously gotten rid of his WMDs. None of that made any difference to the Iraqi insurgents. What they saw was a hated American enemy that needed to be stopped at all costs. They pounded the security contractors, just like the American soldiers, with everything from rocket-launched grenades right on down to knives.

PMCs licked their chops at the money to be had in Iraq. The U.S. government had not planned well; it had thought the Iraqi enemy would cave quickly; it would be a grateful, docile population to work with. Instead, Iraqi insurgents, fuled by their hatred of Americans, fought back long after President Bush declared the war officially over. With American forces strung out across the globe, security contracting companies came in to plug the gaps.

Supply lines are essential in war. Hannibal found that out when, after defeating the Romans, they got him back by severing his supply lines, forcing a hasty retreat. So it was in Iraq. Foodstuffs, medicines, hardware, replacement parts for vehicles, you name it, all had to be dispatched by armed convoy through Iraq's dangerous interior. And it made no difference whether said supplies were strictly humanitarian. As far as the insurgents were concerned, the convoys and everyone in them, were fair game.

Many PMCs got contracts with the American and British governments to provide armed security for various clients involved in rebuilding the Iraqi infrastructure. One of those was Blackwater USA.

Up until mid-2004, Erik D. Prince was the anonymous founder of Blackwater USA, a PMC that operated out of Myock, North Carolina. Then Prince found himself unwillingly thrust into the limelight when four of his mercenaries were shot, burned, and hung with coverage on worldwide 24 hour a day, 7 day a week television. Suddenly a company that deliberately operated anonymously, was thrust into the limelight.

Sandy haired and blue-eyed, Prince hails from Holland, Michigan. Prince grew up in Holland, attended private schools and the United States Naval Academy, and then resigned before graduation, opting instead to enlist in the Navy. Eventually he was selected for the elite SEALs. Despite the fact that he didn't have to work, after his hitch was up, Prince became a civilian and started Blackwater, USA.

Born into a wealthy, well-connected family, his mother was one of the Republican Party's largest fundraisers in the state, as well as a steady personal contributor. Prince's father, Edgar, was friends with Gary Bauer, a conservative evangelical Christian, who ran George Bush's campaign in the southern states during the 2004 election. For Prince's future plans, it helped that Edgar was the co-inventor of the car visor with lighted mirror. The product took off, and Prince Corporation became one of the auto industry's largest parts suppliers, producing 60,000 visors a day. Prince Corporation is also Holland's largest employer, with approximately 4,000 workers.

When Edgar Prince died of a massive coronary in 1995, he left behind a company that his family eventually sold for $1.4 billion. Late in 1996, Prince started Blackwater. Sparing no expense in building his North Carolina training facility, he bought 6,000 acres and put in a 1,200-yard firing range, one of the country's largest, as well as a bunkhouse, lodge, and small-arms ranges.

Seeing an opportunity after 9/11, Prince decided to expand Blackwater. He even built a mockup of an airplane cabin in Myock to train future air marshals. "Before the events of Sept. 11, I was getting pretty cynical about how people felt about training," Prince told the *Virginian-Pilot* shortly after the attacks. "Now the phone is ringing off the hook."

Since 2001, Blackwater has been raking it in. In February 2004, Blackwater recruited 60 Chilean soldiers who had trained under the military dictatorship of Augusto Pinochet. The company took them to their Myock facility for training and then assigned them to duties in Iraq, paying them $4,000 monthly.

In England's *Guardian* newspaper, Gary Jackson, the president of Blackwater, said: "We scour the ends of the earth to find professionals—the Chilean commandos are very, very professional and they fit within the Blackwater system. We have grown 300% over each of the past three years and we are small compared to the big ones. We have a very small niche market; we work towards putting out the cream of the crop, the best."

In response to the loss of many of their trained soldiers to the private sector, Chilean Defence Minister Michelle Bachelet told the *Guardian*, "If the [U.S. military] is going to outsource tasks that were once held by active-duty military and are now using private contractors, those guys [on active duty] are looking and asking, 'Where is the money?'"

The answer, of course, is going private, just like mercenaries have realized since the ancient world. As one former soldier working in Iraq told the paper. "This place [Iraq] is a goldmine. All you need is five years in the military and you come here and make a bundle."

By April 2004, Blackwater had more than 450 contractors in Iraq and millions of dollars worth of contracts. Its crown jewel was the $21 million Blackwater got for guarding L. Paul Bremer, the top U.S. official in Iraq. Things were going well, until Fallujah.

No battle involving by mercenaries since the ancient world has been covered more by the media than the Fallujah massacre of four Blackwater mercenaries on March 31, 2004. While much of the coverage at the time focused on the atrocities, little if any reporting actually focused on who the mercenaries were, what their mission in Iraq was, and why they were killed. With the passage of even the brief period of time since their deaths, Blackwater USA, combined with an investigation by the *San Francisco Chronicle*, revealed what really happened to the four Blackwater mercenaries that last day of March 2004.

(AP/Wideworld/Khalid Mohammed)

Iraqis chant anti-American slogans as charred bodies hang from a bridge over the Euphrates River in Fallujah, west of Baghdad, Wednesday, March 31, 2004. The dead were security contractors in the employ of Blackwater USA.

Wesley J. Batalona, 48, was a Filipino Hawaiian. A native of Kauai, he joined the army and became a member of the U.S. Army Rangers. He fought in Panama in 1989, and in Iraq in 1991. Retiring from the service in 1994, he went back to Hawaii, but the longing for military duty seems to have lured him to Iraq, where Blackwater employed him to provide security for a food convoy. Batalona was joined by three other men.

Scott Helvenston had 12 years of experience as a Navy SEAL and had left the service for a variety of jobs. A top pentathlete, Helvenston made his own workout video. Somehow he managed to get the job training Demi Moore to play an onscreen Navy SEAL in *GI Jane*. Helvenston craved action, and he found it when he signed up with Blackwater.

Jerry Zovko, 32, was a Croat who changed his first name when he became a naturalized U.S. citizen. A former member of the US Special Forces, Croatian journalist Marina Seric says in an Interpress News Service article, "One cannot establish the exact number of Croats who have been contracted to work as security personnel in Iraq. But the bottom line is that they all used to be professional soldiers. They are aged between 30–45. Depending on their experience they do different jobs—simple protection, logistics, training."

The last man in the Blackwater security team that day was 38-year-old Michael Teague, an army veteran who served with a special operations aviation unit. The four mercenaries comprised what Blackwater refers to as a mobile security team. Their mission was to provide armed escort for a convoy of trucks carrying foodstuffs through the most dangerous town in Iraq.

According to the *San Francisco Chronicle*, the contract for the job had been taken over from Control Risks Group. The latter told Blackwater that Fallujah was not a safe place to travel through. There would later be speculation that Blackwater was determined to show it was a better company than Control Risks and could get the convoy through Fallujah, but as of this writing, that could not be confirmed.

What is clear is that either through hubris or ignorance, the food convoy blundered into Nightmare Alley, the two-lane highway that travels through Fallujah's shabby downtown, flanked on all sides by buildings in which the enemy could easily set up ambushes. The Blackwater contractors were lightly armed, despite the fact they knew that they were going to be passing through Iraq's most dangerous area. Making matters worse, the mercs drove two to a car, which meant only one man could return fire.

In a *New York Times* interview, Patrick Toohey, Blackwater's vice president for government relations, said the Iraqi Defense Corps or imposters wearing their uniforms appeared to have promised the Blackwater mobile security team safe passage through the city. Believing them, the convoy proceeded forward. When the contractors were well within Fallujah's Nightmare Alley, the road was blocked. Never having time to react, the soldiers of fortune didn't know what hit them when their cars were hit by rocket-propelled grenades (RPGs). The cars blew up and the people of Fallujah ran amok.

The type of RPG used to kill the four Blackwater security contractors in Fallujah is a shoulder-mounted, inexpensive, one-shot weapon, common in insurgent arsenals. Originally manufactured in the Soviet Union and distributed around the world, the launcher weighs roughly 10 pounds, with the grenade weighing an additional 5. This 15-pound weapon was used to devastating effect by the Vietcong and North Vietnamese army in the Vietnam War and the Afghans during the Soviet occupation. Later, RPGs were used to down an American helicopter in Mogadishu, leading to the slaughter of American soldiers.

RPGs are extremely effective against soft or unarmored targets such as a car or bus. With little or no training, anyone, including a child, can operate it. It's not surprising how it has found itself a niche among smaller armies and poorer countries of the world. It has become the weapon de rigueur of guerilla forces worldwide and, it was being used extensively against American forces and security contractors in Iraq.

Even with the car blown up and burning, the bloodthirsty mob fired shot after shot into the Blackwater corpses, making sure that the bodies were fried to a crisp before they removed them, and then hung two of them over a bridge in the middle of the town. All of these images were captured live by photographers and broadcast on world television. An international furor erupted, condemning the murderers and the bloodthirsty Iraqi mob. There were calls to patriotism afterward, despite the fact that the dead were not soldiers in the U.S. Army.

All of the media attention just served to confirm Tim Spicer's worst fears about what happens when mercenaries go into a hotspot without a clear plan of what is to be accomplished and what is necessary to accomplish it. Clearly, the Blackwater security mobile team had ventured into a prohibited area. The company's story that the team was lured in by a good-conduct pass makes sense because the alternative is they were just foolish. But it is also clear that they were too lightly armed for their job, considering that they knew the enemy had the kind of powerful weapons that eventually killed them.

In the wake of what the media called the Fallujah massacre, PMCs became front-page news. As if to confirm their newly found importance, Blackwater's Erik D. Prince briefed key members of Congress, including Sen. John Warner (R-Va) about the massacre and the work of his company. Prince also hired Alexander Strategy Group, a well-known Washington, D.C. company with strong Republican ties, to represent Blackwater when it faced questions from congressional members about its activities in Iraq.

Back in Iraq, nothing stood still. Just days later, Blackwater operatives were once again in mortal danger.

Later estimates would place the attacking Iraqi militia members in the hundreds. Armed to the teeth, they attacked the U.S. government's headquarters in Najaf on Sunday, April 4, 2004. Military assistance would not be readily forthcoming.

Blackwater had gotten the contract to protect the U.S. government headquarters in Najaf, Iraq. Stationed there were eight Blackwater contractors along with four army military. Their job was to protect the U.S. headquarters, its environs, and its charges. When the Shiite militia attacked in force, there was no time to summon the U.S. military for help; Blackwater had to handle the situation itself until the American military came to the rescue.

In the intense firefight that ensued, the contractors were continually pounded by RPGs and AK-47 gunfire; all four U.S. servicemen were wounded. Blackwater dispatched two of its helicopters to resupply ammunition to its men and ferry out one of the wounded soldiers. Video was shown worldwide of the contractors firing their automatic weapons side by side with the servicemen. They held off the Shiites until U.S. troops finally arrived to relieve them. The contractors emerged unscathed.

The next day, Brig. Gen. Mark Kimmitt, spokesman for the top U.S. commander in Iraq, Lt. Gen. Ricardo Sanchez, said, "I know on a roof-top yesterday in An Najaf, with a small group of American soldiers and *Coalition soldiers* (author's emphasis) … who had just been through about 3½ hours of combat, I looked in their eyes, there was no crisis." He continued, "They knew what they were here for. They'd lost three wounded. We were sitting there among the bullet shells—the bullet casings—and, frankly, the blood of their comrades, and they were absolutely confident."

While not mentioning the contractors by name, Kimmitt had referred to them as "Coalition soldiers." The U.S. military had acknowledged their contribution. For Blackwater, the positive publicity quickly diverted attention away from the Fallujah massacre. Their capital in the security game rose instantly because of Najaf, and the contractors' heroism against overwhelming odds.

(AP/Wideworld/Karim Hussein)

Fijian security guards are seen in the streets of the northern Iraqi city of Mosul.

Contractors working for British firms also found themselves in the heat of the action. In March 2004, Iraqi insurgents attacking the gates to the Basra palace were greeted by the incongruous site of a lone British officer barking commands to six Fijians, as these security contractors with Global Risk Strategies, a London-based PMC, defended the palace.

British PMCs are the other major player in post-war Iraqi security. David Claridge, managing director of Janusian, a London-based security firm, claimed in an article in the *Economist* on March 25, 2004, that "Iraq has boosted British military companies' revenues from £200m ($320m) before the war to over £1 billion, making security by far Britain's most lucrative post-war export to Iraq."

Because it's such a lucrative business, British military contractors, like their American counterparts, live in luxurious villas complete with swimming pool and fully stocked wet bar. These same villas were once occupied by Saddam's Baathist Party leaders. And demand has outstripped supply.

The war provided a ready market for military outsourcing. Established security companies expanded while new ones sprung up. In the former group, for example, Control Risks Group, which prior to the Iraq War was a consultancy firm, retooled and became more of a PMC. They now have more than 1,000 security contractors in Iraq, more than the Coalition forces of Germany and Japan combined.

British PMCs maintain a distinct pecking order. First and foremost, it is based on class and education. At the top will always be those formally trained at the British military academies, such as Sandhurst, and who served in the British armed forces, particularly the heralded SAS. Caucasian former officers from Third World countries get paid about $15,000 a month. Third-country nationals (TCNs), specifically Fijians and Gurkhas, get paid approximately $2,250 per month. The British class system extends to British PMCs, although some don't like to play that game. For example, Control Risks prefers westerners.

In contrast, rival British PMC ArmorGroup employs 700 Gurkhas to guard civilian employees of Bechtel and KBR who are rebuilding the Iraqi infrastructure. Erinys, still another British PMC, employs Iraqis to protect the Iraqi oil pipeline. Clearly, Third World soldiers of fortune are much cheaper than their western counterparts, which accounts for one of the reasons PMCs are raking it in.

"Why pay for a British platoon to guard a base when you can hire Gurkhas at a fraction of the cost?" asks one executive with a British PMC.

The American Program Management Office (PMO), which currently has an $18.6 billion budget for Iraq, initially estimated that 7 percent of that money would go for security. They then increased their projection to 10 percent when Iraqi insurgents dug in for the long haul. But those are the public figures. Privately PMCs expect the PMO budget to hover conservatively around 20 percent.

A private contractor involved in prisoner interrogation enters an interrogation room as an Iraqi detainee squats outside in a processing center at the Abu Ghraib Prison on the outskirts of Baghdad.

What has ultimately created problems for all the PMCs, regardless of nationality, is the lack of government regulation. As events unfolded in 2004, it became obvious that some of the military contractors working in Iraq were poorly trained. Some of these incompetents actually erected checkpoints within the country without proper authorization and functioned as a law unto themselves. One South African company guarding a Baghdad hotel actually put guns to the heads of a reporter's guests. These, of course, were minor incidents compared to the abuse contractors heaped on Iraqi prisoners in Abu Ghraib Prison.

When the story broke about the torture, interrogation, and humiliation of Iraqi prisoners in the infamous prison, the first blast of publicity centered on the American soldiers who actively participated in these human rights abuses. But as the story continued to play out, it was revealed that at the center of it were contractors working for PMCs, who allegedly did the same things the military men have been convicted of: torture and humiliate the Iraqi prisoners.

Taking a page out of the American legal playbook, on June 9, 2004, eight Iraqis filed a federal class-action lawsuit claiming that employees of two American contractors subjected them to abuse, including electric shocks, rape, and torture that led to one death. The lawsuit alleges that the Virginia-based PMC, CACI International, and the San Diego-based PMC Titan Corp, all worked under government contract.

Systematically, they tortured prisoners with the goal being to extract intelligence, which could help the companies gain additional contracts. None of the plaintiffs, though, can identify their torturers, who they say were hooded. Instead, the lawyers based their suit on the identification by military authorities of civilian contractors who contributed to the abuse at the prison.

The companies involved have denied any wrongdoing. The class-action suit seeks to represent all Iraqis who were victims of abuse by contractors in U.S.-run Iraqi prisons. Meanwhile the Iraqi eight are asking for unspecified monetary damages. Yet, even if the contractors did commit the crimes, there can be no justice. Non-Iraqi private-security personnel contracted to the Coalition or its partners, including TCNs, are not subject, as mentioned earlier, to Iraqi law. As for American law, it does not extend to Iraq.

One big problem for the countries where the higher-end contractors are recruited, particularly the United States and Britain, is how to keep their soldiers from defecting to PMCs for the money. Why should a soldier risk his life for a fraction of what he could get as a contractor? The only reason, of course, is love of country.

The British are concerned that many of their SAS soldiers are asking to be discharged early so they can take advantage of the market in Iraq for contractors. Patriotism is fighting a hard battle. As for the American army, they are not talking. How many soldiers have left to become contractors is unclear.

Even when the need for contractors in Iraq is reduced, they will be needed someplace else. It is a new world order in which contractors will continue to perform vital security functions for their clients in hotspots worldwide. For the contractors, the pattern has been set in Iraq for how much their services are worth. That will continue in their participation in future conflicts.

In a world increasingly defined by the dollar, or the dinar, whoever has more can certainly buy their own army. In that way, things haven't changed very much from the ancient world.

CHAPTER 4

THE DISTANT PAST

Thousands of years ago, swords, knives, daggers, and other metallic implements of death did not yet exist. The discovery of how to make soft metal hard had not yet been made. Therefore, weapons of war were made out of stone, wood, or any number of naturally available substances.

About 3500 B.C.E., early metallurgists discovered that copper can be made harder by melting it together with tin, thus forming the harder metal called bronze. This revolutionized warfare because previously, only soft metals like copper, as well as stone, or wood, could be made into weapons. The discovery of bronze meant that edge weapons and other tools of the military trade could now be made in a stronger, tempered metal that would withstand the rigors of the battlefield.

Stone, especially in the hands of skilled slingers, would remain popular. But bronze enabled frontline combatants to kill more efficiently than ever before. It is during this time, the beginning of what came to be known as the Bronze Age, that some of the earliest recorded instances of mercenary activity occurred. It is no surprise that in Africa, the cradle of civilization, the first recorded instances of mercenary activity occurred.

Located in North Africa, Egypt in pre-antiquity employed Libyan mercenaries. The Egyptians respected the contributions of the Libyans and later absorbed them into Egyptian society.

The descendants of the Libyan mercenaries came to power during the XXI to XXV Egyptian dynasties (ca. 1100–664 B.C.E.)

Over the following century, Egyptian military strength waned while its reliance on mercenaries increased. During the XXVI Saite Dynasty (ca. 664–525), Egypt established a precedent that would last for centuries—an alliance with Greek mercenaries. Under the Egyptian ruler Neco II, the Egyptian army, fortified with the Greek mercenaries, campaigned in north Syria and dominated Palestine (present-day Israel) for four years. But in 525 B.C.E., Egypt was defeated by Persia and became part of the latter's domain. Although Egypt regained some independence between 404 and 342 B.C.E., it still relied on the Greek mercenaries to staff its army.

The Greeks were proficient with many weapons, including the sling. In the ancient world, the sling was popular as a great leveler of men. David, the future king of Israel, slew the Philistine giant Goliath with his sling. Had he chosen hand-to-hand combat with the giant, David surely would have been killed.

Instead, he used his shepard's sling the way it was meant to be used—as a projectile weapon. The weapon itself was popular with ancient armies because it was inexpensive and took up almost no space. David would have loaded a stone into a pouch that extended out on both sides into long sturdy strings. Made from braided hemp or wool twine, the sling was whirled overhead.

At the last moment, David would have extended his arm, aiming the sling at the same time at Goliath's forehead. Because of his experience with the weapon, David knew how to coordinate the movements of his body to put the most amount of force behind the throw, which struck Goliath dead on the forehead and felled him.

The sling was used in all battles, including the Battle of Gela in 405 B.C.E. In many ways, the Battle of Gela presaged the twenty-first-century development of a professional, paid army. At the time, what it presaged was political turbulence in the Mediterranean region for years to come.

What had happened was that Himilikon, a general of Carthage, laid siege to Gela, the only city on Sicily's southern coast still in Greek hands. Dionysios I, the ruler of Syracuse, raised a substantial army in an effort to break the seige. His army confronted Himilikon's to no notable effect; it was a stalemate. Changing tactics, Dionysios decided to take the fight to the Carthaginians. The conflict that followed is notable not so much for who won, but for who fought the battle.

According to contemporary accounts, the Syracusans employed 2,450 mercenaries out of a total force of 50,000. The majority of the mercenaries, 1,700, were from Campania. Campania is a section of Italy that comprises present-day Naples and Salerno. It is located on the instep of the "boot" that Italy describes on the map. Seizing on the opportunity provided by the instability in the region, Campanian mercenaries threw themselves into the conflict.

On the Carthaginian side, the reliance on mercenaries was even heavier. Iberian, Balearic, Campanian, Phoenicians, Libyans, and Moorish mercenaries totaled the majority of the 300,000 Carthaginian troops. As for the Battle of Gela itself, the Carthaginians beat the Syracusans.

On both sides, Campanian mercenaries died for their employers.

Among the mercenaries of the ancient world, the Greek hoplites were among the most feared. They were heavy infantry, armed with among other things, long spears. Their favorite method of engaging the enemy, and the most popular of the era, was to engage the enemy in a phalanx formation. They would move toward the enemy in tight, shoulder-to-shoulder formation, spears measuring 12 to 15 feet outstretched, ready to impale the enemy's body before a juggernaut of men and steel.

The hoplites were natives of and fought for Athens, Sparta, and other Greek city-states that warred constantly, supplying an unending stream of winners and losers. If you happened to be in the losing camp, you'd find yourself out of a job and looking for employment elsewhere. For hoplites, that could be any number of Middle Eastern and North African kingdoms looking for well-trained mercenaries to swell its ranks and the professionalism of its armies.

By 401 B.C.E., hoplites were unemployed after 30 years of war between the nation-states of Greece. Hostilities had ceased, and hoplites went out into the world looking for military work. They found it in Persia. Cyrus the Great had in mind an attempt to overthrow his brother, Artaxerxes II who ruled Persia. Acknowledging the temporary political stability and cessation of hostilities in Greece, Cyrus hired the unemployed Greek hoplites to form up the center of the army he wanted to throw against his brother's. To make certain he won, Cyrus hired Clearchus, the Spartan general and living legend, to command the troops from his own country.

Cyrus's army contained 50,000 men, of which 13,000 were the Clearchus-commanded Greeks. Moving from the coast of the Aegean Sea through Anatolia, the army came to the plains of Babylon, where Artaxerxes II was waiting. The latter commanded 100,000 men, a two-to-one advantage over Cyrus. But Cyrus had something better—the Greeks.

The Greeks immediately formed up to meet the challenge into rectangular blocks of men—the feared phalanx. Lined up 12 to 16 deep, 100 yards across, spears outstretched and lowered, the marched slowly forward, into the left flank of Artaxerxes' infantry. The Greeks were unstoppable. They rolled over the Persians like buzzards feasting on flesh. The Persian left flank collapsed.

Marching into the left flank rather than the right was a deliberate move by Clearchus. In the ancient world, the left flank tended to be weaker than the right. The reason for this is that most people are right-handed, just as the Persian warriors were. In hand-to-hand combat, soldiers move forward toward the side of the body in which they are holding the weapons. Constantly pivoting toward the right made the left side that much more vulnerable. What all this maneuvering meant was close battle formations and battlefield action rarely too far from where it started.

With Artaxerxes left flank in ruin, the Greeks pivoted and started marching in the opposite direction intending to do the same to the Persian right and finish up the battle. Their employer Cyrus, who had been staying back from the line as any good ruler should, foolishly decided to join in the fray. Charging, he raced his horse across the plains of Babylon ... and promptly fell off his horse. The arrow that killed him had been fired from one of his brother's archers.

Cyrus's death left the Greek mercenaries without an employer. Their "brother" Persians, fighting under Cyrus's banner, quickly deserted the field when they realized their leader had died. That left the Greeks to face Artaxerxes superior force. Alone. But Artaxerxes men had had enough. Even with superior numbers, they chose to leave the field of battle.

If the Persians had chosen to fight, the Greeks would either have beaten them or seriously compromised their army. Either way, Artaxerxes would have found himself in a hole. Instead, by withdrawing, his army was free to regroup, recruit, and, if necessary, fight a rear-guard action against the mercenaries should they choose to follow. Artaxerxes figured they wouldn't do that for the simple reason when that arrow struck his brother, it also struck down their employer.

Artaxerxes was right. The Greeks stayed put, trying to decide what to do. Artaxerxes sent a messenger with an offer to discuss peace. It was a generous move considering the kind of just-finished conflict tended to provoke feelings of revenge rather than peace. Clearchus had 10,000 men he was responsible for, so when Artaxerxes invited him to discuss peace, Clearchus accepted.

Under a flag of truce, Clearchus and his generals embarked for the enemy's camp. Once inside, Clearchus was summarily executed. The rest of his staff, having watched their general's demise, were then separated from their heads. Artaxerxes then sent a simple message back to the Greeks: Become slaves or die the same way. Battle-hardened mercenaries in any age are not likely to take up such an offer, and the Greeks did not disappoint.

Instead of panicking and accepting the Persian "offer" of safety in slavery, the junior Greek officers reviewed the situation. With the high command dead, they were now in charge. Far from home and without friends, their ranks were filled with men from Sparta and Athens who considered each other mortal enemies. It was not just a question of whether or not they could escape from Persia with their heads on. Could they act as a single, fighting unit without sectional disputes? If they didn't, their ranks would be corrupted from the hatred within.

To their credit, the Greeks realized the problem. Quickly, they established a unified joint command composed of officers representing their home country's various city-states. Among them was Xenophon, who would later record all of the battle and the actions that followed in the *Anabasis*. Xenophon began his life as a mercenary and ended it as one of history's greatest historians.

As a teenager, Xenophon knew Socrates. Xenophon's friend was going with Cyrus to fight Artaxerxes. He asked Xenophon to go, too.

A thoughtful young man, he talked the matter over with Socrates who recommended that he consult with the Oracle at Delphi. Heeding the great man's advice, Xenophon went to Delphi. On the way, he made up his mind to accompany his friend. When he finally met the Oracle, he did not ask what to do because his decision was made. Instead, he asked what sacrifices he should make and to which Gods, to insure a safe journey. After he made the sacrifices the Oracle advised, Xenophon accepted the invitation and marched into battle against the Persians. Later in life, Xenophon settled down in Sparta and Athens and became a historian. The detailed account of the Battle of Cuxana exists because Xenophon took it all down and later published it in the *Anabasis* ("Up Country March"). Taking eight years to write it, Xenophon saw the *Anabasis* published in 371 B.C.E.; it survives to the present day.

Xenophon died some time around 357 B.C.E. when he was approximately 87 years old. It was amazing that he died of old age and not on the March of the Ten Thousand.

After refusing to surrender to the Persians, Xenophon and his colleagues took out a map and pondered their course of action. There seemed only one solution to their predicament—they would have to fight their way out as they moved north for the Greek colony of Trapezus (Armenia today) and sanctuary. Of course, if they did that, it was a thousand-mile trek through mountainous, enemy territory. There was no other choice.

Thus began what became known as the March of the Ten Thousand, one of the greatest forced marches in history.

Xenophon and the new Greek high command led the mercenaries up into the mountains of Iraq. Marching through freakishly fluctuating weather conditions, everything from sandstorms to freezing cold, while traversing the treacherous mountain terrain, the Greeks fought a constant rear-guard action against the relentlessly pursuing Persian troops. At the end of five months of forced march and battle, six thousand Greeks survived and reached the safety of Trapezus. There the soldiers said goodbye and went back to their city-states.

The next time some of them saw each other, it was once again as combatants during subsequent Greek-against-Greek conflicts. But the achievement of Xenophon and his officers stands the test of history.

They managed to take once-hated enemies and make them into true professional soldiers who could put their personal feelings aside in pursuit of a common goal—escape from enemy country.

Mercenaries were making an impact on the history of the ancient world at a rapid rate. Less than a century after the March of the Ten Thousand, the Messanan Crisis occurred, the first time in recorded history that mercenaries controlled an entire city.

In 310 B.C.E., Agathocles, the Tyrant of Syracuse, was fighting a losing battle with Carthage. The greatest naval power of the Mediterranean, Carthage was located in North Africa, near modern-day Tunis. In desperation, the Tyrant launched a secret counterattack and took Carthage by surprise. The defeated Carthaginians would not mount another successful attack against him until 307 B.C.E. Even then, Agathocles hung on to power until he died in 288 B.C.E.

The Tyrant may have been dead, but he still had a large group of Campanian mercenaries under his banner. With no one to pay them, the Campanians found themselves unemployed. Rather than leave Sicily, the Campanians seized the Greek city of Messana on the northeast tip of the island. Naming themselves Mamertines (or "sons of Mars"), they became the law in the region and proceded to plunder the surrounding countryside.

Hiero, the new Tyrant of Syracuse, looked at the Mamertines as a threat: Messana was only miles from Syracuse. After securing his power base at home by marrying the daughter of one of the most influential Carthaginians, Hiero led his troops toward Messana. Within Hiero's army were other disaffected and mutinous mercenaries. Instead of putting his own people into the frontlines, Hiero had something else in mind.

Thrusting the mercenaries to the front as a shock column, he allowed them to be completely cut to pieces by the enemy, while he used the moment of their rout to effect a safe retreat for himself and the citizens into Syracuse. The Tyrant rid himself of many of his mutinous mercenaries without shedding a drop of Syracusian blood.

The Mamertines, of course, had not been defeated. They still controlled the city; they still pillaged the countryside. The Tyrant finally forced the Mamertines' hand in 264 B.C.E. by blockading the harbor. Realizing they were badly outnumbered, the Mamertines split into two parts.

"Some of them betook themselves to the protection of the Carthaginians and were for putting themselves and their citadel into their hands; while others set about sending an embassy to Rome to offer a surrender of their city, and to beg assistance on the ground of the ties of race which united them," Polybius, a contemporary historian, wrote.

It wasn't a bad idea. The Mamertines were actually Italian mercenaries, and it made sense to believe that the Romans, also Italian, would help them. To the Romans, it was clear that Carthage could be a deadly menace to the empire. Carthage was already "mistress of all the islands in the Sardinian and Tyrrhenian [Mediterranean] sea. If the Carthaginians became masters of Sicily too, they should find them very dangerous and formidable neighbours, surrounding them as they would on every side, and occupying a position which commanded all the coast of Italy. If the Mamertines did not obtain the assistance they asked for, the Carthaginians would very soon reduce Sicily," said Polybius.

The Romans debated over the crisis the mercenaries had brought about. They realized that if they "avail themselves of the voluntary offer of [the Mamertines], and become masters of it, they were certain before long to crush Syracuse also, since they were already lords of nearly the whole of the rest of Sicily."

The Roman Senate took its time debating what to do. While it did, the Syracusans and Carthaginians had some diplomatic conversations in which they realized that the Mamertines were their common enemy. There was no way they could let them control as important a port as Messana.

Carthaginian and Syracusans forces united and marched to Messana. Seeing the handwriting on the wall, the Mamertines surrendered. Quickly a Carthaginian garrison secured the city while its fleet sailed into Messanan Harbor. Carthage now controlled Messana with its ground troops and its fleet. Thus did Carthage become a clear danger to Rome.

Directly across a narrow channel of water from Messana was Italy. Worse, the exhibition of the Carthaginian fleet was not just a show of power. Those ships gave Carthage control over the Straits of Messana, an important waterway. As a result, the Roman Senate, although unwilling to start a war with Carthage, sent an expeditionary force to return control of Messana to the Mamertines. Among them were the slingers.

Roman representatives had traveled to the Balearic Islands, an archipelago in the Mediterranean. An autonmous community off the Spanish coast, the archipelago is composed of four islands: Majorca, Minorca, Ibiza, and Formentera. The Romans proceeded to sign up Balearic shepherds as mercenaries, whose prowess as slingshooters was legendary.

When they got to Messana, the Romans found the Carthaginians attacking the Mamertines. The Roman Consul Appiyus first attempted to "relieve the Mamertines from the contest altogether by sending embassies to both attacking forces." Neither Syracuse nor Carthage would entertain any Roman proposals. The Romans then arranged a parlay with the admiral of the Carthaginian fleet. The Romans betrayed the admiral and captured him. The Carthaginians were immediately forced to withdraw from Messana to save the admiral's life. The Romans, though, won a Pyrrhic victory because both Carthage and Syracuse declared war on Rome.

Not knowing which way to turn, or what to do, but clear that he had to do something, Appius made the decision to attack the Syracusans, who were more vulnerable. The Syracusans and Romans engaged in battle, and the Syracusans were defeated in no small measure because of the contributions of the Balaeircic slingshooters whose deadly projectiles killed many a foe. The Tyrant was forced to march home a defeated man. But for Rome and Carthage this was only the beginning.

The Mamertine Crisis provoked the Punic Wars, three wars fought between Carthage and Rome in the third to second centuries B.C.E. The First Punic War lasted from 264 to 241 B.C.E, the second from 218 to 202 B.C.E., and the third from 149 to 146 B.C.E. When the first one ended, it was really a draw with neither side winning, though the Carthaginians suffered the most terrible loss of all: The Romans destroyed their navy.

For the first time since the Carthaginians formed their trade empire, they had lost power over the waterways that were the lifeblood of their trading empire. Attempting to reassemble an army, they quickly realized that unlike Rome, they did not have a large enough civilian population to draw from. Carthage was forced to buy mercenaries, many of whom came from Spain.

The Carthaginian colony of Spain was commanded by Gen. Hamilcar Barca. After his assassination in 221 B.C.E, his 26-year-old son Hannibal was forced to take over. Hannibal was destined to become history's greatest leader of mercenaries. The first display of his later battlefield brilliance came when Hannibal immediately recognized his own weakness as a Carthaginian commander—he could not find among his own troops either the numbers nor the expertise to fight the Roman legions.

Hannibal proceded to "beef up" his army with Numidian cavalry from Africa and Spanish swordsmen who agreed to fight under the Carthaginian banner. Hannibal's newly hired mercenaries included everything from light infantry armed with swords and slings, to archers and mounted cavalry. Native Carthaginians were now in the minority.

Because they did not have the nationalistic fervor of the Carthaginians, Hannibal promised his mercenary army that whatever booty they obtained in battle would be divided evenly. That was enough to ensure their loyalty, at least until after the first battle. Hannibal was ready now to do the last thing the Romans expected. He devised a daring plan: to scale the Alps and attack the Romans on the other side. The Romans would never think anyone would be crazy enough to go over the mountains for a "backdoor" attack. But Hannibal had method to his madness.

Rome was the world's most ruthless conqueror and had made many enemies. Hannibal was counting on those ill feelings to swell his army, and he turned out to be right. As he traveled across southern Gaul and scaled the Alps with his pacyderms hauling the heavy freight, many local tribes flocked to his banner. Out of pure hate for Rome and the opportunity to make a profit, the Gauls joined up. Hannibal promised them, too, an equal share of the booty.

After scaling the Alps, Hannibal's mercenaries started pouring out of the mountains on the other side into the upper Po Valley. There they were confronted by Roman legions that they beat in two successive battles. Because of his success, Hannibal recruited even more mercenaries, this time the Celts of northern Italy.

The Celts were a wild and crazy people who preferred head-long charges rather than studied deception. Hannibal put them at the point, in the lead of his army. When they engaged the enemy, Hannibal used them as shock troops, the first to fall, thus preserving the lives of the Carthaginians in the rear.

CHAPTER 4: THE DISTANT PAST

Moving south, crossing over the Apennenes, Hannibal headed for the shore of Lake Trasimene. He was being chased by two Roman armies. The larger of the two, commanded by Flaminius, almost caught up, but every time it did, the Numidian cavalry and Spanish swordsmen kept them at bay.

Arriving at Lake Trasimene, Hannibal surveyed the ground. Looking up, he saw cliffs that sloped at a 45 degree angle over a narrow defile that ran in front of the lake. Properly exploited, this could be a tremendous tactical advantage in battle. He would also be able to stoke the fires of hate within the mercenaries, all of whom detested Rome with a passion. Every single one of them came from a country that had had some relations with Rome, and always to the negative, usually in body count.

Hannibal had his Numidian and Spanish mercenaries allow the Romans to get close enough before dark to see Hannibal enter into camp for the night on the far side of the road that ran by the lake. Then he had the mercenaries push the Romans back just as night fell. The Romans, Hannibal knew, would not attack at night, and so they would have all night to smell the blood of their enemies on the far side of the lake.

The trap had been baited.

Besides the element of surprise, Hannibal was counting on the Romans own superciliousness to defeat them. The Roman force that wanted to kill him was primarily composed of heavy infantry, similar to the Greek hoplites. Besides bearing heavy lances, they wore heavy body armor. Although their strength was superior to that of light infantry, they could not move easily. It was that lack of mobility that Hannibal hoped to exploit at the dawn. First, however, he had work to do.

Hannibal's light infantry blocked the road on the northeast side of the lake. His heavy Carthaginian and African infantry were placed at the eastern end of the defile. He positioned archers, slingshooters, and light infantry up on the steep, overhanging cliffs. Cavalry were sent west to deploy on the other side of the Roman camp. If they tried to escape, the cavalry would drive them forward into the trap.

The earth had cooled at night, and so the sun was fighting its way through early morning mists and failing to make much of a dent. It was a cool, gray dawn. At points along the defile below the mercenaries' position, all was shrouded in dense fog. But weather did not matter to the reckless

Roman commander Flaminius. As soon as gray appeared in the sky and surmounted black, he had his men marching forward with the intention of passing along the lake shore and trapping Hannihbal at his camp on the other side.

Visibility on the ground was not much better. Legionnaires could see maybe 50 feet in front of them. As for overhead, *what overhead?* At ground level, there was nothing but dense fog up there. Even had there not been, Flaminius probably wouldn't have deployed scouts up on the cliffs. Climbing them was difficult enough. Besides, Flaminius was convinced Hannibal still lay in camp on the other side of the lake.

The Romans marched forward, through the defile and then, at the far end of the defile, the mercenaries showed themselves. Hannibal ordered these troops forward to block the Roman advance. The mile-long column had to stop to engage them. That caused a chain reaction through the column, with one Roman legionnaire marching into the man in front as he attempted to put on the brakes.

Up on the cliffs, it was hard to tell what was happening on the ground below. The fog was still too thick to see much of anything. The mercenaries peered down into the murk, estimating when the entire army was in the defile by the sounds of their confused marching, the clanging of armor together as man stumbled into man and the occasional poking of a lance above the ground fog.

On the ground, Flaminius continued to move forward, thinking that if he broke through Hannibal's heavy infantry, he would just be able to waltz in and capture Hannibal himself. That's when the arrows started to fly. Back in the ranks man after man sank to the ground with arrows through the parts of their bodies that the armor did not protect.

Hannibal now unleashed his slingers and lancers.

As death literally rained down on them, the Romans broke ranks but were so tightly packed together in formation, they had nowhere to run. The Romans tried to place their shields over their heads to counter the stones, arrows, javelins, and other projectiles raining down on them. It didn't work; the thousands of mercenaries on the cliffs were overwhelming them.

Some Romans wheeled and if they were lucky enough before they were cut down, ran into the lake. Others sank to the bottom with arrows in their backs. Some of the Romans turned west and attempted to get out that way. They were met by Hannibal's Numidian, Celtic, and Spanish cavlary charging from the opposite direction and forcing them back into the defile.

The bloodthirsty Celt infantry took over, slashing their way into the Romans, who bore more of a resemblance to an undisciplined mob than a Roman legion. The Celt's packed them tighter and tighter until finally, they were back in the killing zone. Once again arrows, lances, stones, and all manner of detris and death rained down on the Romans. A group managed to get through the eastern end of the defile, only to be surrounded and forced into surrender the next day.

The Romans had finally had it; they had finally met their match in Hannibal. Some rid themselves of their weapons and attempted to surrender asking for that which they as Romans never supplied: mercy. That was a matter Hannibal wisely considered. When the fog finally lifted that morning, Hannibal on horseback gazed down on the defile from the cliff.

On the blood-soaked ground were more than 30,000 Roman dead and wounded. Hannibal's losses were relatively minimal: several thousand dead, many the barbarian Celts. It was now time for Hannibal to make good on his promise to his men to split the booty equally. There were the possessions the Roman legions carried into battle, including armor, weapons, and money to be split up. When it was, and his men were happy, Hannibal turned to the issue of his prisoners, 10,000 from the Roman army.

Making clear his contempt for Rome, he only kept as prisoner Roman citizens. The rest, who came from Roman-occupied provinces and territories, he set free with a clear message: He waged war against Rome and no one else. One can only imagine the joy the mercenaries felt as they finally, after ages of war with the mighty Roman Empire, beat them to a pulp.

Hannibal's brilliance that day shoots through time to the present, where his tactics are taught at major war colleges. But it is just as important to remember that a general is only as good as his men. Hannibal's use of light cavalry to defeat a more heavily armored foe could not have been achieved with anything but a professional army of mercenaries. Had Hannibal had to rely on the Carthaginians themselves for troops, the battle would surely have been lost.

After the Battle of Lake Trasimene, the armies of the Romans and the Carthaginians remained encamped facing each other, licking their respective wounds and plotting the other's demise. Hannibal had to refit and regroup his army. His supply lines stretched all the way back to Spain, so this took some time. For their part, the mercenaries wanted more action. They were more than willing to follow a commander who not only treated them well, but who also respected their abilities and accomplishments. In fact, Hannibal had so much confidence in their military training, he believed that they could withstand the worst that the Romans could throw against them.

History was fortunate that among the Romans, while they were fighting Hannibal, was Polybius, one of history's first great historians. He wrote about the Mamertines, the Punic Wars, and many other facets of Roman life in the ancient world.

Born in 200 B.C.E. in Greece, as a young man he was taken prisoner by the Romans during one of their many arch encounters with the Greeks. Politically aware, Polybius became friends with Scipio Aemilianus, the scion of one of Rome's most prominent families. Scipio found him good company, became Polybius's patron, and took him on military campaigns. The latter included the Third Punic War, which Polybius witnessed and wrote about first hand. In between the military campaigns, Scipio introduced the budding historian to Roman high society.

As an historian, Polybius wanted to explain how Rome was able over a period of many years to conquer the Greeks. What was it about Roman culture that was so superior? In his writing, Polybius said that Romans had moderation, integrity, valor, boldness, discipline, and frugality in much greater amounts than other peoples and nations. As a result, Rome could close ranks when faced with danger and act united against a common foe, which other civilizations, he claims, could not. But he was also a realist who wrote about real things.

Polybius readily admitted that Roman discipline was a key component of their ability to conquer. He cited such examples as executing a sentry for neglecting his duty, a soldier being beaten for throwing away his weapon, and beating a soldier for homosexuality. The historian thought it a sign of strength that Rome was willing to punish by decimation—the killing of every tenth man—any military unit that had displayed cowardice.

Polybius wrote:

> When the season for the new harvest was come, and making up his mind that it would be to his advantage to force the enemy by any possible means to give him battle, [Hannibal] occupied the citadel of a town called Cannae.

The town of Cannae from whence the Battle of Cannae took its name "had been reduced to ruins the year before: but the capture of its citadel and the material of war contained in it, caused great commotion in the Roman army; for it was not only the loss of the place and the stores in it that distressed them, but the fact also that it commanded the surrounding district."

The Romans were concerned that the mercenary army was gaining a foothold right in the middle of their empire. Deciding it was time to act, "the Senate passed a resolution that they should give the enemy battle." The Romans then put into the field 80,000 soldiers, more than it had ever dispatched to fight an opposing force.

The Roman army consisted of 55,000 heavy infantry; 9,000 light infantry; 5,000 cavalry; and 10,000 guarding their camp that could also employed, if necessary, as light infantry. The Carthaginian/mercenary force opposing them was 32,000 heavy infantry, 8,000 light infantry, and 10,000 cavalry. Comparatively, the Romans had an advantage of 30,000 men, which in the ancient world under any other commander but Hannibal would have meant certain defeat.

Hannibal studied the enemy's deployment. Following conventional battle wisdom of the era, the Romans split their cavalry for battle, positioning them on the flanks with the infantry in the center. In turn, the infantry had extra depth in the center column, providing what the Romans thought would be a more effective strike force. Hannibal realized this made them especially vulnerable to a strong frontal attack, coupled with a pincer movement, essentially surrounding the enemy from the flanks and driving them toward the middle.

Hannibal deceived the Romans by placing his slingers and spearmen in the center, directly in the front of the infantry. Behind them, where the Romans couldn't see, he positioned the wild Celts and Spanish swordsmen. On the right wing, he placed his Numidian cavalry, on the left his Celtic and Spanish heavy cavalry.

As they advanced toward the Romans on the open field, the moving Carthaginian column slowed just enough to allow the slingers and spearmen to turn and move toward the rear, where they would actually act as reserves. The Romans, still not suspecting anything amiss, attacked first, throwing their legions into the center of the Carthaginian line.

Had the Romans been thinking instead of preening, they would have wondered why it was so easy. The Numidian and Spanish mercenaries fell back readily. To the Romans this appeared to be due to their powerful drive. They were wrong; the troops had been told to retreat when pressed by the Romans.

The Roman cavalry on the right flank engaged the Spanish and Celtic heavy cavalry on the Carthaginian left. The Roman infantry kept up its drive into the Carthaginian lines. They appeared to be winning. Moving forward steadily, with the mercenaries withdrawing, the Romans suddenly became aware that light infantry on the Carthaginian side was moving around the Roman flanks to attack.

Hannibal's Celtic and Spanish heavy cavalry began driving the Roman cavalry back. Because the Roman infantry had been allowed by Hannibal to move so far forward, there now appeared a breach in the Roman line. Implementing the pincer, a large part of Hannibal's cavalry separated from the Carthaginian left wing and charged across the field toward the right wing, where it fell onto the rear of the Roman cavalry.

Looking down on the battlefield from a far-off hill, an observer would have seen the devastating effects of Hannibal's strategy. The Roman legions, shaped in a battle square, had been forced to halt on the open plain, surrounded by Hannibal's mercenaries. And now the killing began in earnest. Not one of the mercenaries had failed to feel the Roman lash at one time or another, either through battle, servitude, or economic control. Here was an opportunity to once and for all get revenge on the cruelest army on Earth.

Arrows, javelins, pikes, swords, slings, and every manner of inflicting death in battle known to humanity was thrown against the trapped Roman army. And as the Romans fell and continued to fall, even as Hannibal rode around the perimeter, shouting to his men to continue the slaughter, the Romans were herded into a smaller and smaller killing space. It was slaughter of the highest magnitude.

When Hannibal finally gave the order for his men to stop, in the killing field laid 48,000 bloody Roman corpses. Hannibal took 3,000 Romans prisoners and proceeded as he had before to grant instant freedom to non-Roman combatants. Only 15,000 escaped death or capture. Those who did were reviled by the Romans and placed in two special legions confined to Sicily for the remainder of the Second Punic War. As for Hannibal, he lost 6,000 men, mostly Spaniards and Gauls.

Members of the Roman legion wore gold rings that signified their rank. After the battle, Hannibal had his soldiers carefully strip the corpses of their gold rings. The rings were very carefully packed and sent back through the lines. Escorted by Hannibal's mercenaries, the ring caravan arrived back in Carthage weeks later. As instructed by Hannibal, the caravan went to the floor of the Carthaginian senate.

Watching carefully, the Carthaginian senators saw the thousands and thousands of rings emptied from the sacks out onto the Senate floor. The mound of gold grew and grew, brighter and higher, until it nearly topped the ceiling. The Carthaginians could only watch awestruck at their good fortune to have Hannibal as their commander, and mercenaries as their true fighting force.

Many military historians believe that the Battle of Cannae was an even greater victory for Hannibal than the Battle of Lake Trasimene. If it isn't, it's a close second. One thing is for certain: The Battle of Cannae was the greatest defeat the Roman Empire suffered in its entire history, inflicted as it was by a mercenary army.

The Roman general Scipio Africanus studied Hannibal's successes and determined to attack the source of his supplies and therefore cripple the replenishemnt of his forces in the field. Hannibal's supply lines stretched all the way back to Spain. Knowing this, Rome sent Scipio Aemilianus to Spain as proconsul. Rome thereafter refused to engage Hannibal in battle, even when Hannibal literally beat on the gates of Rome for a fight. Rome had finally realized that it had met its match. Instead, Scipio led a Roman army in conquering Spain, thus severing Hannibal's supply lines.

Hannibal's army was forced to withdraw from Roman soil because it lacked supplies. Scipio opened a second front and took the war to Carthage itself, threatening to lay siege to the city. Hannibal had already returned to defend Carthage. He knew the Romans outnumbered the Carthaginians and mercenaries combined. The Romans won siege warfare because of their force of numbers.

Forced into defeat, the Carthaginians sued for peace and finally admitted defeat. Part of the deal included the Romans taking over former Carthaginian holdings, including much of northern Africa, Spain, and the major islands in the western Mediterranean.

Knowing how dangerous Hannibal was, the Romans tried to capture him. Hannibal fled and lived in exile for a number of years before he poisoned himself in 183 B.C.E. rather than fall into Roman hands. He was 65 years old. The next time a general commanded a mercenary army as large as Hannibal's would not be until 2,187 years after his death, when Col. Tim Spicer took overall command of the security contractors in Iraq in 2004.

CHAPTER 5

THE ORIGINS OF THE MODERN CONTRACT WARRIOR

In the ancient world, the force of law was the force of arms. Whoever had the larger army could wreak revenge and justice on his enemies. As civilization evolved, and with it man's understanding of how to exploit his physical environment, new technology began to evolve that supplanted the old.

Metals could be made stronger through various physical processes; gunpowder was invented by combining various naturally occurring substances; and the English invented the longbow. As trade routes continued to evolve and civilization spread out across the world, possession of the technologies could give a civilization an advantage. But the weapons of the new technology were only as good as the hands that wielded them, and the more professional, the better. And in the ancient world, the professionals were the Thracians.

The Thracians were a warrior people whose ancestors lived on the Balkan Peninsula during the New Stone Age. Numbering more than a million on average during the first millennium B.C.E., spreading out all across eastern Europe, Africa, and the Middle East, they were daring and courageous, ideal characteristics for a warrior. This did not go unnoticed by the rest of the world that looked on the Thracians as the ideal mercenaries.

Seeing a market for their services, Thracian warriors readily hired themselves out to the highest bidder. Throughout the ancient world, Thracians became popularly known as mercenaries. They were the only people of the epoch to have this distinction. Frequently, the highest bidder for their services was Rome, which always knew a good soldier when it saw one.

It had been more than 160 years since Rome had endured its greatest defeat at the hands of Hannibal and his mercenaries. Rome had the hubris to believe that nothing close to that could ever happen again. Enter, Spartacus.

Most generations believe him to be a fictional character played by Kirk Douglas in the classic 1960 film. The reality is that Spartacus came from the province of Thrace. Freeborn, he, like his brethren, hired himself out as a mercenary and served with the Roman forces in Macedonia. But Spartacus came to hate his employers and deserted before his contract was up. The Romans outlawed him, then captured him and sold him into slavery. They made the mistake of sending him to Batiatus, the gladiator school in Capua. There he became the leader of his fellow slave gladiators. The Thracian decided he would not accept his fate as bait for the tigers in the Coliseum.

In 73 B.C.E., Spartacus led a rebellion of approximately 75 gladiator/slaves from the gladiator school. They escaped to Mount Vesuvius and camped at the base of the volcano. Rome soon sent a force of 3,000 raw recruits to bring Spartacus back. Escaping down the opposite side of the mountain, Spartacus and his men came up on the rear of the Romans and routed them. Seeing his success, 70,000 Roman slaves including Gaulic and German mercenaries, left their masters and flocked to his banner.

Spartacus's goal was freedom for his men. To achieve it, he planned to lead them over the Alps. Unfortunately, the Gauls and Germans had other ideas. They insisted on plunder and pillage, much to Spartacus's frustration. Many separated from Spartacus to indulge their baser instincts. They subsequently took the brunt of the force of two Roman legions that had been dispatched into the field to bring Spartacus to heel. They stopped

Spartacus's rebellious troops and then set their sites for the biggest prize of all.

When the Roman legions caught up with Spartacus, they made the mistake of engaging him. They were roundly defeated. Spartacus took 300 men as prisoners, but they didn't last long. As punishment for their defeat, the former gladiator had the men fight in pairs until they were all killed.

Spartacus fought more battles, each time defeating the Romans until, finally, he had a clear path to the Alps. And once again, the Gauls and Germans among his troops insisted on plunder rather than escape. Spartacus changed strategy, heading for southern Italy where he hoped to board ships for Sicily.

By the fall of 72 B.C.E., Spartacus's slave-led rebellion was at its height. More than 200,000 slaves and other followers had flocked to Spartacus's banner. Again the Romans sent legions into the field to attack Spartacus and again, the Thracian mercenary defeated them. The Romans then staged a successful counterattack. Spartacus lost the battle and headed to the south of Italy to lick his wounds and perhaps escape to Sicily. He contracted with Sicilian pirates for transport to Sicily, but at the last minute the Sicilians betrayed him; he was left with leaky boats. Spartacus had to once more fight the Romans on their home ground.

In 71 B.C.E., Spartacus started north. The remaining Gauls and Germans separated from him and were attacked by the Romans, who almost defeated them until Spartacus rescued them. Then, in a major battle in southern Italy, near the headwaters of the Siler River, the Romans finally defeated Spartacus and his army by sheer force of numbers.

Some historians believe that Spartacus died in this battle. There were so many gladiator/slave corpses that his body was never positively identified. About 5,000 slaves escaped from the battlefield and headed northward. Captured by Pompey's army north of Rome as they were marching back from Spain, they were returned to a life of servitude. It is much easier, then, to believe that Spartacus died nobly in battle rather than what happened next.

Crucifixion was the worst manner of execution in the ancient world. The Romans saved this heinous method of death for those who politically challenged the status quo. Spartacus and his men met these criteria. So the

Roman commander had the 6,000 surviving gladiators crucified, their crosses placed at methodical intervals on the Apian Way from Capua to Rome. Despite his death or perhaps because of it, either in battle or on the cross, the legend of Spartacus the Thracian mercenary and slave was formed and continues to this day.

In the twentieth century, actor Kirk Douglas's performance as Spartacus in the eponymous 1960 film defined the man and separated him from the myth. The way he did this was through one of history's epic moments of life imitating art.

Douglas, who was also producing the film, hired blacklisted writer Dalton Trumbo to write the script. The practice at the time was to use a pseudonym for a blacklisted writer. When the film was completed and it was time to submit the names that would appear in the film's credits, Douglas decided to defy the blacklist. He submitted Trumbo under his own name. In so doing, Douglas was taking the chance that he would be blacklisted himself. He was betting everything on his own integrity.

Kirk Douglas won. Not only didn't the government or the movie industry come after him, Douglas single-handedly broke the blacklist. Into the movie business pored thousands of people branded Communists by the House Un-American Activities Committee and unable to work in the movie and TV business.

Surely Spartacus would have been proud of the man who not only played him, but became him, if even for a short while.

To the Greatest Generation, Cleopatra was actress Claudette Colbert, who played the Egyptian queen in a 1934 film. To the Woodstock Generation, Cleopatra was actress Elizabeth Taylor, who played her in the 1964 role. What has gotten lost in the emphasis on her romances with Caesar and Antony is that Cleopatra was actually the name of each of the seven queens of ancient Egypt.

The one known best today, the queen actually played by the latter two actresses, is Cleopatra VII, who was born in 69 B.C.E. Eighteen years later in 51 B.C.E., her father died and left his kingdom to Cleopatra and her younger brother Ptolemy XIII. To take sole power, Cleopatra needed to marry or take a consort. She therefore took her own brother Ptolemy XIII as her consort and ascended to the throne.

In 48 B.C.E., Cleopatra presaged the trouble she would later bring to the Roman Empire when she met with the sons of the Roman governor of Syria. They had a request from their father for Cleopatra to send soldiers to fight in their conflict with the Parthians. Cleopatra's reply was to have her mercenaries kill the Roman governor's sons.

Rome was infuriated, of course, but more so the Egyptians, who did not want to bring the Roman wrath down on their already shaky kingdom. Cleopatra was then overthrown in favor of her younger brother. She would, of course, rise from the ashes to once again rule Egypt as well as have affairs with Marc Antony and Julius Caesar.

And never were her mercenaries far from her side.

Across the world from the Roman Empire, in Asia, the T'ang Dynasty ruled China. In 755 C.E., An Lushan revolted against the T'ang in one of the dynasty's strongest tests of power.

An Lushan was a general of "non-Chinese origin," probably from Turkey, who served in the Chinese army. Although Western texts have been careful not to identify him as a mercenary, his foreign origins and faithful, well-paid service to the T'ang Dynasty make it clear that he was.

The T'ang knew talent when they saw it. An Lushan quickly rose through the ranks of the Chinese army in the 740s. He became a military governor and one of the favorites of Emperor Xuanzong. What An Lushan's exact motivations were to turn on his employers is hard to say, but turn he did in 755.

An Lushan led his troops to the eastern capital city of Luoyang and conquered it. While his men celebrated, An Lushan proclaimed himself emperor. It took only another six months before An Lushan had also seized the western capital of Chang'an. At that point, An Lushan had become more than a pain in the neck to the T'angs; he was threatening their very existence.

Therefore it comes as no surprise that in 757 An Lushan was murdered. But the T'angs did not completely put down the rebellion until 763. As a result, the T'ang Dynasty was forever weakened by its struggles with An Lushan and had to cope thereafter with recalcitrant warlords. Those warlords were aided in their wars by the modern invention of gunpowder.

The invention of gunpowder forever changed warfare. Its effects are still being felt to the present day when gunpowder or some derivative is still the primary explosive propellant used by the military and mercenaries alike.

In the eighth century C.E., Chinese scientists, who were vastly superior to any in the world at that time, discovered that an explosive mixture was produced when you combined sulfur, charcoal, and saltpeter (potassium nitrate) in very specific amounts. The Chinese military immediately had the scientists produce primitive rockets and guns using bamboo tubes. The latter made sturdy launch platforms for whatever projectiles were inserted into the hollow interior. Centuries later, the invention made its way to the European battlefields where it ignited history.

The story of El Cid, the Spanish knight who fought against Moorish influence in Spain, has become legend over the centuries. However, like much in myth, there is just as much falsity as there is truth.

One in a long line of Spanish mercenaries, what really distinguished El Cid, and made him one of history's greatest mercenaries, were his origins, education, and connection to the Spanish throne. El Cid was born Rodrigo Diaz in 1045 into a politically explosive situation.

When King Ferdinand I died in 1065, he divided his dominions between his three sons, Sancho, Alfonso, and Garcia, and his two daughters, Elvira and Urraca. In turn, they promised not to argue among themselves and not to protest the division. Sancho, though, had other ideas. He thought he should have inherited everything because he was the oldest and decided to find a way to get what he wanted.

At the time, Rodrigo was at Sancho's court. Out of gratitude for services Rodrigo's father had afforded him, Sancho mentored Rodrigo. He made sure that the boy got as good an education, including military training, as any noble. Later as an adult, Rodrigo distinguished himself on the battlefield when Sancho warred with Aragon. It was during this campaign that Rodrigo was made *alferez*, standard bearer or commander in chief, of the king's troops.

After the war with Aragon ended, Sancho turned, in 1070, to gaining possession of his siblings' kingdoms. He added Leon and Galicia to his holdings, but not without a vicious fight in which Rodrigo's bravery on the battlefield each time turned the battle in Sancho's favor. Together they took the city of Toro, which belonged to his sister Elvira. Then Pancho laid siege to the city of Zamora, owned by his sister Urraca. It turned out to be one city too many when one of his sister's soldiers slew him before the gates of the city.

Brother Alfonso, exiled to the Moorish city of Toledo, quickly came home to claim Sancho's dominions and succeeded him on the throne as King Alfonso VI. According to the Catholic Encyclopedia, "The story is told, though not on the best historical authority, that the Castilians refused Alfonso their allegiance until he had sworn that he had no hand in his brother's death, and that, as none of the nobles was willing to administer the oath for fear of offending him, Rodrigo did so at Santa Gadea before the assembled nobility."

If the story is true, it could account for the bad feeling Alfonso subsequently showed toward Rodrigo that would, ironically, seal Rodrigo's fate as El Cid the mercenary. But that bad feeling did not manifest itself immediately. Instead, Alfonso adopted the Sicilian manner of dealing with an enemy by keeping him closer than his friends; Alphonso gave him his niece Jimena in marriage in 1074.

Not long after, Rodrigo was sent by his patron to collect tribute from the king of Seville, Alfonso's vassal. Seville's king gave the money over readily, and Rodrigo returned with it immediately. Upon his return, Alphonso claimed that Rodrigo had pocketed part of the money for himself. The charge, of course, was trumped up, but it served its purpose. Finally showing his hate, Alfonso banished Rodrigo from his dominions in 1076. Thus began Rodrigo Diaz's new career as a soldier of fortune.

Over time, poets would write of his chivalrous exploits. Rodrigo was hailed as the champion of Christian Spain against her Moorish invaders. The truth was different. With no way to make a living save as the soldier he had trained to be, Rodrigo offered his services and those of his followers to one petty tyrant after another. He didn't care whether his employer was Christian or Moor. He fought hard for the highest bidder and gained a reputation as a successful, honest, ruthless mercenary who was christened El Cid by the Moors.

So successful was Rodrigo that Alphonso put his hate aside and later hired him to fight Yusuf, the founder of Morocco. Unfortunately, he didn't arrive fast enough to please the king's sycophants, who told the king he should be punished for his insolence. Once again, Alphonso gave in to his baser instincts. He took from Rodrigo all of his possessions, then imprisoned his wife and children. Adding insult to injury, he again banished Rodrigo from his dominions.

With no options, Rodrigo once again turned to the mercenary's trade, looting, plundering, and fighting for whoever would give him a contract. After completing one of his contracts, he heard that the Moors had not only driven the Christians from Valenci, they had taken possession of the city. Seeing a golden opportunity for money and power, determined to recapture it and become lord of that capital, Rodrigo used the kind of siege warfare that had made Rome so successful in battle. Capturing Valenci in 1094, he took the throne.

Rodrigo had finally achieved power, money, prestige, and position. His two daughters married Spanish nobility, the Infante of Navarre and the Count of Barcelona respectively. When he died five years later, he was buried in Valenci, where he lay until the Moors conquered the city in the next century and Rodrigo's remains were transferred to the monastery of San Pedro de Cardena near Burgos, where they now rest.

During the Italian Renaissance, from the late thirteenth century until the French invaded in the 1490s, the Italian *condottieri* served their Italian masters.

The country was broken up into a series of feuding city-states that warred continually with one another. Pisa and Florence, Milan, Genoa, whatever armies these feudal states possessed, were readily supplemented with outside forces that became known as the condottieri.

Condottieri were mercenary captains hired by these feudal states to wage war under their banner. It was strictly business. The condottieri served their feudal princes for a price. The only allegiance they offered was that usually contained within the written contract that every condottieri signed. In the contract was a provision in which they swore *not* to serve an opposition leader or leaders for a set period of time after they leave their prince's employ.

The name *condottieri* derives from the contract, or *condotta*, that each condottieri was required to sign that included the term of employment, how much they would be paid, and the number of men the captain would command. Drawn up by lawyers, condotta were broken down into three separate types.

- *Condotta a soldo disteso.* A contract between a mercenary and a native-born Italian general, under whose command the condottieri served.

- *Condotta a mezzo soldo.* A contract between mercenary and an Italian ruler in which the condottieri was only answerable to his employer, but no other soldier. Under this contract, the mercenary was also free to plunder the enemy's land at his own convenience.

- *Condotta in aspetto.* In time of peace, a retainer paid to the condottieri in return for their loyalty to their employer.

Regardless of the type of condotta signed, the condottieri would also have to agree to another common feature of these contracts: the no-compete clause. There was no way that a ruler wanted his condottieri, when their term was up, to defect to the other side. Therefore, the condotta usually contained a provision that bound the condottieri to their employer after their term of employment was up.

During this "rest period," the condottieri could not work for the opposition. But after this time period was up, they could do as they pleased. It therefore fell to the Italian princes to keep the length of the no-competition clause as long as possible. Because this was all a business arrangement, the condottieri even got paid for this "rest period."

Niccola Machiavelli, the Italian political philosopher, historian, writer, statesman, and diplomat, distrusted and despised the condottieri. In *The Prince* (1513), his classic treatise on political corruption and machination, he writes:

> I want to show more clearly what unhappy results follow the use of mercenaries. Mercenary commanders are either skilled in warfare or they are not; if they are you cannot trust them because they are anxious to advance their own greatness by coercing you, their

employer, or by coercing your enemies more than you intended. If however the commander is lacking in prowess, as often as not he brings about your ruin … Experience has shown that only princes and armed republics achieve solid success, and that mercenaries bring nothing but loss.

As history has shown, Machiavelli was wrong. But because he writes so brilliantly in other parts of his book, his opinions about mercenaries went unchallenged and became part of popular belief.

The Battle of Crécy took place on August 26, 1346, near Crécy in northern France. The defining battle of the Hundred Years' War, it was at Crécy that warfare changed for the first time in more than 500 years. The condottierie from Genoa, serving with the French army, were the first victims of that change.

What had happened was that Edward III invaded France in the summer of 1346. Attacking and sacking Caen, he made it almost to the gates of Paris before a counterattack forced a retreat to the coast, where the French ruler, Philip VI, caught up with him. Philip had approximately 35,000 men under his command, Edward 12,000, giving the French ruler an almost 3 to 1 advantage. Edward, however, was a masterful tactician. He arranged his forces in three groups.

The first was under the command of his son, the Black Prince. One of the Black Prince's soldiers was 26-year-old, John Hawkwood, who would later make a name for himself as the Renaissance's preeminent mercenary. The second unit was under the command of the Earl of Northampton, and the third, Edward commanded himself.

Philip was impetuous. So were his troops, who craved battle. Unfortunately, his noblemen felt differently; they wanted to wait until the morrow to attack, when they would have the best chance of winning. Philip might have agreed, but as soon as he came in sight of the English, his blood began to boil. Reason deserted him, replaced with hatred for the foul-smelling English.

The French began their attack late in the day. The shock troops in the frontline were condottieri from Genoa. They marched headlong into English longbow attacks. When one thinks of a longbow now, it is usually in concert with memories of one version of the Robin Hood legend or another. In all of them, Robin and his men were longbow marksmen. That legend is based on fact.

The longbow was a weapon that, indeed, originated in the forests of England. Up to the moment of its popular introduction at Crécy, knights in battle felt confident in their chain mail armor that covered most of their bodies and that of their horses. There were, of course, vulnerable points— in the ribs where the armor had seams, in the neck, in unprotected parts of the leg, and, of course, the head. It had to be a well-aimed blow to really get under the chain mail and do damage. The longbow changed that.

Five to six feet in length, with a pull over 100 pounds, the English long-bow took years to master. Unlike conventional crossbows, it had a greater trajectory. A skilled bowman was capable of unleashing six arrows a minute, with as much force as any hand-operated projectile then known on the planet, and from a greater distance than the longbow with the same kind of accuracy. That's why the longbow archer did not have to aim for the exposed crease in the armor. Instead, with that kind of power, his arrow could penetrate chain mail and go inches into the body underneath.

The condottieri at Crécy went down en masse, arrows penetrating not only their body armor but their horses as well. This infuriated the French, who started to kill their own mercenaries out in front to get to the English. The French attacked repeatedly, some historians claiming as many as 15 times, and each time the longbows cut the French down. Finally, Philip withdrew. By that time, it was dark.

The English did not realize the extent of their victory until morning when they gazed out on the battlefield and saw thousands of arrow-riddled corpses. Edward and his army continued their march to the sea and even-tually captured Calais.

The Treaty of Bretigny in 1360 stopped the Hundred Years' War tem-porarily while the respective dukes and barons and kings of each country tried diplomacy. Good businessmen, they saw no reason to maintain a wartime army while they talked, so many soldiers on both sides were let go pending future hostilities.

What does an unemployed soldier with no other prospects do when let go by his native country? He seeks the company of those like himself, skilled in battle but also unemployed. Bretons, Gascons, English, and

Welsh soldiers let go after the treaty's signing drifted south down the Rhone Valley. They made their way to Italy where they formed the White Company.

The White Company, named after their shiny, almost white armor, received employment in Pisa, at war with Florence. Rather than engage the Florentines immediately, the White Company tarried in Pisa, enjoying the wine, women, and song. It was in Pisa, where the White Company was living on its reputation as the brave soldiers of Crécy, that John Hawkwood found them.

Sir John Hawkwood was born to a prominent working-class family in Colchester, England in 1320. An adventurous youth, he fought with the Black Prince as one of his soldiers at Crécy. After the Treaty of Bretigny he, too, found himself unemployed. He drifted across Europe and one day found himself in Pisa just as the White Company arrived.

Hawkwood's father had been a tanner and a good businessman; part of that business acumen had rubbed off on the son. Realizing that the White Company had a contract with Pisa that they needed to honor, he cut himself in on the action. Hawkwood organized the White Company into a tight military unit. Because of his obvious leadership skills and charisma, the men of the White Company made him their captain-general.

In 1364, Hawkwood and the White Company moved against Florence. Facing them was a band of German mercenaries that Florence had hired to do its fighting, under the command of Henri de Montfort, another well-known mercenary of the era. Outnumbered, the White Company was beaten by Montfort and the Germans during the early battles of the campaign. The Pisans hired 3,000 more mercenaries, including Germans and Swiss, under the command of another mercenary general, Annechin Bongarden.

Reconnoitering the terrain in and around Florence, Hawkwood noticed that Florence was a walled city outside of which were newer homes. These villas did not have the protection of walls and instead relied on man-made barricades made from overturned carts, lumber, and anything else that could be scrapped together and heaped in a pile. Hawkwood decided to postpone his counterattack until May Day. In the Middle Ages, this was a festival that celebrated the beginning of the summer season. Sticking to his word, Hawkwood attacked on May 1, 1364. The engagement became known as the Battle of Florence.

The White Company's archers let loose a barrage of arrows that forced the defenders at the barricades to retreat. Storming them, the Hawkwood-led White Company moved against the walls of Florence itself, only to encounter an old foe: the Genoese crossbowmen. The latter had acquitted themselves well at Crécy, but this was another fight on different ground.

Whereas Crécy had been an open-field contest where the longbow, with its greater range, was clearly superior to the crossbow, things were different at Florence. Now the Genoese were firing down at their enemies, and therefore had the advantage. This was a war of snipers. When the arrow was in the slot and ready to fire, the crossbow was easier to maneuver and fire.

While the archers dueled, Hawkwood and the rest of the White Company postured in front of the gates of Florence. To attack was suicide, Hawkwood knew, because to gain the gates was one thing; to maintain safety inside the city of the enemy, and live long enough to plunder and loot while the enemy closed around you, was indeed a fairy tale. Instead, Hawkwood showed his might without so much as one swing of the sword, letting the Florentines know what was in store for them if they came out of hiding.

Like Hannibal, Hawkwood knew his men expected plunder. At the end of the day, the White Company withdrew to divide up the day's spoils. There was gold and silver taken from the villas they had sacked; armor, leather, food, wine, anything that wasn't screwed down, and perhaps some that was, the White Company pilfered. The men were delighted and held a feast and partied long into the night. The wine had piqued Hawkwood's playful side. Playing a practical joke on the Florentines, he sent drummers and trumpeters to Florence's southeast gate. The terrified Florentines ran around in a panic when they heard the drummers and trumpeters signaling for the attack. Eventually realizing Hawkwood was just playing a joke, the Florentines hurled insults from the parapets; the White Company good-naturedly took up the verbal harangue.

History does not record what kind of hangover the White Company had the next day, but it must have been a good one. Still, these were fighting men used to violence and debauchery, and Hawkwood knew he could rely on them to finish the job. He insisted that they fulfill their end of the contract and defeat the Florentines.

Hawkwood realized that if the Florentines could be fooled by his drunken revelry, what if he feigned real attacks? During the following week, until May 8, Hawkwood set about harassing the Florentines with what would later be called psychological warfare. He had his men begin surprise attacks at all hours of the day, and then suddenly withdraw, leaving the Florentines in a tizzy.

The Florentines had a businesslike response. Their counterattack was to simply buy the mercenaries off the field. Annechin Bongarden negotiated a deal for his German and Swiss mercenaries. His men divided up 35,000 florins while he pocketed 9,000 for himself. Their pockets bulging with money, they left the battle to Hawkwood and his White Company. Hawkwood, though, refused to be bought and thus established his legend. Countering the prevailing wisdom that mercenaries had no scruples and would turn sides for a penny, Hawkwood told the Florentines that he was under contract to the Pisans and that he would honor it. If, however, a truce could be negotiated, that would be acceptable. If not, Hawkwood and his men were ready to begin battle again. That's what Hawkwood thought. And hoped. But he was soon to find out that few men, mercenaries or otherwise, had his scruples. The previous commander of the White Company, a German mercenary named Albert Sterz, managed to convince, quite readily, the majority of the White Company to accept the Florentine offer of 100,000 florins. The German mercenaries agreed to switch sides. That left Hawkwood and only 800 men of virtue still in the field, fighting to honor the Pisan contract.

Realizing he could not win with just the 800, Hawkwood told the Florentines that he would be back and retreated to try and gather more troops. Soon after, the Florentine mercenaries took the battle right to the gates of Pisa, where Hawkwood was forced into a defensive action. With his 800, Hawkwood defended Pisa adequately enough that the city could sue for peace and get favorable terms. That left Hawkwood out of the money because he and his men had still not been paid.

Yet, as far as his reputation was concerned, Hawkwood's would now precede him. In a profession never known for its honesty and virtue,

Hawkwood had shown both in refusing the Florentines generous offer and sticking with his conscience. Hawkwood and his men were finally paid when Bernabo Visconti, Milan's strongman, fronted the money for the Pisans to pay off. But Pisa was smart enough to keep Hawkwood in their employ. As part of his settlement, and some additional monies, Hawkwood agreed to stay on as a Pisan hired general for an indeterminate period. His services were immediately loaned out to the Visconti, who was badly in need of them.

Charles IV was the ruler of the Holy Roman Empire. He expected northern Italy to owe him its allegiance, although few of his predecessors had actually set about making this a functioning reality. The prevailing feeling among the empire's aristocracy had been to look the other way and let Italy do what it wanted as long as it didn't stand in opposition.

Deciding to change the status quo, Charles invaded Italy with a huge force and demanded that the Italian city-states and their rulers swear undying allegiance. The Visconti of Milan would not bow down to Charles and so decided to fight. His secret weapon was John Hawkwood.

The Visconti's idea was to stop Charles before he could gain a foothold. Knowing that Charles's army was descending from the Alps and would have to cross the Po River, Visconti figured that if he could build fortifications at Borgoforto, across the river from Milan, it would make it difficult for Charles to ford it. Unfortunately, the Visconti had sent German and Burgundian mercenaries to do the job. They immediately began arguing among themselves and couldn't get any real work done until Hawkwood showed up.

Hawkwood organized the troops into cohesive units. He built up the fortifications that the Visconti had requested. Advance scouts told Hawkwood that Charles had mercenaries from Poland, Serbian Bohemia, and other countries serving with him in an exceptionally large force. A huge battle was imminent.

Charles, whom Hawkwood had last seen as a combatant at Crécy, came down the Po, stationing his massive army between Borgoforto and Mantua. He attempted to outflank Hawkwood, whose back was to the river, by sailing rafts down it and coming up from behind. Hawkwood could abandon his position and retreat into Milan, but if he did that he could be caught with his pants down in the middle of the water. Surveying the terrain, Hawkwood realized there was a better way.

Charles had camped downstream. He was directly next to a raging river whose flow was controlled by a series of old dikes. When it was dark and the enemy was thoroughly encamped, Hawkwood led a party of White Company mercenaries downstream. There, under the cover of darkness, working stealthily, the men pounded through the earthen works of the dikes. Finally they created a small breach that with thousands of tons of water pressure behind it, would only get worse. Hawkwood, probably with a smile, withdrew to watch the fun.

Sometime in the middle of the night, the breach opened wide and the dike fell apart. The Po River began to flow through the hole with the force of a cannonball. Charles awakened to the screams of sentries trying unsuccessfully to shout arnings above the sound of the roaring torrent.

As Hawkwood watched from the safety of the far bank of the Po, the wall of water slammed into the Holy Roman Emperor's camp. Knights in armor were thrown about like pebbles in the current. Swords, bows, arrows, slings, everything, washed away or sunk to the bottom of the river. Horses struggled in the waters, some drowning. Soldiers tried to get as many horses as possible to higher ground; they knew if they didn't they would have to walk instead of ride from the battlefield.

By the time the waters had receded, the army of Charles IV had been routed by the dual forces of nature and Hawkwood's strategy. They escaped to the city of Manua and there sought dry succor. But Charles IV had had it. He made peace with the Visconti and then rode south. Hawkwood would go on to serve the Visconti for the next 10 years, during which time he also briefly served at the behest of Pope Gregory XI.

The pope turned out to be Hawkwood's most penurious and dishonest employer, cheating him out of his pay constantly. Hawkwood actually had to kidnap and hold ransom a cardinal. Pope Gregory still refused to pay. Hawkwood finally let him go when the pope paid him off with a group of rundown estates that Hawkwood was forced to restore with money out of his own pocket.

It was while working for the pope that Hawkwood was manipulated by the papacy into almost abandoning his principals.

The pope had sent Hawkwood to Cesena to be paid for his services by a papal legate there, Clement IV, who had already convinced the Cesenians to surrender with little resistance. Upon his arrival, Hawkwood was informed by the legate that Cesena was to be punished because they were not loyal to the pope. Punishment, in this case, meant death, specifically a massacre of unarmed men, women, and children in the city. Hawkwood protested. His protests were met when Clement IV unleashed the pope's merciless Breton mercenaries on the city. The Bretons began massacring people from one end of the city to the other.

Once again, Hawkwood would not give up his honor. He and his men managed to spirit more than 1,000 women out of the city into the countryside, where he set them free. Hawkwood had had it with the papacy. He told Gregory he was quitting and left his employ.

Clement IV would go on to become pope. As for Hawkwood, he returned to Milan. In 1377, he married one of the illegitimate daughters of the Visconti and settled down to have a family and live the life of a country gentleman on his estates.

Hawkwood established a network of informers throughout Italy. These informers enabled Hawkwood to keep track of anyone plotting against him, and to reach the ripe old age of 60 in 1387 with his scalp and all his organs intact. It was through his intelligence network that Hawkwood discovered a major plot against the government of Florence and determined to make an honest profit on the information.

An envoy from Florence came to Milan to meet the mercenary captain-general who gave the Florentine a choice. If he paid 50,000 florins, he would reveal all the details of the plot, save the identities of six of the traitors. It was thought that these might be some of Hawkwood's former associates. On the other hand, if the Florentine paid 20,000 florins, Hawkwood would give him enough information to prevent assassination of Florence's strongmen without revealing names.

Over the course of the next few days, Hawkwood and the Florentine negotiated. In the end, the Florentine drove a hard bargain that Hawkwood agreed to: 12,000 florins for enough details, sans the conspirators' names, to foil the plot. Hawkwood had his informer brought before the Florentine. They were in a darkened room that served to preserve the man's identity. The informer gave the Florentine enough information to foil the plot against the rulers of Florence. Grateful to the old mercenary they gave him a contract to provide military services.

Had this been any other time, Hawkwood might have stayed where he was. But he had not lived to the ripe old age of 66 without knowing when the wolves were yapping at his heels. Indeed, within the walls of Milan, trouble was afoot. As soon as Hawkwood left to assume his new commission, he realized how right he was.

The Visconti, Hawkwood's father-in-law, was removed by his nephew. The Visconti then died of what his family said was natural causes, but which they suspected was actually foul play, perhaps poisoning. One of Hawkwood's brothers-in-law was also the victim of a plot, but Hawkwood found out from his informers in time and rescued him.

Sir John Hawkwood had come out of retirement for one last, great battle. He was 67 years old, an ancient age when the average was closer to 30, let alone for a man who had led his entire life by the strength of his sword and an unerring sense of when to use guile to achieve his ends.

Marching out of Florence with 500 mercenaries of various nationalities, plus his prized 600 mounted English longbowmen, Hawkwood was offered command of the Paduan army, which he accepted. That brought his regular troop strength up to 8,000. From his informers, Hawkwood knew that Verona would be putting at least twice that many men into the field.

Hawkwood had initially conceived of the idea of besieging Verona, and sent his troops forward with that intention. Changing his mind because he was concerned about overextending his supply lines, Hawkwood retreated. Smelling blood, the forces of Verona poured out of their city. There were 2,500 crossbowmen, 9,000 soldiers, thousands of militiamen, and even a special piece of artillery the Prince of Verona had reserved for the occasion.

The only way to compare this invention to anything close to modern day would be the Gatling gun of the nineteenth century, a rotating series of barrels that fired hundreds of rounds of ammunition. The Prince had actually tried to improve on an invention that hadn't even been invented yet: his gun had 144 barrels! They were placed across a frame so what Hawkwood and his men would see were 12 evenly spaced rows of gun barrels, piled 12 high. It was a massive gun and it depended for its success on three ifs: If it could be wheeled to the frontline; if the fuse could be lit; and, most important, if it worked, the wholesale slaughter resulting would be the greatest in history.

Hawkwood had seen just about everything. He wasn't surprised that Verona was throwing such a weapon into the mix. Evidently Hawkwood intuitively had little or no confidence in the gun's success because he began mapping out a campaign that never once considered the gun's impact.

Surveying the ground he found himself on, Hawkwood noticed that in front of his position was a long irrigation ditch. Beyond that were fields made soggy by the spring rains. On Hawkwood's right flank was a canal. His back was to the river. The old mercenary prepared his troops for battle by making sure they had plenty to eat and sleep. He was up before dawn and began showing his general's art for the last time. He placed his men in front of the irrigation ditch. Broken into three battalions in the front, three in the second, and one in the rear, he was ready.

When the Paduans on the march got to the irrigation ditch, they broke front ranks and like worker bees began constructing bundles of wood. They would be tossed into the irrigation ditch to make it a dryer crossing. Their work lasted until late afternoon, when finally they were ready to attack. The wooden bundles were thrown en masse into the ditch and spears lowered; the Paduan army charged.

As the battle progressed, Hawkwood saw that his own line was about to break. He got on his horse and rode into the fray, followed by mounted archers and cavalry. He outflanked the Veronians and let loose his archers. As the English archers continued to move in closer to the Veronians, their longbow-launched arrows had as much velocity as a bullet. Arrow shafts buried deep into flesh, and men screamed out in agony and death.

Hawkwood led the charge into the Veronian ranks. He had already instilled fear through his flanking maneuver. Now, seeing Hawkwood himself leading the charge, the Veronians panicked and broke ranks. They fled over the marshy ground with Hawkwood and his mercenaries in hot pursuit. They gave no quarter and killed all they came upon. As darkness fell, Hawkwood gave the cease-fire.

Assessing the situation, Hawkwood noted that all the Veronian generals were dead, wounded, or prisoners. In addition, 800 Veronian troops were dead and 6,000 taken prisoner. Hawkwood lost less than 100 men. It had been a very good battle.

Afterward Hawkwood let loose the dogs, and his men swarmed over the Veronian booty, which included the 144-barrel gun found stuck in the mud. It had proven too heavy to cart and had therefore been abandoned.

In medieval Italy, nothing was what it seemed.

Verona and Padua were actually minor players in the major conflicts that existed between Florence, Milan, and Venice. Both cities eventually fell to Milan. But by that time, Hawkwood had quit the field for good.

For the rest of his life, Hawkwood would remain in Florence's employ. The grateful city gave him honorary citizenship, the highest honor it could bestow on a foreign-born knight. Full citizenship would be bestowed, however, on Hawkwood's heirs and family for all time.

In 1394, at the age of 74, Hawkwood sold off part of his real estate holdings and decided to return to mother England. Before he could fulfill this last wish, he died from a stroke on March 16, 1394. While Florence offered Hawkwood's family a state funeral with full honors, England decided to chime in. King Richard II requested that Hawkwood's body be put on ice and returned to England for final burial. The Florentines could not turn down such a request, and so Hawkwood, in death, made one final trip across the English Channel.

Hawkwood now rests in the parish church of his youth. He may have missed out on seeing the colonization of much of the world by the European powers, but there were others who followed in his profession, particularly in the eighteenth century, when opportunities abounded.

During the eighteenth century, the European powers expanded their spheres of influence to India. European mercenaries came to India to see whether they could earn money by fighting for one kingdom or another. The European mercenaries, with their warrior training and expertise, became highly valued within Indian society. The mercenaries, in turn, saw a place where they could grasp and gain power. Some conquered kingdoms, others ruled provinces, and still others fought for princes. One of the most powerful was the Dutch mercenary Willem Hessing.

Born in 1739, Hessing served as a mercenary in Ceylon in 1752. After returning home to the Netherlands for awhile, he went to India, where he really made his mark. He served two different kingdoms, finally settling on Scindia. By 1799, when he was 57 years old, Hessing had risen to command the Agra Fort and the city of Agra, which the fort guarded. Hessing died four years later at his post, a revered man in Indian society.

Beginning with the *samurai* or "knights" who served twelfth-century Japanese royalty, the samurai were a warrior caste who served their master. On occasion, samurai renounced their clan or were discharged by their lord. Sometimes they were uprooted by the death of their master. When that happened, the samurai became a *Ronin*, or wandering samurai.

Ronin were outcasts in their own society. Some became farmers, some monks, but more often than not Ronin turned to the one thing they really knew: soldiering. Roaming the countryside, Ronin sold their services to the highest bidder. Perhaps the most famous in Japanese history are the Forty-Seven Ronin.

In 1703, the Forty-Seven Ronin avenged the disgrace and ritual suicide (*seppuku*) of their master, Lord Asano, by assassinating Lord Kira, the man responsible for their master's death. When they were finished, the Forty-Seven committed seppuku themselves. The Forty-Seven Ronin have since been honored as cultural heroes, their loyalty celebrated in Japanese art and literature.

A mere 73 years later, another group of mercenaries would become as reviled as the Forty-Seven Ronin are revered. If history has ever cast a group of mercenaries as the "bad guys," it would have to be the Hessians. The Hessians are best known to Americans as the infamous German mercenaries who fought for the British during the Revolutionary War. But in Europe, they are better known as, literally, the Continent's most respected hired guns, born out of an extraordinary geographical mosaic.

Across northern Germany—east to west, but not in a straight unbroken line—stretched the territories of the king of Prussia. The other distinct area was the Austrian hereditary dominions. Smaller in size, they occupied Germany's southeastern corner.

"Beyond the boundaries of these two great powers, all is confusion," says Edward J. Lowell. Lowell's 1884 book, *Hessians and the Other German Auxiliaries of Great Britain in the Revolutionary War*, was written barely 100 years after the actual historical events.

"There were nearly three hundred sovereignties in Germany, besides over fourteen hundred estates of Imperial Knights, holding immediately of the empire, and having many rights of sovereignty. Some of these three hundred states were not larger than townships in New England, many of them not larger than American counties. Nor was each of them compact in itself, for one dominion was often composed of several detached parcels of territory," Lowell continues.

The feudal princes who ruled these German kingdoms maintained armies to protect their interests, armies that were not always engaged in indigenous military activities. In the twelfth century, some members of German royalty adopted the term *landgrave* to separate themselves from the inferior counts under their jurisdiction. By the eighteenth century, the rank of landgrave signified a German nobleman equivalent to a British earl or French count.

Like many of the feudal German rulers, the landgraves of Hesse-Cassel made money in between wars by renting their troops out to the highest bidder. Among the Germans, the landgraves were the most successful at it. They maintained professional armies like well-trained gladiators to go and do battle honorably with anyone put in front of them. These mercenaries simply had to knock down those who rose against them and move on to collect their pay.

Lowell notes that one of the first recorded instances of the landgraves' mercenary transactions was in 1687, when Hesse-Cassel rented 1,000 soldiers to the Venetians fighting against the Turks. In 1706, 11,500 Hessian troops were sent to Italy. Patriotism and politics played no part in it; it was simply a business arrangement all the way around.

The landgraves' best customer was the British crown. Through most of the eighteenth century, the ever-pragmatic English employed the Hessians to help fight its wars. And the landgraves had no problem either with pitting Hessian against Hessian and making a profit on the deaths of their own soldiers.

In 1743, at the Battle of Dettingen, the Pragmatic army, commanded by England's King George II and comprising British, Hanoverians, and Austrians, fought against the French army of Emperor Charles VI. On each side were 6,000 Hessians the landgraves had thoughtfully rented out.

Born in 1716, Frederick II, landgrave of Hesse-Cassel, was the Catholic ruler of a Protestant country. His first wife was an English princess, King George II's daughter. When Frederick converted to Catholicism, the princess separated from the landgrave and went to Hanau with their young son. That left Frederick to enjoy a bachelor's total debauchery.

He took a "cast-off mistress of the duc de Boullion," and then openly cheated on her. Later he married again. By the end of his life, he had more than 100 children. In 1776 when the English colonists were revolting, Frederick was still in his prime at 60 and ready to make a profit. He began negotiating with King George III. Although much has been written about his mental illness, when he was not ill, George was a smart ruler, smart enough to get the Hessians to fight for Britain against the American rebels of the thirteen colonies. If the Americans were so intent on their freedom from England, they would have to go through the Hessians to achieve it.

As negotiations progressed, one thing soon became clear—both sides were anxious to reach a deal. England needed the men to supplement their own army. The previous year, after the Revolutionary War began, the British had tried to get 30,000 mercenaries from Russia and failed. They tried buying the services of Scots mercenaries, but that didn't work either. The British turned to the Hessians, the Continent's best.

"The Landgrave of Hesse-Cassel was to furnish twelve thousand men, completely equipped, and with artillery if desired. He was to be paid levy-money at £7 4s. [7 pounds, 4 shillings] for every man. His subsidy, however, was larger in proportion, amounting to 450,000 crowns banco, or £108,281 5s. per annum, to be continued for one year after the actual return of the troops to Hesse," Lowell writes in *The Hessians and the Other German Auxiliaries of Great Britain in the Revolutionary War*.

In other words, Frederick II had struck a good bargain for himself. The treaty with Hesse-Cassel, dated January 15, 1776, specifies that the Hessians were to serve together under their own general, unless "reasons of war should require them to be separated." Their sick were to stay in the care of their surgeons. They were to be treated as well as the king's troops.

Under subsequent agreements the landgrave furnished an additional 2,992 troops; other German feudal princes supplied a total of 13,075. But because the majority of the German mercenaries, 14,992, came from

Hesse-Cassel, all German mercenaries came to be known as *Hessians*. The Hessians would eventually make up about one third of the forces the British arrayed against the Americans.

Each Hessian was armed with smoothbore musket and a full complement of powder and musket balls. Artillery included 3-pound guns. Sent to America on British warships, about 18,000 Hessians arrived at Staten Island on August 15, 1776. The Hessians faced battle immediately, against Gen. George Washington's Continental army during the Battle of Long Island.

When they landed at Staten Island, the Hessians were immediately impressed by what they perceived as the colonists' wealth. Coming from a poor, feudal society, to them the colonists' comfortable houses surrounded by cultivated gardens and orchards bespoke wealth. Under German standards, the colonists lived like German country gentlemen. The Hessians were astonished that they had therefore decided to revolt against the British. Did they really think they could do so much better for themselves?

Across the Verrazano Narrows, in the Brooklyn section of Long Island, General Washington had his army defending the coastline. The Hessians were determined to attack his positions. To get there, the Hessians had to march across Staten Island and then take boats across the narrows into Brooklyn.

Marching on the roads, the Hessians maintained strict discipline and close ranks. Sometimes they stopped for rest or sleep in homes still occupied by those colonists who had stayed despite the Hessians advance. The Americans were angry and obviously put out by the Hessians, but had to capitulate given that Washington's troops were not there to defend them. The Hessians, in turn, did not take advantage of their superior military might. They took provisions as they needed, but no more. Still, looking around at so much wealth, the Hessians wondered how they could get some of it for themselves.

Fording the narrows on August 22, 1776, the British and Hessians made a beachhead on the other side. Washington, defending the coast, was quickly pushed back inland. An anonymous Hessian mercenary kept a diary that was published in 1777. In it, the Hessian describes the action a few days later on August 27:

Our colonel had been promised that he should make the first attack, and he heard that the English were to attack today, but he had not received any orders either last evening or this morning. About ten o'clock we were all put under arms, and about eleven we were all in order of battle.

On our left and right the English advanced on the flanks, and destroyed those that we drove back. On the left wing, where I commanded the advanced guards (thirty chasseurs and twenty grenadiers), stood Colonel Block, with his battalion. Behind me I had Captain Mallet with one company, as a reserve. In the centre Captain von Wrede attacked, and had the battalion von Minnigerode behind him. On the right Captain Lory pressed on, supported by the three remaining companies of Linsig's battalion.

During this first, crucial part of the Battle of Long Island that the Hessian soldier describes, the Hessians formed the center of the British force. The right, under Clinton and Lord Percy, with Sir William Howe, had begun its advance early in the morning and had already succeeded in turning the left flank of the American position.

When General von Heister heard the British cannon pounding away on the right, he ordered his Hessians to advance. Seeing the implacable Hessians advancing with muskets firing and rapiers flashing in the sun, the Americans retreated. A few fled so fast that they fell in Gowanus Creek and drowned. Two whole American regiments would have been captured were it not for the quick thinking and bravery of General Stirling, who covered the American retreat with the firepower of five companies of Marylanders.

The Hessians waded into the fight against Stirling and his men.

"My chasseurs were so eager that I had hardly got into the wood when I found myself alone with my command," the Hessians soldier continues. "I came into the middle of the rebel camp, where they still were, saw on my left their great camp, on my right a fortification, and fifty or sixty men were forming in column before me. But we left them no time and beat them completely. Many were shot and still more taken prisoners. I did not lose a single man, so much had the rebels come to be afraid of the chasseurs.

"Things went equally well on the other wing. We lost few men, and, except one chasseur, who was shot in the village, not a single one was killed. On the other hand, we made on the first day more than five hundred prisoners, among whom were General Stirling."

A new American line formed on the Brooklyn Heights, where Howe decided to lay siege to the Americans, surrounding their position. But Washington was too wiley for Howe. In a dense fog formed at dusk on August 29, Washington had a group of Marblehead, Massachusetts fishermen turned soldiers ferry the troops across the East River to Manhattan and safety. By the time the sun burned off the fog in the morning, the British were astonished to find empty trenches that used to be occupied by 8,000 armed men who had vanished!

"One thing I must remark in favor of the Hessians and that is, that our people who have been prisoners generally agree that they received much kinder treatment from them than from the British officers and soldiers," Washington later wrote.

But the Hessians had nothing but contempt for the Americans who had fled rather than fight.

"The enemy [are a] frightful people who deserve pity rather than fear. It always takes them a quarter of an hour to load, and meanwhile they feel our balls and bayonets," wrote Colonel von Heeringen, commanding a Hessian regiment.

For the next couple of months, the British kept the Americans on the run, the Hessians leading the drive against the rebels throughout present-day New York City. Finally, in full retreat against the overwhelming force, Washington led his men across the Hudson to Fort Lee, New Jersey. Washington continued his retreat south, intent upon keeping the remnants of his army intact, and with good reason: Washington lost approximately 2,000 men in the battle, roughly one quarter of his fighting force. As for the Hessians and British, they had used their overwhelming numbers to good effect. They lost a total of only 400 men.

Pursued by the dogged mercenaries and their British employers, Washington and his army finally crossed the Delaware River in December 1776, and settled into winter quarters at Valley Forge. The Hessian garrison took up position at Trenton in New Jersey.

When the winter was over, hostilities would begin again, and this time, the Hessians were expected to crush the Continental army with their superior numbers and superb military training. Among the Hessians, Col. Johann Rall was the most accomplished mercenary.

A dashing officer of the old school, Rall enjoyed kicking the rebels out of New York and into the Pennsylvania countryside. That's where they belonged; to him, they were rabble. Victory against the colonists had come easy; he did not take them seriously as a fighting force. Previously Rall had volunteered to fight with the Russians against the Turks.

Rall never believed to his dying day that the Americans could seriously attack a Hessian brigade. When he later commanded the Hessian garrison at Trenton, he told a British subordinate, "Earthworks! Let them come on! We'll meet them with the bayonet." When the same officer asked him to have some shoes sent from New York for the troops, Rall replied that the request was nonsense. He and his brigade would run barefoot over the frozen ground to Philadelphia, kill Adams and Jefferson and Franklin and all the rest, and litter the city with their Continental carcasses.

It was this appetite for battle that made General Howe confident enough to retreat for the winter while leaving Cornwallis in command of the British and Hessians in New Jersey. Cornwallis meanwhile did not stop the impatient Hessians from looting and plundering the New Jersey population. He believed it prevented desertions.

As for the Hessians, before they left Hesse-Cassel, they were told that they could come to America to establish their own private fortunes. To the Hessians, plunder was a matter of principle. They had withheld that privilege on Staten Island but had been in America long enough to have their greedier instincts massaged by the abundance around them.

What the Hessians did not know was that by December 14, Washington was already thinking about a surprise move to route the enemy and dramatically improve morale of his beleaguered men. It became of utmost importance to strike a blow before the enemy should be ready to move, and before the last day of December, when the term of service of many of his men would expire.

Washington believed that the Hessian garrison at Trenton was vulnerable. The last thing they would expect would be a surprise assault by the

Americans. And just to make certain that the Hessians were even more overconfident than usual, he decided to begin his assault on Christmas night, December 25, 1776. While the Hessians celebrated, Washington had the Marblehead fishermen row his soldiers across the icy Delaware. Once on the other side, they marched toward Trenton in a blinding snowstorm.

The rough weather delayed Washington's attack until daybreak. The Hessians, recovering from the late-night Christmas celebrations, were still in their bunks, their perimeter lightly guarded by sleepy sentries. The two columns of Washington's force, led by Maj. Gen. Nathaniel Greene and Maj. George Sullivan, quickly overran the Hessian outposts on the north and west of Trenton.

After a night of debauchery, Rall was sleeping it off when his adjutant woke him from a deep sleep. Hanging out his window in a nightshirt Rall shouted down, "What's the matter?" His adjutant asked him in disbelief had he not heard the firing. Meanwhile Washington's soldiers, pressing the advantage, were invading the town, and the surprised mercenaries didn't know what to do. Their commander had told them not to worry; the colonists were nothing. Now what?

Part of Rall's regiment succeeded in forming up. Soon after, Rall, in stiff, pressed uniform, appeared at their head on horseback. Rall ordered his men to advance, but the order was given in a dazed, albeit drunken manner, and his men hesitated. Rall took some men and tried to repulse the enemy on the outskirts of town, but to no avail. Then he tried to fight his way back into the town, to obtain his plunder and escape.

Soldiers fired from every doorway, outbuilding, roof, and alleyway. The Hessians tried to fire back, but their powder was still wet from the storm; the Americans had made sure, under Washington's orders, that theirs was dry. The Americans formed up into ranks and charged the Hessians, who were finally forced to retreat.

When the smoke cleared, most of the Hessians mercenaries laid their weapons on the ground and surrendered. Only 162 escaped. In his first report to the Continental Congress regarding the Battle of Trenton, Washington wrote the number of those who surrendered at 23 officers and 886 men. A few more were afterward found in Trenton, raising this number to about 1,000.

"Colonel Rahl [sic], the commanding officer, and seven others," Washington wrote, "were found wounded in the town. I do not exactly know how many were killed; but I fancy not above twenty or thirty; as they never made any regular stand. Our loss is very trifling indeed, only two officers and one or two privates wounded."

Washington knew that his forces were still smaller in number to that of the English and the Hessians to the south of him. Discretion was the better part of valor. That same evening, December 26, he retired across the Delaware with the prisoners and artillery he had taken, leaving in his wake the colonists' greatest victory against a mercenary army.

In Germany, the landgrave of Hesse-Cassel was furious. How could his crack troops be beaten by the American rabble? The only thing possible, he believed, was for all discipline to have broken down. The landgrave ordered an investigation to be made as soon as the officers, who were then prisoners in American hands, were exchanged. He threatened to hold accountable to his justice those guilty of misconduct.

The landgrave swore that no Hesse-Cassel regiment defeated by the rebels would have their colors restored unless they took an equal number of American lives. But that was not to be. The Battle of Trenton proved that the Hessians were not invulnerable. The sight of them on the battlefield literally seemed to inspire the Americans. Although Hessians fought in every campaign during the Revolutionary War, after 1777, the British mainly used them as garrison troops.

The numbers totaled up after the war indicated that 5,754 Hessians died from battlefield wounds, infection, and illness. In addition, 5,000 succumbed to American propaganda to desert, and joined the indigenous German American population in the United States and Canada. The majority, 17,313 Hessians, returned to Germany. For the services of the German mercenaries, the British crown paid more than £1,770,000 sterling, a fortune in those days; the equivalent of a tidy $275 billion today.

As for the landgraves' mercenary practices, they would soon end.

In 1872, Otto von Bismarck unified Germany. The feudal system collapsed. The power of the landgraves and their aristocratic cousins was broken. The Hessians were absorbed into a larger, nationalistic German army that culminated in the twentieth century with the rise of the National Socialist Party.

The eighteenth century would yield yet another popular revolt, this time in France. In the middle of it was the Swiss Guard. Any history of mercenaries that does not at least mention their honorable service during the French Revolution to King Louis XVI does them an injustice.

Trained in the Prussian military tradition, with superb skills as soldiers—proficiency in hand-to-hand combat, logistical planning, and most of all, loyalty—the Swiss Guard began in 1505 as servants to the pope. Pope Julius II first used them as bodyguards, beginning a tradition that has lasted to this day. Wearing Renaissance helmets and blue, red, and yellow tunics, the colors of the Medici family, the men of the Swiss Guard have always stood out in bold fashion.

The very idea of a foreign mercenary protecting an indigenous ruler goes back to the ancient world. Whether it is the Egyptians, Greeks, or Romans, it always paid to have a foreigner to guard royalty, a *loyal* foreigner who would not be subject to internal pressures. None were more respected and trusted than the Swiss Guard.

Occasionally the Swiss Guard would work for other European powers, including France. In 1792, the Swiss Guard found themselves protecting the Bourbon dynasty. France was bursting at the seams, ready any day to overthrow the crown and establish a democracy. Events in America, where the previous 16 years had seen the establishment of the new United States of America, had fueled the French freedom movement. Thomas Jefferson would later write that the tree of liberty needed to be refreshed occasionally by the blood of tyrants. And he meant that literally. Eventually all that stood between the Bourbons and death by the Paris mob was the Swiss Guard.

On the night of August 9, 1792, the French Revolution was in full swing when a French mob got ready to storm the Tuilleries. The latter was the palace where King Louis XVI and his family had taken refuge since the

Swiss Guard had spirited him away from Versailles. That was after the mob tried to get him the first time.

For the Swiss Guard, it was simply a matter of honor. They had been paid to do a job and they were not going to desert simply because the odds had turned against them. A few did cave in to their baser impulses and did indeed cross lines to save their skins, but approximately 750 Swiss Guard decided to stay and fulfill their contract to the king. Before the battle, King Louis addressed the troops and rallied them. They cheered for their employer, who promptly deserted the palace and took refuge in the nearby Assembly chamber out of harm's way.

From the castle's parapets, the Swiss Guard turned their muskets on the approaching mob and fired, bringing down a hundred men. Within the mob were trained soldiers fighting for the revolution. They organized into battalions and began a concerted assault. Using 50 artillery pieces, they lobbed cannon balls at the castle. Infantry were lined up 10 deep and fired continuous musket volleys at the castle. Despite the odds, the Swiss Guard held out. Their deadly aim kept back the steadily encroaching mob from storming the gates. In the end, they defeated themselves, or rather Louis had.

The king had neglected to supply his own guard enough ammunition to defend themselves. They did not have enough ammunition to hold out against a numerically superior force. If they'd had what they needed, there is good reason to believe the Swiss Guard could have repelled the mob with their superior fighting abilities. But that was not to be.

When they ran out of ammunition, the Swiss Guard was reduced to fighting with their bayonets. By that time, the crowd had broken through the perimeter defense, and the Swiss had been forced to retreat. But even as they did, they managed to keep the enemy at bay with deft use of the sharp weapons that left many of the mob killed or wounded.

Realizing that all was lost without a full retreat away from the palace, a detachment of Swiss Guard was sent to the Assembly, where they sought out the king. They found him cowering in a stenographer's booth. For Louis, all was lost, though he wouldn't acknowledge it. Instead, he stubbornly refused to leave, and then ordered the Swiss Guard to surrender.

Some historians believe he did this to save their lives, others that it was an offering to the mob to save himself. For the Swiss, though, it made no difference. The only thing they had to decide was whether to follow their employer's last order.

Well paid and well taken care of, the Swiss Guard knew they were about to die. There was no way to reason with the mob; they knew that. Death was imminent. The only question was whether to disobey their employer's final order and go out fighting or give up their arms as a way of showing honor and obeisance to their employer.

A few chose to strip off their uniforms and try to melt into the crowd. Others chose a last armed stand before the crowd got to them. But the vast majority did lay down their arms and surrender. The mob fell upon them. Like soldier ants, they picked away at their bodies until finally, body parts littered Paris's streets. Their beaten, bludgeoned, lanced, vivisected corpses were finally consigned to a huge bonfire the mob lit in front of the palace.

The death of the Swiss Guard that day represents not the greatest mercenary defeat in history. Rather, within the mercenary culture, it is a celebration of the mercenary ethic. Today the Swiss Guard continues their 600-year tradition of guarding the pope.

The pope has a Swiss Guard of 100, including 23 noncommissioned officers and 1 chaplain. Recruits are Swiss Roman Catholics, single, under 30 years of age, and at least 5'8" tall. Each man must have received his initial military training in the Swiss army and must produce certificates from religious and civil authorities attesting to his upstanding character.

Each man signs up for a 2-year "hitch," with a maximum renewable option of 25 years at their employer's request. Residing during their service in a Vatican City barracks, their training includes hand-to-hand combat, marksmanship, and lessons in the Italian language and the culture of the Vatican. After their first year of service, they take an exam to show their proficiency in each area.

CHAPTER 6

THE MODERN AGE OF WAR FOR HIRE

By the end of the eighteenth century, Spain and Portugal had divided up South America, with each having various areas of the continent under its control. Inspired by the example of the United States, and then the French, South America soon experienced its own independence movements. Oppressed for generations by their European brothers and sisters, the South Americans yearned for freedom, too.

Simon Bolivar, the great South American revolutionary, had looked on from afar during the recently completed Napoleonic wars. Many of the Irish who had fought during those struggles were now at liberty and without contracts. Bolivar had his European agents recruit them for service in his army of liberation. In August 1819, 1,000 Irish mercenaries made the 4,500-mile voyage from Dublin to Venezuela, and Bolivar immediately placed them into the line. They helped Bolivar liberate Venezuela, Columbia, and Ecuador from the Europeans.

Bolivar's respect for the Irish mercenaries was so high that Arthur Sandes, from County Kerry, rose to become brigadier general and later had a street named after him in the city of Cuenca, Ecuador. Another mercenary, Lt. Col. William Ferguson from County Antrim, died while defending Bolivar from assassins. But it was a third Irish mercenary, County Cork's Daniel Florence O'Leary, who would make the most lasting impact on South American history by writing it.

O'Leary, who served as Bolivar's *aide de camp*, later published a 32-volume set of his memoirs that details the history of the South American independence movement from an eyewitness perspective. O'Leary's writings have become de rigueur for any historian studying the South American independence period and the life of Bolivar.

O'Leary, the historian/mercenary, died in 1854, after which he was honored with a bust of his likeness overlooking a plaza in Bogotá. In 1882, the Venezuelan government disinterred his bones and transferred them to the National Pantheon, where they lie today near Bolivar's.

Irish immigrants in the tens of thousands arrived in America throughout the 1830s and 1840s. They were escaping famine and lack of economic opportunity in their own country and hoping for better in America. Many found it; many didn't. But among the ones for whom the argument can go either way are the Irish immigrants who, seeing no other way to support themselves, enlisted in the U.S. Army.

The U.S. Army had not progressed much since the revolutionary period. Weaponry was still confined to the musket, bayonet, and cannon. Frontal attacks, where row upon row of infantry were sent against entrenched artillery and infantry, was still the norm. What was different was the U.S. Cavalry.

Since cavalry had gained popularity fighting the Indians, cavalrymen had become more proficient at mounted attack just to survive. Fresh off the boat from Ireland, many of the Irish were more than willing to fight for their new country by climbing back in the saddle … again. Like the native-born Americans, the Irish came from an agrarian society, where horsemanship was common. Some had fought the British who, it seemed, had occupied their country forever. To a starving soldier, three squares and regular monthly pay in service of the United States was infinitely preferable to starvation or a boring clerk's job in a dry goods store. Enlisting in the Army, the Irish immigrants would soon have their hands full when their adopted country decided to go to war against Mexico.

By 1846, America was enveloped in its mantle of Manifest Destiny. Believing itself God-driven to own part of the northern part of Mexico—the reason being that it happened to have the misfortune to abut the southern border of the United States—the United States declared war. In turn, the Mexican government decided to use propaganda to help itself win.

The Mexican government was well aware of the kind of prejudice Irish Catholic immigrants faced when they came to the United States. Nativists such as William "Bill the Butcher" Cutting, who controlled New York's legendary Five Points, believed that their Irish brethren were lower-class rabble. Simply because their families had arrived generations earlier, Cutting and the Nativists wanted nothing to do with their Irish brothers.

The Protestants, who were a majority in all facets of American society, also despised the Catholics. There was regular animosity between the two religious groups that played itself out in social and class differences, with the Irish Catholic soldiers someplace at the bottom of the heap. Knowing all this, when the Mexican-American War started, the Mexican government urged Catholic immigrants in the U.S. Army to desert and fight for them. The Mexicans concocted a helluva "pitch."

They told the Catholics in the U.S. Army that the United States intended to destroy Catholicism in Mexico. Leave the United States and flock to their banner, the Mexicans said, to a Catholic country that the Protestant Americans were attempting to destroy. The Mexicans hoped to convince (eventually) some 3,000 soldiers in the U.S. Army to change sides.

It's not good for soldiers to have a conscience about whom they kill. Once they do, their effectiveness as soldiers decreases dramatically. That's why military training in all ages focuses on dehumanizing the enemy, making him easier to kill. Unfortunately, John Riley was one of those soldiers who did have a conscience and couldn't look the other way when he believed his religion was being trampled on by his adopted country.

A devout Irish Catholic, Riley couldn't make sense of the United States attacking, for no reason except an expansion of its boundaries, a Catholic country. It bothered him deeply. A lieutenant who served in Company K of the Fifth U.S. Infantry, Riley was one of those who listened to the Mexican propaganda machine and deserted.

In November 1846, Gen. Antonio López de Santa Anna, the same Santa Anna who laid siege to the Alamo 10 years earlier, put Riley and his Irish compadres into a special unit that Riley named the Saint Patrick Brigade. The Mexicans hailed them as the San Patricios. Reilly's San Patricios became mercenaries. For them, it was a very good deal.

In the U.S. Army, they were the frequent butt of jokes by the Protestants who ruled the military. The Catholic Mexicans treated them like heroes. Turning sides, the San Patricios were happy to fight under the Mexican flag. During the next two years, the San Patricios saw action at Monterrey, Saltillo, and Buena Vista. They fought the Americans with so much verve and professionalism, their resourcefulness became legendary in their adopted country. Then came the Battle of Churubusco in August 1847.

Santa Anna had decided to make a stand against the advancing American army at Churubusco. He fortified a strategic bridge with two 100-man companies of San Patricios and a battery of five cannons. Behind them was a convent, where they could take shelter if forced to retreat. Riley outfitted its sturdy walls with cannon, too, just in case.

American forces advanced from the south and the west and suffered heavy casualties under the guns of the San Patricios. But ammunition began to run low under the continued American advance. Santa Anna ordered one company of San Patricios into the convent, along with another infantry company and a wagon of ammunition.

Inside the convent, the San Patricios fired their cannon at the Americans who continued their bloody frontal assault. The second company of San Patricios was also forced to retreat into the convent. By sheer force of numbers, the Americans finally succeeded in breaching the walls until, finally, the San Patricios surrendered.

During the Battle of Churubusco, 83 San Patricios were captured, and the U.S. Army subsequently court-martialed 72 of them for desertion. Of those court-martialed, 50 were found guilty and sentenced to be hanged, because they had deserted after the war started. Another 16 were flogged and branded on their cheeks with the letter "D" for deserter.

John Riley, who deserted before the war, could not be hanged. Instead, he received 50 lashes and the letter "D" branded on his cheek. Held prisoner in Mexico City, he wrote to a friend back in Michigan, "Be not deceived by a nation that is at war with Mexico, for a friendlier and more hospitable people than the Mexicans there exists not on the face of the earth."

After the war ended, the surviving San Patricios stayed on with their Mexican employer. They hired themselves out as gunfighters, patrolling the more rural sections of the country, killing bandits and Indians endangering the encroaching civilization. Politics, though, was an even better way of making money, or at least political alliances.

It therefore comes as no surprise that the San Patricios became involved in the country's internal politics until a presidential order of President José Joaquin de Herrera stopped them. He dissolved the San Patricios in 1848. The survivors, who could not return to the United States and had no desire to return to Ireland's poverty, stayed on in Mexico, where they are celebrated to the present day for their exploits on behalf of the Mexican state.

Were it not for the efforts of a late-twentieth-century writer named Milt Gelman, the story of the San Patricios might have been lost to history. Gelman, a screenwriter, was obsessed by the Irish battalion. He wrote a screenplay about it that wasn't produced until after his death. The film, called *One Man's Hero*, starred Tom Berringer as Riley. Once again, newspapers around the country carried stories about the legendary battalion.

During the second half of the nineteenth century, Egypt had aspirations to empire building in Africa. Toward this end, the Egyptians negotiated contracts with former officers of the Confederate States of America to help staff their army. Egypt then went to war against Ethiopia, which climaxed with the Battle of Gura. The Confederates who fought during the battle of Gura left behind their notes of what happened there, which have since been combined with other eyewitness accounts:

On November 6th and 7th, the Egyptians were attacked by the Ethiopian army, (which was estimated at 60,000 men) and sur-rounded. Most of the Ethiopians were armed with firearms, and although they had only one field-gun, it is said to have had no effect in deciding the action. The accounts of the American officers are silent on the point; but it is said that [their Egyptian employers] insisted on the ramps of the trenches which had been erected being razed, so that the artillery could have a clear zone of fire.

The gunners and infantry were enfiladed by the Ethiopians from higher ground, and the slaughter was so great that several regiments became completely demoralized. Those officers, who attempted to rally their men and the survivors, were accused generally of joining in the panic, and of cowardice in the field.

The Egyptians were defeated. The Confederates, though, had been defeated a decade before but refused to accept it. This time, they had no choice. But unlike most mercenaries, they had no nation to go back to. Making matters more difficult for gainful, mercenary employment, by the end of the nineteenth century, the tactics of war had finally changed. The frontal assaults and unimaginative battlefield tactics that had changed so little since the Roman phalanxes had evolved into a more intelligent way of making war.

The elements of surprise and intelligence in battlefield maneuvers that sought to conserve rather than diminish troops, to become superior over the enemy in the air and on sea as well as land, this all changed the way wars were fought over the next 50 years.

Mercenaries knew they had to change their fighting methods. They began to adapt their skills to the changing technologies. No longer just proficient with handheld weapons, mercenaries became experts with all manner of killing devices, from airplanes to dynamite. But what doesn't change during this era is the unusual ability of the mercenary in combat to improvise and his inherent cockiness. No matter the enemy's advantage, the mercenary is better trained and better suited to not only do battle but do it well.

The Battle of San Juan Hill is rarely if ever thought of as a victory achieved with the help of mercenaries. Like most things in his celebrated life, President Theodore "TR" Roosevelt's involvement cast a giant shadow over this fabled fight that served to obscure the true nature of the combatants.

By 1898, war with Spain was inevitable. The United States had fulfilled its Manifest Destiny of spreading from the Atlantic to the Pacific coast. It was time to look elsewhere for a burgeoning superpower. The country was fortunate to have Theodore Roosevelt, TR to his friends, as the chief advocate of imperialism.

Like Jefferson before him, he saw war as sometimes inevitable. But unlike Jefferson, TR saw war as a chance to win glory and a true test of manhood.

America had strong business interests in Cuba and the Philippines. Both happened to be Spanish possessions. It was a perfect opportunity to start a war. Somebody did when the United States battleship *Maine* was blown up in Havana Harbor on February 15, 1898. Spain always denied taking part in the sabotage, but that made no difference. President McKinley declared war on Spain on April 25, and the battle was on.

Serving as the Navy under-secretary, TR had deliberately built up the nation's fleet to make it into a world power. When the war started, TR resigned his job to form a volunteer unit of elite cavalrymen to fight the Spanish in Cuba. Their official designation was the First United States Volunteer Cavalry. They became better known as the Rough Riders.

No clear record exists as to how many foreign mercenaries joined the Rough Riders and fought with TR. Anecdotal evidence, though, abounds of English and German mercenaries who became Rough Riders. Certainly there are many "foreign" names among the discharge records of many of the Rough Riders in the National Archives, although it is not clear how many were not U.S. citizens. What is not in dispute is that Congress made it easy to recruit mercenaries for this particular war.

What had happened was that with war declared, McKinley suddenly realized he didn't have the troops to fight in two theaters of operation. In fact, that had never been done. He needed troops in the Pacific and he needed them in the Caribbean. To help resolve the problem, on April 22, 1898, Congress passed a law allowing for the formation of three regiments of volunteer cavalry. Mercenaries could be recruited.

When TR was putting together his regiment, advertisements went out all over the world that he was looking for men. TR's reputation preceded him, and the Rough Riders got many more volunteers than they needed. In the end, the unit consisted of "twelve hundred as separate, varied, mixed, distinct, grotesque, and peculiar types of men as perhaps were ever assembled in one bunch in all the history of man and one—possibly two—Democrats," one of the Rough Riders later wrote.

The first American troops to land in Cuba were U.S. Marines (landing on June 10). The Rough Riders left Florida on the 14th, arriving in Cuba on the 22nd. The regiment's first battle came soon enough, at Las Guasimas on June 24, when TR's men, trained in and proficient with Krag-Jörgensen carbines, defeated a detachment of the Spanish army that was holding back the invaders' penetration to the interior of the island.

Falling back, the Spaniards regrouped on San Juan Hill, which they proceeded to fortify. On July 1, 1898, TR led the Rough Riders on the famous charge up that famous hill. Supported by the 9th and 10th U.S. Cavalry, the 1st U.S. Volunteer Cavalry seized the Spanish fortifications at the top, pushing the Spaniards back yet again into Santiago de Cuba.

The attack cost 1,000 American and mercenary casualties. No attempt was made to separate out the figures for the mercenaries because to TR, they were all part of his unit. TR knew good soldiers when he saw them. He didn't care where they came from as long as they could fight and fight well.

By July 16, the Spanish had had enough and surrendered. TR and the Rough Riders went back to the United States, where they became legend, and TR became vice president and then president after McKinley's assassination.

Since 1661, the East Indian Company maintained a private militia of two regiments of seasoned mercenaries: the 102nd Royal European Madras Fusiliers and the 103rd Bombay Fusiliers. In 1881, the East Indian Company's two regiments were finally integrated into the British army as the 1st and 2nd Battalions of the Royal Dublin Fusiliers (RDF). By then, the regiment consisted mostly of Irish mercenaries fighting for the crown. When Word War I broke out in 1914, three reserve battalions were added, bringing the unit's complement up to five.

The 2nd RDF first went into battle on August 25, 1914, at the French town of Le Cateau, with a full complement of 22 officers and 1,023 troops. On August 26th, many soldiers cut off from their battalions were taken prisoner by the Germans. They were held at the Limburg prisoner-of-war camp, where hundreds of Irish died.

By September 14, after 20 days of fighting, the 2nd RDF had just 10 officers and 478 other noncommissioned officers and enlisted men left. The British Expeditionary Force was practically wiped out, as was the French army, which lost 40,000 men in just four days—27,000 on August 23 alone. Six months later, in February 1915, the 1st Royal Fusiliers were among the troops the British deployed to take Turkey's Gallipoli peninsula. It was to be another failed operation. By January 1916 when the British retreated, they left behind 214,000 dead. Of that number, 4,777 were RDF mercenaries.

In 1922, when the Irish Free State was created, the Royal Dublin Fusiliers was disbanded, its members were free to serve in the Irish army.

The Spanish Civil War was an internal conflict that played itself out on the world stage, complete with mercenaries fighting for both sides. It began in 1936 when the Popular Front or Republicans, composed of liberals, socialists, and communists, tried to institute a series of leftist reforms in Spanish society. As a response, the so-called Loyalists, led by Gen. Francisco Franco, decided to fight to gain control of the government. Franco immediately led a revolt of the Spanish army in Morocco.

As the war intensified over the next three years, Italy and Germany, fascist states, backed the Loyalists, while the Soviet Union backed the Republicans. So did the Americans with occasional arms shipments and, most important, manpower.

The Abraham Lincoln Battalion consisted of mercenaries who decided to fight for the Loyalist cause of a free and liberal Spanish government. Around 30 percent were Jewish, and 70 percent were between 21 and 28 years of age. The majority were members of the American Communist

Party, whereas others came from the Socialist Party of America and the Socialist Labor Party. They were given the minimum in military training—basic conditioning and target practice and the rudiments of battlefield tactics—before they were rushed into the line, to Spain's Jarama Valley to block Franco's advance. Engaging the Loyalists on February 23, 1937, the men of the Lincoln Battalion fought hard. On the first day of battle, 20 men were killed and nearly 60 wounded.

On February 27, the Lincoln Battalion was ordered to attack the Nationalist forces now entrenched at Jarama. Of the 263 brigade mercenaries who fought that day, 113 were killed and only 150 survived. "The battalion was named after Abraham Lincoln because he, too, was assassinated," one soldier said afterward. That was the last battle the Lincoln Battalion fought. The survivors were later reconstituted as the Lincoln-Washington Battalion.

Although artists, especially Ernest Hemingway in his novel *For Whom the Bell Tolls*, celebrate the American contribution to the Spanish Civil War, at best it was doomed from the start because of a severe lack of proper training. However, it remains the most ideologically driven mercenary group in history, which probably accounts for its failures.

Robert Merriman, the man who commanded the Lincoln Battalion in battle, was neither an experienced soldier nor mercenary. He had never been on active duty, never served in battle. Instead, Merriman was a well-meaning, left-leaning intellectual who happened to have spent two years in the Reserve Officers Corps. He didn't like what the Fascists were doing in Spain and so volunteered to fight for the Republican cause.

When he got to Spain, Merriman was put in charge of training the Lincoln Battalion recruits because he had the most military experience of anyone present. Promoted to battalion commander, he led his men into battle, and slaughter. Shot in the shoulder in February 1937, he was replaced by Oliver Law as battalion commander. Soldiers today looking at Merriman's troops could easily wonder, considering their lack of training, how any of them survived at all.

Long before American mercenaries arrived in Iraq, they got to China first as members of the Flying Tigers.

CHAPTER 6: THE MODERN AGE OF WAR FOR HIRE

The idea of the Flying Tigers began when Madame Chiang Kai-shek, the wife of the Chinese ruler, became the leader of the Chinese Aeronautical Commission. Noting immediately the inferior nature of the planes that comprised the Chinese air force, not to mention the training, she determined with the strength of character that characterized everything in her life, to make changes.

In April 1937, Madame Chiang Kai-shek made a proposal to Claire L. Chennault, then a captain in the U.S. Army Air Corps. She needed an expert airman to make a confidential survey of the Chinese air force, to specifically make recommendations for a way to modernize it. Because Japan and China were on the verge of war, and air power could bring supremacy to either side, the situation was dire enough to bring in a mercenary from the outside to help. Seeing Japan as an imperialistic and militaristic threat, Chennault was more than willing to do the job.

Retiring from active duty, he accepted an offer for a three-month assignment in China to survey the Chinese air force and make recommendations for change and improvement. So began Chennault's three-month China "hitch," which turned into a full eight years.

It was while he was helping the Chinese form their new air force, and combat the Japanese, that he developed the knowledge that would later be used when he organized and commanded the American Volunteer Group in 1941, better known as the Flying Tigers.

Chennault was born in 1890 in Commerce, a small, rural Texas town. A few years later, his parents moved to the backwoods of northeastern Louisiana. From the moment the Wright brothers flew in 1904, when Chennault was 14 years old, he knew that his future lay in the sky. He wanted to pilot an aeroplane.

When the United States finally decided to enter World War I in 1914, Chennault was 26 years old and deemed too old for the newly formed Army Air Corps. Relegated to backwater duty as an infantryman in San Antonio, it was there within the shadow of the Alamo that Claire Chennault learned to finally fly, convincing flight instructors at Kelly Field to teach him how to fly. Chennault quickly mastered flying, but not in time to get into the war.

That seemed to be Chennault's problem—lack of timing. He always seemed to be in the right place at the wrong time—that plus his natural affinity for candidness, boldness in strategy, and a willingness to carry it out, qualities prized in a military commander during wartime but despised during peace.

The post-World War I U.S. Army had gone with a plan of building fast bombers to strike at the heart of the enemy's homeland, wherever that enemy might be. Chennault violently disagreed, believing steadfastly that a well-flown fighter could bring down and decimate an enemy bomber fleet. With an attitude like that, Chennault's superiors saw no reason to advance his career beyond aerobatic pilot.

By 1937, when Chennault was 47 years old, he suffered from bronchitis, blood pressure fluctuations, and chronic exhaustion: all the result of his years in the cockpit flying at high speeds doing all kinds of aerobatic maneuvers. Finally grounded by the air corps for his poor condition, Chennault was, in effect, being forced out. Looking around for a means to support himself, luck finally smiled on Claire Chennault when Madame Chaing Kai-shek hired him.

The deal proposed to Chennault would pay him $1,000 a month plus expenses, a fortune in those days. His rank was civilian advisor to the secretary of the Commission for Aeronautical Affairs, first Madame Chiang and later T. V. Soong. Chennault was not only selling the Chinese his expertise, he had convinced them how important an air force of fighters really was in repelling the Japanese bombers.

No matter his fictitious rank, Chennault was hired to be the commander of the Chinese air force. His responsibilities included recruiting, equipping, and training before going into battle. During this three-year period, from 1936 to 1939, when Chennault was following through on his contract to China, time after time Chennault and his fighters swooped low over Japanese convoys. Using their wing guns, they blasted them to kingdom come.

In between "kills," Chennault revolutionized aerial-to-ground warfare with his invention of the early-alert system. The early-alert system as Chennault instituted it throughout China called for Chinese throughout the country to contact a central authority with information about any encroaching Japanese aircraft. Shortwave radio, phone, telegraph, whatever mode of communication happened to be employed, it all found its way back to central command, from which Chennault would dispatch his fighters accordingly.

Chennault's recruits were dominated by mercenaries who already had experience in combat. Those, plus the nationalistic Chinese who came to Chang's banner, filled out an air force that engaged the Japanese from 1936 to 1939. Undermanned and underequipped—the Americans remained neutral and would not sell China modern fighters—the Chinese air force under Claire Chennault carried on. But it was clear to President Roosevelt that without further support, in trained pilots and modern weapons, the Chinese would lose. Such a loss, resulting in the ascendance of Japan as the military power in the Far East, would present a direct threat to the West Coast of the United States, as well as to American interests in Asia.

Determined to act despite his very public position of neutrality, Roosevelt signed an executive order on April 15, 1941 that allowed American pilots to resign their commissions, join a dummy corporation, Central Aircraft Manufacturing Company (CAMCO) that was really a front for the U.S. War Department, and then get assigned to fight with Chennault in China.

To do their job, Chennault's air force needed some modern equipment. He managed to lobby and convince the secretary of the treasury, Henry Morgenthau, to give him just that. Roosevelt approved and soon Chennault had 100 Curtiss P-40 fighters to take back with him to China.

Prior to World War II, the P-40 was America's state-of-the-art plane in aerial-fighter warfare. The plane had a maximum speed of 362 mph, with a cruising speed of 235 mph. It had a range of 850 miles without refueling and could climb to 30,000 feet without stalling. The aircraft was 31 feet across the wings and 37 feet from propeller to tail. It cost $45,000.

Chennault had chosen well. The P-40 was a rugged, reliable workhorse. Even before the United States entered the war on December 8, 1941, American designers had been at work on even newer and better fighters. Throughout the war, the P-40 would be exceeded by planes that could fly faster and were more maneuverable, but none could deliver the reliability of performance that enabled the P-40s, in the hands of the American volunteer group, to become the most famous mercenary flying force in history.

The P-40s and their American general settled in at Kunming. On December 20, 1941, barely 13 days after Pearl Harbor, Chennault's early-alert system sounded an alarm: Japanese Mitsubishi K1-21 twin-engine bombers had entered Chinese air space and were approaching Kunming. They were 300 miles out coming from Hanoi. Chennault quickly scrambled two squadrons and sent them into the air to do battle.

Chennault had a keen intellect and knew the value of intimidation and propaganda. He had let his pilots paint a shark's mouth and teeth on the front of their Flying Tiger aircraft, which is what the Japanese saw as the mercenary force approached. Adopting the Japanese tactic of firing without warning, the Flying Tigers ripped into the Japanese zeros, the tiger's machine guns chattering continuously. With their superior diving speed and maneuverability, the P-40s shot 9 bombers out of a 10-bomber battle group out of the sky. The lone Japanese bomber that survived had been severely damaged in battle and barely made it back to its base in Hanoi.

For Chennault it was a particularly personal victory: He had finally proven the superiority of fighters over bombers that he had been arguing about with his superiors in the U.S. Army for almost a decade. The Chinese were so grateful to Chennault and his battle group that they nicknamed them the *Fei Hou* or "Flying Tigers." The name stuck.

Their subsequent encounters with the Japanese proved that they had an enemy who could adapt and use some imagination of their own. The next time the Americans tried attacking a group of Japanese bombers, the Japanese flew out of formation when the Americans attacked, turned, and did some attacking of their own. The Americans who had faster and more maneuverable planes, but most important better trained and disciplined pilots, began to grind out victory after victory against the Japanese air force.

Had the mercenaries been allowed to continue on their own, there is no telling how well they could have done. But once the United States entered the war, the American presence in the Pacific theater dramatically increased, including American troops being assigned to China. Lt. Gen.

CHAPTER 6: THE MODERN AGE OF WAR FOR HIRE

Joseph W. Stilwell pressured Chennault into integrating the Flying Tigers into the American Air Force. But when Stilwell decided that another officer, Brig. Gen. Clayton Bissel, would assume command of the Flying Tigers, the Tigers had one last say.

Like all good mercenaries, they were devoted to and understood the strategic importance of their leader Chennault. Without him, they just weren't the same. So the pilots of the Flying Tigers chose to voluntarily disband rather than be absorbed into the Army. Many would go on to fight once again for America. Probably the most famous of Chennault's men was Gregory "Pappy" Boyington.

If ever there was a mercenary with a Hollywood lifestyle, it would have to be Greg Boyington. It therefore comes as no surprise that of all the mercenaries in history, "Pappy" is the only one to ever have a TV series based on his exploits. Born in South Dakota, Pappy descended from Sioux Indians and easily had the courage of his forebears.

After World War I, Pappy found himself languishing at the Pensacola Naval Air Station, in the northwestern corner of Florida. With Alabama's border only miles away, locals call the area the Redneck Riviera. Unfortunately, Pappy spent more time for roistering on the nearby beaches, than flying.

The Marines, in their infinite wisdom, had taken a truly daring and original pilot and made him a flight instructor. Unfortunately, Pappy had too much of a tendency to party with alcohol and women, with bar fights thrown in, and that had severely hindered his career. So when one of Chennault's recruiters stopped by Pensacola after FDR signed the executive order giving soldiers a chance to fight in China and reassume their commission, Pappy jumped at the chance. Pappy would go on to become the most famous of Chennault's pilots.

Shortly before July 1942, Pappy saw the handwriting on the wall—the American Air Force was going to assimilate the Flying Tigers. Until that happened, the Americans were giving little if any assistance, including spare parts, to the Flying Tigers. Pappy resigned from the Tigers and rejoined the Marine Corps. Eventually he got his owner fighter squadron in the South Pacific. Boyington went on to win a Congressional Medal of Honor.

It was Pappy's experiences in China and the South Pacific that inspired the 1970s TV series *Baa Baa Black Sheep*, which starred Robert Conrad as Pappy.

As the twentieth century progressed, mercenaries tended to play less of a role in world affairs than they had previously. Killing technology progressed to the point that one individual's finger on the "release" button of an atomic bomb meant devastation for millions. With less opportunity to ply their trade, mercenaries' skills as soldiers diminished. That partially accounted for all the ill-trained men who fought for the Republicans during the Spanish civil war.

World War II was largely fought by warring, militaristic nations that had no need for outside assistance except perhaps in isolated instances. That all changed with the 1950s. The catalyst was communism.

Post-World War II, America and Western Europe were renamed the Free World. Their antagonists were any countries with Communist governments, primarily the Soviet Union and China. Fear of communism so ruled U.S. policy that a government that heretofore fought its own wars began to rely more and more on mercenaries. The operative philosophy was that communism was such a creeping scourge, U.S. Forces no matter how plentiful could not be spread all over the Communist sphere of influence. Therefore mercenaries needed to supplement U.S. regulars.

During World War II, as supreme commander of the Allied Forces, Dwight Eisenhower relied for triumph against the Germans and Japanese on the success of clandestine operations by the Office of Strategic Services (OSS). After the war, the OSS became the CIA. In the 1952 campaign, Ike had attacked Truman's containment policy as "accepting the status quo." The United States needs to "wrest the initiative from the Kremlin, and, if possible, 'liberate' areas from Communist control." So when Eisenhower became president, he had no hesitation in using the CIA for a clandestine operation that involved the use of mercenaries in Guatemala.

In the early 1950s, Guatemala had a left-leaning government led by its duly-elected president, Jacobo Arbenz-Guzman. Afraid Arbenz-Guzman might lean so far to the left that the dreaded Communists would take over, Eisenhower authorized a covert CIA operation using mercenaries to overthrow the Arbenz-Guzman government. The man the CIA picked to lead this counterinsurgency was Carlos Castillo Armas.

A politically astute colonel in the Guatemalan army, he was a graduate of the U.S. Army Command and General Staff College at Fort Leavenworth, Kansas. The CIA selected him to lead the invasion force, which would provide the political cover to show that it was the Guatemalans taking back their government, not the United States.

Subsequently convicted as a Watergate burglar, E. Howard Hunt was a CIA official involved in the Guatemalan insurgency. He later said that Armas was selected because the CIA was "impressed with Castillo [Armas]'s qualities as a military leader."

In the months before military action began, Armas acted as a lightning rod for the U.S. pre-invasion propaganda offensive. Beginning on May 1, 1954, a "liberation army" radio campaign began on Voice of America. Armas was going to lead an overt rather than covert operation. The broadcasts made it clear that across the border in Honduras, Armas was training a CIA-sponsored Guatemalan army of freedom fighters. Knowing the armed forces as well as he did, he knew many were not loyal to Arbenz-Guzman. Armas's hope was they would capitulate readily when the invasion began.

On June 18, 1954, Armas entered Guatemala from Honduras at the head of a force numbering fewer than 300 men. Well armed with mortars, Bren guns, and even flamethrowers, the so-called liberation army stopped its march barely beyond the border, in the town of Esquipulas.

Hedging their bet, the CIA had hired mercenary flyers to bomb the Guatemalan forces and soften them up for the invasion of the 300 Guatemalan freedom fighters. Then the mercenaries in the air took over, among them Whiting Willauer, who had served as Gen. Claire Chennault's deputy in the Flying Tigers. Willauer, along with other veterans of the Flying Tigers and assorted mercenaries the CIA had hired, flew a group of B-26 bombers and three P-47 fighters. Appearing above Guatemala City, they dropped leaflets first, and then flew on to targets selected largely for their psychological effect: ammo dumps, oil storage tanks, and military drill areas. "We blew up the government oil reserves and subsequently when the political situation was up in the air and required decisive action—the main powder magazine of the army," one of the pilots said to a U.S. newsman afterward.

Seeing the odds against them, the Guatemalan army wisely chose not to fight. Without an army to back him up, Arbenz-Guzman's government didn't last long. On June 27, Arbenz-Guzman stepped down, replaced by a military junta. The CIA pressured the junta of colonels into accepting Armas as the leader of a new government. That's how on July 3, 1954, the Guatemalan mercenary Castillo Armas rode into Guatemala City in triumph and became the new Guatemalan president.

Continuing the CIA's war against the Communists, President Eisenhower was convinced that the Communists needed to be contained in Asia. The spread of communism across Asia would harm U.S. interests in Japan and other free countries. Eisenhower readily approved a secret CIA plan for what would prove to be the largest mercenary operation ever undertaken by the agency.

In the small Southeast Asian kingdom of Laos, the CIA established a mercenary recruitment and training center. Although the Vietnam War was eventually lost, no one could blame the CIA for being asleep at the wheel. For more than 13 years, the CIA provisioned, commanded, and dispatched native forces that fought major North Vietnamese units to a standstill. But without Air America, none of it would have been a reality.

Air America was an airline secretly owned by the CIA, staffed primarily by American mercenaries. It was the most vital component in the agency's operations in Laos. It is no accident that Claire Chennault provided the CIA with the means to make Air America a reality. Mercenaries are really entrepreneurs of war, and between wars entrepreneurs still find ways to make money. For Chennault, that meant forming an airline in China after World War II. He called it Civil Air Transport (CAT).

When the CIA decided that it needed a cover airline to conduct its covert air sorties, Chennault secretly sold them CAT. Despite its new owners, CAT continued flying commercial routes throughout Asia, acting in every way as a privately owned commercial airline. But out of the public eye, CAT became Air America. The operation became so big that by the summer of 1970, Air America had two dozen twin-engine transports, two dozen short-takeoff-and-landing (STOL) aircraft, and 30 helicopters, all for operations in Laos.

As for staffing, more than 300 pilots, copilots, flight mechanics, and air-freight specialists worked the planes, which flew from bases in Laos and also Thailand. Although humane tasks were handled by Air America, including dropping millions of pounds of foodstuffs for Laotian consumption, the airline made its "bones" doing dangerous jobs: transporting tens of thousands of troops and refugees; flying emergency medevac missions; rescuing downed airmen throughout Laos; monitoring sensors along infiltration routes; conducting a photoreconnaissance program; and, field testing state-of-the-art electronic equipment, including night-vision glasses.

On January 27, 1973, an agreement in Paris between the United States and North Vietnam formally concluded hostilities. The following year, on June 3, 1974, Air America flew its last mission. In the end, only 111 Air America "mercs" died in Laos. That is a tribute to the CIA's effectiveness, at least in those days, of directing a guerilla war.

The Battle of the Bay of Pigs stands as one of the few instances in American history when the American government secretly financed a massive mercenary force for the express purpose of invading a foreign country. The United States was one of the few world governments that eschewed the use of mercenaries save for sporadic instances when it was just absolutely necessary. For the most part, Americans fought their own wars. But the United States paranoia regarding Fidel Castro was so great, they readily recruited and accepted help.

The story really begins with a secret plan concocted within the inner reaches of the Kennedy administration to use mercenaries to invade Cuba. According to the Inspector General's Survey of the Cuban Operation and Associated Documents, dated February 16, 1962, "The history of the Cuban project began in 1959 and ... ends with the invasion of Cuba by the Agency-supported Cuban brigade on 17 April, 1961 and its defeat and capture by Castro's forces in the next two days."

The "brigade" referred to were Cuban mercenaries recruited and paid for by the CIA to go into Cuba secretly and try to overthrow the Castro government. Castro, a Communist, controlled the strategically important island 90 miles from U.S. shores. America's increasing vigilance about the

Communist pest on its shoreline was well justified considering the 1963 Cuban Missile Crisis. But in 1961, that was still two years in the future.

What is surprising about the Bay of Pigs is that whereas Kennedy bears the historical blame for its defeat, it was Eisenhower who originally approved the crude invasion plan. From the IG's report:

> Formal U.S. Government adoption of the project occurred on 17 March, 1960, when, after preliminary preparations by the Agency, President Eisenhower approved an Agency paper titled "A Program of Covert Action Against the Castro Regime."

The plan the government concocted had three phases to it.

> The initial phase of paramilitary operations envisages the development, support and guidance of dissident groups in three areas of Cuaba: Pinar del Rio, Escambray and Sierra Maestra. These groups will be organized [sic] for concerted guerilla action against the regime.

> The second phase will be initiated by a combined sea-air assault coordinated with general guerilla activity on the main island of Cuba.

> The last phase will be air assault on the Havana area with the guerilla forces in Cuba moving on the ground from these areas into the Havana area also.

In the end, the hope was that the guerilla forces in Cuba would establish a beachhead and "organize, train, and lead resistance groups."

The proposed plan included allocating $1.5 million to recruit and pay the Cuban mercenaries hired by the CIA to do the job. The United States had chosen to fund no less than a Cuban-mercenary takeover of the Cuban government. In the early months of the program, recruitment intensified in the Miami area of Cuban immigrants and dissidents who would be willing to go back to their home country and take it back from the Communists by force. The CIA needed to find a way to recruit the Cubans without doing so overtly.

The answer was the Bender Group, CIA agents who set up "a national organization of American businessmen to provide cover for dealing with the Cubans." The CIA succeeded in placing a storefront recruiting depot in Coral Gables, Florida on May 25, 1961, "under cover of a New York career development and placement firm. Safe houses were also required in the Miami area for various operational uses."

The plan being considered required a combination of infantry and air support. The United States established secret training bases in Panama, Nicaragua, and Guatemala where the mercenaries had their training; the U.S. government also had 25 tank operators successfully trained for the strike force at Fort Knox, Kentucky. On April 12, 1962, President Kennedy told the mercenaries and their leaders that he would not provide overt military support for the operation. Covert action was a different story.

Using eight B-26s supplied by the U.S. government, Cuban mercenaries on April 15 flew from a coastal air base in Nicaragua to Cuba and bombed Castro's air bases, "destroying half of his total air force." When they returned to base, it was announced that the pilots were native Cubans trying to take back their country. Now it was time to invade.

With Castro's air force crippled, the mercenaries felt their opposition had been considerably diminished. Besides, the U.S. government had taken special care to arm them well.

"The armament provided for combat included sufficient numbers of Browning Automatic Rifles, machine guns, mortars, recoilless rifles, rocket launchers, and flame throwers. There were also 5 M41 tanks [and] 12 heavy trucks."

All was in readiness for the invasion.

"The Invasion fleet which had assembled off the south coast of Cuba on the night of April 16 included [seventeen ships]." All the vessels were armed with 50-caliber machine guns.

The invasion brigade comprised 1,511 mercenaries, including five infantry companies, a heavy-weapons company, an intelligence-reconnaissance company, and a tank platoon. During the early-morning hours, Cuban underwater demolition teams, each led by a U.S. "contract" employee, were first ashore on recon work and engaged the enemy in some firefights. They came ashore at the *Bahia de Cochinos* (Bay of Pigs) on Cuba's south coast.

Like many American incursions, this one was marked, too, by faulty intelligence. If half of Castro's air force had been destroyed the previous day, it came as a helluva surprise to the Castro's troops. Suddenly the freedom fighting mercenaries looked up; the sun was blotted out by Castro's B-26s, Sea Furies, and T-33s. Trapped on the Cuban beaches, air attacks on the mercenaries, continued throughout the day. "The eleven B-26s of the Cuban [mercenary] force were no match for [Castro's] T-33 jets." Four of the "merc" B-26s were shot down, seven returned safely.

As for ground forces, Castro sent his army to engage the mercenaries in a series of firefights. The mercenaries were clobbered. For some reason, the United States had clearly underestimated the proficiency of Castro's troops and overestimated the proficiency of their own mercenaries. Then things went from bad to worse.

The Cuban mercenaries were running out of ammunition. But Cuban government planes were patrolling her territorial waters, making resupply difficult. Over the next two nights, three shipments managed to parachute down to the beach, but that was insufficient for counterattack, let alone a strategic defense.

"On the night of April 18, when failure appeared inevitable, the Cuban brigade commander refused an offer to evacuate his troops. And on the morning of April 19th, with ammunition rapidly running out, the brigade was still able to launch a futile counterattack."

The next morning, April 19, three friendly B-26s, including two piloted by Americans, were shot down by Castro's T-33s. In those last hours of fighting, the Cuban commander sent out a series of desperate messages to the task force command, pleading for help:

"We are out of ammo and fighting on the beach. Please send help. We cannot hold."

"In water. Out of ammo. Enemy closing in. Help must arrive in next hour."

The last message was as follows:

"Tanks are in sight. Am destroying all equipment and communications. I have nothing to fight with. I cannot wait for you. Am taking to woods."

An evacuation convoy was headed for the beach on the afternoon of April 19. When it became known that the beachhead had collapsed, the convoy reversed course. There was no sense wasting any more lives in pursuit of what at best was an illusive political goal. During the next few days, "two Americans and a crew of [mercenary] Cuban frogmen succeeded in rescuing 26 survivors from the beach and coastal islands."

In the end, 90 Cuban mercenaries lost their lives, and the rest were taken prisoner. In analyzing the reasons for the failure of the invasion, the Inspector General would later write in his report, "The fundamental cause of the disaster was the Agency's failure to give the project, notwithstanding its importance and its immense potentiality of damage to the United States, the top flight handling which it required—appropriate organization, staffing throughout by highly qualified personnel, and full time direction and control of the highest quality."

What had doomed the project from the start was that the United States had decided to place the ideology of their mercenaries above their ability as warriors.

Africa from 1961 to 1969 was a powder keg that someone kept putting a match to as civil wars roiled the continent. Perhaps the worst of the strife was in the Congo.

"The history of the Congo since independence has been, to say the least, bewildering. It is very difficult to disentangle the mercenaries from the history," writes Anthony Mockler in his 1969 book, *The Mercenaries*.

On June 30, 1960, the Congo, formerly a colony of Belgium, was granted its independence. Barely five days later, on July 5, the Armée Nationale Congolaise (ANC; the Congolese National Army) mutinied. Then, on July 11, Moise Tshombe proclaimed the secession of the Katanga area of the country. The central government of the Congo did not take kindly to this secession. It would eventually invade Katanga several times with ANC units.

Upon becoming prime minister of Katanga, Tshombe realized that he had no real army to oppose the ANC or any of his tribal enemies. He brought in the one man he thought could recruit, equip, and command a modern mercenary army: Michael "Mad Mike" Hoare.

Mike Hoare was born in Dublin in 1920. An accountant, World War II interrupted his studies. He fought in Burma and worked his way up to become a member of Lord Montbatten's personal staff. In 1947, he immigrated to South Africa. He took up accounting again; owned an interest in a used-car business; and organized safaris for hunters who wanted to see "darkest Africa," have some fun, and bag some pelts.

One of Hoare's contacts during this period was a mercenary named Jeremiah Puren. Puren had been friends with Tshombe. When the latter became prime minister, it was to Puren he turned to for help and, in turn, Puren to Hoare. Hoare was given the commission to form an all-white mercenary company called Five Commando.

Five Commando was the elite mercenary unit that Hoare formed. He was the field commander, with Puren as his second in command. The mercenaries were openly recruited in Rhodesia and South Africa, and then flown to Kamina for two to three weeks of training before going into action.

The majority of his recruits, which he was being forced to mold, were young men in their early 20s looking for action. And being young men, they were not very patient when their contacts did not show up when they landed in Kamina. There were no barracks, uniforms, or weapons waiting for them. Many went back to South Africa and told the press how disorganized Hoare's endeavor was. It didn't help Hoare's reputation much when his first attack on Albertville ended with ignominious retreat and the deaths of two German mercenaries.

Hoare went back to the drawing board and got his base organized with barracks, uniforms, ammo, and food; everything he could give his men, he gave them. He drilled and trained his new batch of recruits according to the strict standards of the British army that he had been brought up with. He drew his noncommissioned officers (NCOs) from the British army and colonial police. The soldiers they commanded were primarily South African Afrikaaners who welcomed the opportunity to serve with an elite, all-white outfit that numbered approximately 250 in total. Hoare divided his men into small units of about 30 men and 2 officers. The idea was for each to operate independently as elite strike forces across the country and to come together whenever Hoare believed the situation warranted.

Five Commando was then flown all across the country to recapture towns held by the Simbas, the Congolese rebels. "Simba" is Swahili for "lion," the power of which the rebels hoped to channel. In the fall of 1964, Simba rebels in the Congo seized the city of Stanleyville. They took more than 1,600 European hostages. One hundred and eleven days later, after fruitless negotiations, a combined force of operation launched by American, Belgian, and Five Commando forces liberated the hostages. When the shooting was over and the numbers added up, the attack was a resounding success. Only 61 hostages were killed and 1,572 rescued. Simba casualties were estimated to be high, but an exact count has never been given.

Five Commando then set up shop in Stanleyville. From its base there, the elite mercenary unit was dispatched to the backwater towns and villages in Orientale province. They were able to close the border with the Sudan, while at the same time saving the lives of many of the white missionaries in the area. But this was not done without casualties. During one firefight with the Simbas, a column of 40 Five Commando vehicles under the command of mercenary Siegried Mueller was ambushed. Most of the vehicles were destroyed, and the men killed.

On November 25, 1965, General Mobutu staged a coup and gained power. Tshombe was booted out, and with him went Hoare. Five Commando survived, with another commander, but Hoare's Congolese tenure was over. Hoare faded from the mercenary scene temporarily, but he was determined to return.

CHAPTER 7

THE BLACK OPS WORLD

Leaders of nations do many things in support of their national policies. Hannibal hired mercenaries to help him defeat the Romans; Ronald Reagan did the same, hiring the Contras to defeat the Sandanista of Nicaragua. But where Hannibal's mercenaries were anything but secret, Reagan's defined the term *black ops.*

The term black ops was popularized by the 1993 film *JFK,* a conspiracy dream of a movie by Oliver Stone about John Kennedy's assassination. In it, Donald Sutherland, as a mysterious Pentagon informant, tells Kevin Costner's crusading district attorney about government "black ops" squads that secretly perform incursions, assassinations, and other dastardly deeds in the metaphorical dead of night.

The definition of black ops has come to invoke images of a shadowy government agency leading a covert action against a foreign government, involving any number of ruthless activities, including murder and drug smuggling, in support of that activity. As the old millennium wore to a close, more than one thousand years of mercenary activity was finally changing with the times; black ops were in vogue. Mercenaries became pawns on a world chessboard—anonymous black ops soldiers, but soldiers nevertheless, carrying out national policy goals. While mercenaries had done the same thing in El Cid's time, for example, the difference was twofold.

First, the world was a much bigger place than it had been in El Cid's time. Second, in El Cid's time whoever had the force of arms won regardless of political philosophy. In the twentieth century, it was democracy that triumphed over communism. The Russian transition to democracy after almost a century of communism, and before that monarchical rule, had shown how that the philosophy of democracy could influence the world without force of arms.

Unfortunately, as the millennium wound down, much of this history was simply ignored.

The term *Golden Triangle* was actually coined in the West. Because of its constant repetition, the name stuck and became translated as *jing san jiao* in Chinese and *sam liam thiong kham* in the Thai language.

In any language, the Golden Triangle is where Laos, Burma, and China meet, an area of lawlessness that is ruled by the gun. Because of its physical isolation deep within the jungles of Southeast Asia, the area is not only home to those involved in the drug trade, but also to slave traders, bandits, and arms dealers. Drugs are the driving force of the local economy.

This area contains one of the largest opium-growing regions in the world and has therefore become synonymous with drug dealing, despite the fact that considerable wealth in precious metals, including silver, and jewels, including rubies and emeralds, have also been discovered and mined. There are just more dollars in illegal drug cultivation and distribution worldwide than any other business.

During the second half of the twentieth century, the Golden Triangle became home to drug warlords. They maintain mercenary armies for protection against rival business interests. They are in the business of manufacturing the poppy-derived opiates, including heroin, and cocaine sold on street corners around the world by drug dealers.

Drug warlords are not mercenaries, though. As for those who serve them, their armies are primarily security forces. Film and television have tended to stereotype these mercenaries as wily, Euro-trash types. That has detracted from the story of the true mercenaries in the Golden Triangle.

To the Laotians and Thai, they are known as *Chin Haw*. To the Burmese, they are the *Panthay*. *Star Trek* fans would know them better as Ferengi. In any language, they are the Triangle Traders, a unique group of transportation mercenaries who control trade within the Golden Triangle, an area where transportation is a serious commodity. Their ancestry is centuries old.

Six hundreds years ago, the Mongol Empire stretched across Central Asia, and into the Middle East. The Mongols employed mercenaries to round out their army. Many were Uzbeks from Central Asia. Kublai Khan, the great Mongol leader, eventually sent Turkish mercenaries to conquer the Yuannan region of China. The mercenaries were so successful that many stayed and married Chinese women. The Turkish Muslims were then given the contract by the government to control the roads.

Over the next few centuries, these Muslims had trouble establishing their ethnic identity in China. After many Chinese Muslims were killed during an ethnic-cleansing incident by the Chinese army in 1873, survivors fled into the hills of the Golden Triangle. Making their way south, they came to Chiang Mai, capital of Northern Thailand, Here they created a small trading post. Its name was Chin Haw Village, from which derives the Golden Traders Chinese name.

Other survivors of the massacre made their way into the Wa states of Burma. This took more than a little guts because the residents of the Wa states are headhunters. Warrior enough to survive with their heads on, the Chinese Muslims used their ability to trade to make money. That, combined with a ruthlessness to stop anyone by force who got in the way, made them into the group who controlled all trade in the Golden Triangle. Eventually, the Traders came to control Panglong, which they made into the dominant city of the Wa states. When the British came to Burma in 1886, the Traders made a deal to supply them with mule trains, the dominant mode of transporting goods in that part of the world.

The British, who always notice class, soon observed how wealthy and powerful the Traders were within their own society. As they delved further, they discovered what the Traders' real business was: opium distribution. It was the Traders' mule caravans, protected by state-of-the-art Winchester .73 repeating rifles, that brought them real riches.

The struggle in China in the mid-twentieth century between the Nationalist Chiang Kai-shek and the Communist Mao Tse-tung, led to Mao's People's Liberation Army conquering the Nationalist forces. In Yuannan, the few Nationalist Chinese forces remaining fled over the border, into the Golden Triangle, where they joined the Traders, despite the fact that they weren't Muslims. Seeing brothers in soul against communism, the CIA then armed the Yuannan Traders and paid them as mercenaries to go in and try to retake Yuannan. After two counter-invasions failed, the Traders gave up and got back to what they were really good at: making money.

Here in the twenty-first century, pack trains loaded with opium still make their way out of the Golden Triangle, protected by Traders armed with state-of-the-art automatic weapons. The Traders still have a stranglehold on the transportation of all the drugs that flow in and out of the region. That is not likely to change soon.

Besides the Thracians, another group of people who have made their living for centuries as mercenaries are Thais.

The tradition of Thais as mercenaries goes back to the Middle Ages. As far back as the thirteenth century, Thai mercenaries emerged as a dominant fighting force in Southeast Asia. They set up independent city-states in several places along the country's Menam River. In the twentieth century, and particularly during the Vietnam War, Thai mercenaries worked for the CIA in supporting Laotian rebels fighting the Pathet Lao in their homeland. It cost an average of $300 million annually to recruit and train the CIA's clandestine army in Laos. So prevalent and so much a part of the Vietnam War did the Thai mercs become that many people survived the war with stories of their exploits.

During the Vietnam War, Frank Laughton (name changed), an army helicopter pilot, rescued a group of Thai mercenaries from a small mountain in northern Laos. Soon after, one of the Thai mercs gave Laughton a tiny Buddha, a family heirloom that, he said, had guarded five generations of fighters within his family. The Thai merc was quitting and he wanted Laughton to go home, too. Laughton went on to wear the good luck charm on every mission he had thereafter. Apparently, it kept him safe.

On another occasion, the Moaus (name changed), a Laotian family, secretly made their way down the Mekong River, trying to get out of the Communist-run country. The family's two youngest girls, 8 and 9, were left, by accident on the far river bank with their parents at the near one. That's when the Thai mercs came to the rescue.

"They came paddling up in a boat and offered to take us across. They just told us to get in the boat. We didn't know if they'd kill us or not, but we got in anyway—what choice did we have? Then they asked us for money or they were going to dump us in the middle of the river," the older girl recounted, years later. "We didn't have any money but they finally rowed us across, took the little we had and left us."

As a group, the Thais had a reputation of keeping their word, but always at a price, even for kids.

Hollywood has had a string of B films over the years that speculated on what happened to the youngest Nazis, the members of Hitler's Youth Corps, the Hitler *Jugend*. Usually they become mad Nazi scientists in the jungles of South America where, in the movies, all ex-Nazis seem to go. Not Rolf Steiner.

At the age of 17 in 1950, former Hitler Youth Steiner joined the French Foreign Legion. He later fought at Dien Bien Phu and in Algeria. Unfortunately, as a mercenary, Steiner wasn't much of a politician. He wound up aligning himself with an anti-De Gaulle faction and was discharged from the Legion for his politics. It was the beginning of a great mercenary career.

In the fall of 1967, the small African country of Biafra was suffering through a famine. The country hired mercenary pilots to fly in supplies. They were paid between $8,000 and $10,000 dollars in cash per month for their services. The Biafran government also hired soldiers. Roger Faulques, another well-known mercenary, was paid £100,000 to hire 100 men for 6 months. One of those 100 was Rolf Steiner.

After Faulques had a fallout with the Biafran government and left, Steiner stayed behind. In July 1968, he asked the Biafrans for a group of soldiers to be trained for army ranger/commando-style operations. The Biafrans assented and Steiner trained his men into such an elite fighting unit that when they encountered the Russian-backed Nigerians in battle in Biafra, they quickly overwhelmed them. Steiner was full of himself.

Given command of thousands of soldiers and the rank of colonel, he quickly proceeded to show his losing ways. Various military defeats against the Nigerians followed. Gen. Emeka Ojukwa, the Biafran leader, finally had enough. He removed Steiner from his commando division, and then got rid of him by shipping him out of the country.

Steiner materialized in Sudan in the 1970s. This time he went a bit off the beaten track, selling his services as teacher to the Anya Na, a force of fighting Islamic militants in southern Sudan. There was a power vacuum, and Steiner briefly became an Anya Na leader. Things were going well until Steiner was captured by the Ugandans. He spent three years in a Ugandan prison, during which time Steiner was subjected to numerous episodes of torture. His captors liked to hang him by his feet and stuff hot peppers into his body cavities.

Eventually released, Steiner died in South Africa of kidney problems.

They were 13 men, battle-hardened mercenaries, hired to fight against the People's Movement for the Liberation of Angola (MPLA), in the Angolan Civil War that broke out after Angola gained independence from Portugal in 1975.

The British among them had been recruited in London by a man named, Del Burnett (name changed) who was later quoted as saying, "I don't feel sorry for them. They are soldiers, they knew what they were doing. I would do it again." The reason for Burnett's defensiveness was that the MPLA had captured the 13 mercenaries and put them on trial for mercenary activities in their country, including the killing of Angolan citizens.

Retribution is a common emotion. When your country is roiling with civil war and some men bully their way into the conflict just to make a buck, that does not sit well when the opportunity for revenge presents itself. It therefore should not have come as a surprise to the 13 when the verdicts were delivered.

Ernesto Teixeira da Silva, one of the five presiding judges in the case, said: "Africa feels mercenaries are a danger to the people, the children, and to the security of the state. They spread fear, shame, and hatred in Angola." And then came the sentences.

Costas Georgiou and Andrew McKenzie, both British army veterans, were given death sentences for participating in the killing of two Angolan citizens and fellow mercenaries. Ironically, Georgiou was the only mercenary to actually admit a sort of guilt when he said he was involved with "an organized group on the fringe of the law."

John Derek Barker's role as a leader of mercenaries in northern Angola led the five judges to sentence him to death, too. The lone American sentenced to death was Daniel Gearhart, for advertising himself as a mercenary in an American newspaper and making the mistake of then going to ply his trade in Angola where he, too, was captured.

The People's Revolutionary Tribunal in Luanda sentenced the nine other mercenaries to 16 to 30 years behind bars in an Angolan prison. After the sentences were delivered, lawyers for all the defendants sentenced to death announced an immediate appeal, stating: "In our view there is no crime of mercenary nor was there disclosed such crime in Angolan law."

The case was then immediately referred to the Angolan president, Agostinho Neto. Neto had to sign off on the death sentences in order for them to be carried out. While considering what to do, Neto received an appeal from British prime minister, James Callaghan. Callaghan asked Neto to give all four condemned men clemency and spare them. Neto, instead, signed the death warrants.

Convicted mercenaries John Derek Barker, Daniel Gearhart, Costas Georgiou, and Andrew McKenzie were executed by firing squad on July 10, 1976. And then just as it seemed the 1970s might end without anything major happening in mercenary affairs on the African continent, Michael "Mad Mike" Hoare decided to make a grand re-entrance.

After his adventures in the Congo, Mike Hoare became a media celebrity and wrote books about his adventures. But the lure of adventure seems to have attracted the old mercenary once again. In 1981, someone hired Hoare to take over the Seychelles, a nation of 92 islands off the coast of East Africa.

Hoare had been the last mercenary general to lead an efficient fighting force that was not guerilla based since World War II. No surprise since Hoare's background was the Royal Armored Corps during the war in which he rose to the rank of major. But "Major" Hoare was in for a very rude awakening.

Hoare's job in 1978 was to overthrow the socialist government of Albert Rene, president of the Seychelles. With that done, Hoare was supposed to consolidate power and take control of the government. The plan was for Hoare and his men to fly into the Seychelles under the guise of a visiting rugby team. They picked December 1981 to implement it.

As customs inspectors in the Seychelles checked the mercenaries' luggage, the inspectors discovered heavy weapons in the bottom of their gym bags. Hoare's 52 mercs whipped out guns and shot it out with the Seychellians on the airport tarmac. They hijacked a plane that was preparing for takeoff and made the pilot, under armed guard, fly them back to safety in South Africa.

Ordinarily, hijacking a plane is about as serious an offense as you can get in any country. But the South Africans, who had a growing tolerance for mercenaries because some of their policemen were drifting into "private security," treated the mercs with kid gloves. Forty-four mercs had made it back, with eight dead or left in the Seychelles as prisoners. Their freedom would eventually be bought back by the South Africans.

The forty-four, including Hoare, were charged with kidnapping, which in South Africa had no mandatory penalty. The South African cabinet approved bail for 39, with the provision that the coup attempt not be discussed with anyone. As for Mad Mike, his mercenary career had finally come to an end and he went into retirement. Meanwhile, in America, Ronald Reagan was elected president in 1980, and the world order began to change again.

Much like scientists in the 1980s saw smallpox as a worldwide plague that needed to be eradicated, so did President Ronald Reagan view communism. Reagan was particularly sympathetic to the Contras, a band of revolutionaries in Nicaragua that opposed the Cuban-backed Sandinista government. Contra is a shortened version of the Spanish word *contrarevolucionari*, which means "counterrevolutionary."

The Sandinistas were actually the "hippie" armed rebels of the Nicaraguan 1960s who, upon toppling the dictator Somoza in 1979, nationalized the country's industries, postponed free democratic elections, and politically continued to move to the left. The Sandinistas became internationally known for their Marxist/Leninist rhetoric.

Within Nicaragua, a small group of insurgents known as the *Contras* were formed. They were a grassroots rebel group with no money, little training, and even less direction. They were the perfect front for a CIA-controlled mercenary army that would oppose the leftist Sandinistas.

President Reagan wanted to help the Contras. To him, they were one more Communist nation on America's doorstep that needed a change to democracy for America to feel comfortable again. But a Democrat-controlled Congress had tied his presidential hands. Congress passed the Boland Amendment, which made it illegal for the United States to intervene in Nicaragua.

President Reagan then told National Security Adviser Robert McFarlane, "I want you to do whatever you have to do to help these people [the Contras] keep body and soul together." Thus began a shell game of gigantic proportions that involved the use of guns, hostages, drugs, and, of course, mercenaries.

That money would eventually be sent to the Contras; there was no question within the upper echelon of the Reagan administration. The money would pay for the Contras to fight the Sandinistas as mercenaries fighting in support of U.S. interests. The question was how to get the money to the Contras under the table while Congress wasn't looking. The answer, strangely enough, was Iran.

In 1985, Iran still held seven Americans hostage. The United States had cut off diplomatic relations with the Iranians. But the Iranians proved more political than the Americans. They approached the American government with a secret request for the United States to sell them weapons. They knew what the United States would think: that by doing so, it would help win the release of the hostages. Although there was no specific quid pro quo with the Iranians, Reagan made the deal, despite a very public policy of never negotiating with terrorists.

Adolfo Calero was the man picked by the CIA to be the leader of the Contras. Robert Owen, one of Lt. Col. Oliver L. North's White House Contra contacts, described Calero as "a creation of the USG [United States government] and so he is the horse we have chosen to ride."

By birth a Nicaraguan, he was educated at Notre Dame, where he graduated in 1953. An outspoken opponent of the Somoza regime, he ran a Coca Cola bottling plant in Managua before the Sandinistas took over. According to an affidavit filed with the World Court on September 15, 1985 by former *Fuerza Democrática Nicaragüense* (FDN; the Nicaraguan Democratic Force) director Edgar Chamorro. Calero "had been working for the CIA in Nicaragua for a long time. He served as, among other things, a conduit of funds from the U.S. embassy to various student and labor organizations."

Testimony during the Iran-Contra hearings revealed that Calero received $12,500 a month from the CIA while he was serving as the Contra's political leader. Former Contra leader Eduardo Pardo-Maurer says in his memoirs that Calero held "the key position between the Contras and the Americans. He remained the pivot around which the military and civilian wings of the Contra movement turned. He controlled the cash, the stores, the camps, and the bureaucracy in Miami."

The arms for hostages deal became public in 1986, when a Lebanese newspaper, *Al Shiraa*, broke the story. By that time, more than 1,500 missiles from U.S. stockpiles had wound up in Iranian hands. While later investigating the secret deal, Attorney General Edwin Meese discovered that while the Iranians had paid the United States $30 million for the missiles, but only $12 million had made it into the U.S. coffers.

Where was the missing $18 million? It was then that Lt. Col. Oliver North, a relatively unknown member of the National Security Council who operated out of the White House basement, revealed the truth. He had deliberately defied Congress and the Boland Amendment by funding the Contras. He was certain that he was carrying out the president's strategy.

Oliver North was born on October 7, 1943, in San Antonio, Texas. Graduating as a Marine officer from the U.S. Naval Academy in 1968, he served honorably as a combat commander in Vietnam. Throughout the 1970s and into the 1980s, North advanced his career, becoming a lieutenant colonel and national security expert. After Ronald Reagan was elected president in 1980, Reagan appointed Adm. John Poindexter as his national security advisor. In turn, Poindexter appointed North as assistant deputy director for political military affairs.

Deep within the bowels of the White House, in his nondescript office, North would come to direct what became known as the Iran-Contra Operation. According to national security documents, North coordinated the covert sales of weapons to the government of Iran, and then funneled the profits to buy weapons for the Contras in Nicaragua.

North kept detailed notes about his activities in a series of notebooks. Those plus declassified memos sent to North detail how he ran the Contra war. For example, an April 1, 1985 memo from Robert Owen (codename: TC for "The Courier") to North (codename: "The Hammer") reported that the officials in the new southern-front FDN units include "people who are questionable because of past indiscretions," including José Robelo, who is believed to have "potential involvement with drug running" and Sebastian Gonzalez, who is "now involved in drug running out of Panama."

In a July 12, 1985 entry, North summarized a call from retired Air Force general Richard Secord during which the two men discussed a Honduran arms warehouse from which the Contras planned to purchase weapons using the arms for hostages money. According to North's notes, he told Secord that "14 M [million] to finance [the arms in the warehouse] came from drugs."

Under an entry dated August 9, 1985, North writes in his notebook of a meeting with Robert Owen, in which they discuss a plane used by Mario Calero, the brother of Adolfo Calero, head of the FDN. The plane was being used to transport supplies from New Orleans to the Contras' base in Honduras.

"Honduran DC-6 which is being used for runs out of New Orleans is probably being used for drug runs into U.S.," North wrote.

On February 10, 1986, Owen wrote to North regarding a plane being used to carry "humanitarian aid" to the Contras; it had previously been used to transport drugs. The plane belonged to Vortex, a Miami-based company run by Michael Palmer, one of the largest marijuana traffickers in the United States. Palmer had a long history of drug smuggling, and a short time later, a Michigan grand jury would indict him on drug charges.

Despite his criminal background, Palmer received more than $300,000 from the Nicaraguan Humanitarian Aid Office (NHAO) to fly in supplies for the Contras. February 1986 State Department contracts detail Palmer's work to transport material to the Contras on behalf of the NHAO. The NHAO was run by Oliver North, Assistant Secretary of State for Inter-American Affairs Elliott Abrams, and CIA officer Alan Fiers.

In February 1987, a Contra sympathizer in California named Dennis Ainsworth told the FBI that he believed FDN officials were involved in the drug trade. The bureau's debriefing states that Ainsworth "has certain information in which he believes the Nicaraguan 'Contra' organization known as FDN (Frente Democrático Nacional) has become more involved in selling arms and cocaine for personal gain than in a military effort to overthrow the current Nicaraguan Sandanista Government." Given the new critical look at current and former FBI operations, further investigation would be needed to fully support the Bureau's conclusion in such an important event in national history.

In 1987, the Senate Subcommittee on Narcotics, Terrorism, and International Operations, chaired by Senator John Kerry, began an investigation of allegations of Contra drug links. The subcommittee report concluded that "senior U.S. policymakers were not immune to the idea that drug money was a perfect solution to the Contras' funding problems."

The following year, on July 28, 1988, two DEA agents testified before the House Subcommittee on Crime regarding a sting operation conducted against the Medellin Cartel. The two agents said that in 1985, North had wanted to direct $1.5 million in cartel bribe money that was carried by a DEA informant and intended for the U.S. Treasury, where it belonged, to the Contras. DEA officials rejected the idea.

The Contras should have been an effective mercenary army. The problem was that despite the training they received, the Contras never were a physical force to be reckoned with. Part of that was due to the CIA using a primarily indigenous army; they imported few, if any, professional soldiers. Nor did the Contras have any clear goals except a democratically elected government. It didn't help that the Sandanista regime that it opposed had a more clear-cut Marxist political philosophy.

On March 23, 1988, Costa Rica mediated a cease-fire agreement. Additional agreements in February and August 1989 provided for internationally monitored elections, which were subsequently won on February 25, 1989 by an anti-Sandinista center-right coalition. The Contras themselves, by agreement, were allowed to reintegrate into Nicaraguan society and politics without penalty.

Back in the United States, the fallout from Irangate, as the press now called it, reached a crescendo. Admiral Poindexter resigned and Lieutenant Colonel North was fired. Fourteen people were charged with either operational or "cover-up" crimes. Although the government obtained a conviction against North initially, his conviction was subsequently overturned on appeal. North has since gone on to become a highly paid conservative radio talkshow host.

As for President Reagan, no direct evidence linked him to the diversion of funds to the Contra mercenaries. When he died in June 2004, his obituary in many newspapers downplayed Irangate in favor of the more positive aspects of his presidency.

As soon as you see a few aliases (or "also known as's") next to someone's name, chances are it's not because that person punches a time clock and lives in the suburbs. It certainly isn't in the case of Bob Denard (a.k.a. Said Mustapha Mahdjoub, Colonel Denard, and Gilbert Bourgeaud), who along with Mike Hoare and Tim Spicer comprise a trio of the three most influential mercenaries of the past 50 years.

Gilbert Bourgeaud was born in Bordeaux, France, in 1929. Changing his name to Bob Denard, he joined the famed French Foreign Legion, serving in Indochina and Morocco, and then went into the mercenary business in the 1960s. Business, to say the least, was booming.

Between Europe's decolonization of Africa and the CIA-funded battle against communism in Asia, Denard never seemed to lack for work. Zimbabwe, Yemen, Iran, Nigeria, and Zaire are just a few of the countries where he sold his services as a soldier of fortune. His critics claim he is responsible for "untold numbers of deaths and contributed greatly to the destabilization of Africa that continues today."

What even his critics can't deny is that Denard was one of the first mercenaries, if not the first, to finally figure out how to take not only a piece of the action, but the whole kit and caboodle. To compare Denard to Kipling's mercenary/emperor Peachy Davenport in *The Man Who Would Be King* would be accurate. But in the mercenary world of the latter twentieth century of which Denard is a big part, there are very few established facts about wars and battles that mercenaries participate in.

Because their very activities are frequently clandestine, it's always hard to find out what happened except from the participants, who are frequently rather closed mouthed because their actions resulted in prosecutorial deaths. What has become clear is that Bob Denard had a "thing" for the Comoros Islands.

The Comoros is an island nation in the Indian Ocean, northwest of Madagascar. The nation's major export is ylang-ylang, a flower, rare in nature, that is used in the making of various aromatic oils. A native of the Comoros who happened to look out to sea on May 13, 1978 would have been greeted with the sight of Bob Denard in command of a trawler that had been turned into a troop ship. Accompanying Denard were 46 heavily armed, black-clad mercenaries.

Not long before, Denard had been in the Comoros after Marxist strongman Ali Soilih had overthrown Abderemane Ahmed Abdallah's government. Denard had been hired by Soilih to train his army. Abdallah, in Parisian exile, turned around and hired Denard to put him back in power. He offered to cut Denard in on a piece of the action, reportedly $6 million. Denard realized there was real "juice" in being the power behind the thrown.

Denard and his 46 mercenaries came ashore quietly at night. They made their way quickly to the palace, where they found the young ruler Soilih in bed with three girls watching a porno film. There are two different stories about what happened to Soilih.

The first is that Denard killed him and drove his jeep through town the next day with Soilih's body sprawled across his hood. The people loved it and readily accepted Denard's rule for the next 11 years. The second is that it was never proven that Denard killed him, but that Soilih did die under mysterious circumstances. What is clear is what happened after Soilih died.

Former vacuum cleaner salesman and mercenary Bob Denard became the head of Abdallah's 500-man presidential guard and effectively ran the country using Abdallah as the figurehead. Denard was attracted to the island and its Islamic culture. He converted to Islam and married a Comoran woman. He also had significant influence and business interests in the archipelago, and eventually became a citizen of the country. He developed a close working relationship with French intelligence, who used his islands to ship arms to the rebel force that fought in the Mozambique civil war.

Denard's sojourn came to an abrupt end in 1989 when he allegedly shot Abdallah during an argument. The French arranged for his resignation, and Denard went back to South Africa, planning his next coup in the country he so loved. Denard also had a tremendous love of family. Married seven times, he had eight children who kept him busy, but he still wanted to go back to his newly found paradise of Comoros. It was, to him, like Shangri-La in James Hilton's novel *Lost Horizon*.

On October 4, 1995, Denard (at that time 66 years old) and a group of 33 mercenaries, most of them French, set sail in a leaky fishing trawler for the Comoros. Landing at night, they quickly took possession of two airports, troops barracks, and a radio station. Then they went after the man who had taken over for Denard, Comoros's 80-year-old president, Said Mohammed Djohar. The president awoke out of a sound sleep to find a gun pointed at his head. Consolidating power, Denard became president and claimed that Djohar was a "bad guy" who had looted the state treasury and betrayed his people.

The French had had enough. Denard was becoming a menace to international law. Two days later, on October 6, the French landed 600 troops that tussled with Denard and his mercs. No one was killed, but Denard and his men were deported. Denard wound up in France.

In 2004, he was 75 years old.

There is only one Western nation that has maintained its own mercenary army as part of its armed forces. Of course, that nation is France. No stranger to employing mercenaries, including the Scot Guards of

Charles VII, the Swiss Guard of the Bourbon kings, and Napoleon's Polish Lancers, King Louis Philippe created the French Foreign Legion on March 10, 1831.

From the beginning, the Legion was an all-volunteer army of anyone, between 18 and 40, "with or without means of identification, who was willing to fight for pay under the French flag." That meant anyone, including criminals, could join up (even to avoid police), and they did. For young men seeking adventure, professional soldiers from other countries, anyone who wanted to make a buck soldiering, the Legion was the place to go.

Over the years, the French Foreign Legion has had a distinguished record. It was involved with the French conquest of Algeria in 1835, and later fought in the Crimea (1855), in Italy (1859), and in Mexico (1863). In Mexico, it won one of its greatest claims to fame: On April 30, 1863, at the Camerone Hacienda near Puebla, 3 officers and 62 Legionnaires resisted 2,000 Mexicans. After a day of heroic fighting, the last five survivors fixed bayonets and charged. The name of the battle adorns every Legion flag to the present day, and remains the symbol of a mission carried out to the bitter end.

During World War I, many Legion regiments suffered heavy casualties, some to the point that the regiment itself was disbanded. The Legion merged these disbanded regiments into a new regiment, the Regiment de Marche, which was headed by the famous Colonel Rollet (a.k.a., the Father of the Legion). They fought subsequent military campaigns in Morocco and the Middle East. During World War II, the French Foreign Legion of mercenaries was once again there to aid in the fight. The 13th Half-Brigade (Battalion) of the Foreign Legion fought at Narvik and Bjervik in Norway, and then aided in the Bir-Hakeim victory in Libya in 1942. The entire Legion was then reunited and fought victorious campaigns in Tunisia, Italy, Provence, Alsace, and Germany. In Indochina, the 5th Foreign Infantry Regiment even managed a close escape from imminent Japanese entrapment.

In 1945, the French Indochina war began, and the Legion was once again sent to the line. Every Foreign Legion regiment was represented on the battlefield, particularly in Phu Tong Hoa, the Colonial Road 4, and Dien Bien Phu, where they fought to the last man. But the Legion continued to recruit. Foreign Legion recruitment posters were ubiquitous throughout France. Soon her depleted ranks were replenished, and the French Foreign Legion was again ready for action.

In 1954, the Legion found itself again in Algeria. At first its regiments were in charge of security, but soon they manned the frontlines facing Algerian rebel fire. After finally leaving Algeria in 1962, the Legion's regiments regrouped in the south of France and Corsica or overseas in Djibouti, Madagascar, Tahiti, and French Guyana. From 1969 through 1970, the 2nd Foreign Parachute Regiment and the 1st Foreign Regiment of the Foreign Legion participated in military operations in Chad. In May 1978, the Foreign Legion made headlines again when the 2nd Foreign Parachute Regiment saved thousands of European and African civilian hostages in Kolwezi, Zaire, from certain death.

Since 1831, 902 officers, 3,176 NCOs, and more than 30,000 Legionnaires have died for France; one third of them while fighting directly for the defense of the country. On the French ambassador to the United States website, the ambassador states, "Foreigners by birth, the Legionnaires have become Frenchmen by the blood they have spilled."

Today the French Foreign Legion is still recruiting foreigners who want to fight under France's banner for pay. What they are looking for? The website states the following:

As an integral part of the French army, the French Foreign Legion is a professional fighting unit using the same equipment and with the same missions as any other infantry, tank, or engineer unit of the French army. They are volunteers of any nationality, race or creed, always ready to serve France. Men of action and elite soldiers with a young and dynamic spirit, they are capable of doing their duty anywhere anytime.

Enlistment requirements are as follows: age between 17 and 40 years old (parental or legal tutor authorization is required for minors); a valid official identity card; physically fit for duty wherever he may be needed. Knowledge of the French language is not necessary because it will be acquired during the contract.

There are a number of enlistment centers throughout all of France. After enlistment, a preliminary medical checkup is required. Passing that, the enlistee is transferred to the selection center of the Legion Headquarters in Aubagne, 15 kilometers from Marseille, where he undergoes medical, IQ, and physical fitness tests. Upon passing those, the enlistee is then asked to sign a five-year contract that calls for service wherever the French Foreign Legion needs him. As for those who fail the selection process, "The unsuccessful candidate is immediately returned to civilian life to rejoin his country of origin without any financial aid," states the French website succinctly.

Because in years past, the Legion did not require enlistees to provide personal identification, many enlistees joined to escape a criminal past. Others joined perhaps because of a personal/family crisis or upheaval in their social/political life. It is not an exaggeration to state that the lax requirements for joining the Legionnaires over the years was tacit French encouragement for enlistees to change their identity so that no one would come after them, for whatever reason.

Examples of this include the mass enlistment of Alsatians after 1871, of Spaniards in 1939, and of Eastern Europeans after 1945. For others, who are unable to deal with the limitations of a middle-class life, the Legion represents a life of adventure. Upon joining up, under a real or assumed name, the Legionnaire enjoys unequaled protection for as long as he serves, because of the anonymity rule. Only the Legionnaire himself can decide when to break the rule and reveal his true identity.

Coming from all over the world, with such different origins, languages, and ideals, it would seem that they have nothing in common, but there is one thing: Legionnaires have broken with their past (and many, with their own families). This state of mind binds the Legionnaires together and explains their "unrivaled cohesion sealed with discipline, solidarity, and respect for traditions."

During his first four months of serving in the Legion, the new Legionnaires receive basic military instruction at the 4th Foreign Regiment, located in Castelnaudary, after which he is posted to a regiment, depending on his capabilities and the needs of the Legion at the time. Promotion through the ranks depends on his physical capacities as well as his IQ, service record, and leadership abilities.

Although the archetypal image of the Legionnaire is that of an individual dressed in desert kit, complete with a cap that shades the neck, today's Legionnaire is not a specialist in desert fighting. World events make it common that they are deployed in a range of environments. A Legionnaire can choose to become expert in areas as diverse as diver sniper or paratrooper and can obtain a qualification in one of these following branches:

- Administrative department (secretarial, accounts)
- Signals (radio or mechanic-exchange operator, telephonist)
- Transportation (light vehicular tracked-vehicle driver)
- Engineers (heavy-equipment operator)
- Building trades (bricklayer, plumber, electrician, carpenter, painter, etc.)
- Maintenance (mechanic, car electrician, welder, car painter)
- Others (musician, medical assistant, cook, photographer, printer, sports instructor, computer operator)

The following table, with information provided by the French embassy, shows what a Legionnaire gets paid.

Grade	Pay
Legionnaire	£975.67/$1,206.08 per month
Corporal	£1,219.59/$1,508.50 per month
Chief Corporal	£1,372.04/$1,697.51 per month

After three years of service, a Legionnaire can ask for French nationality and may also be entitled in the meantime to a French resident permit if he has obtained a certificate of satisfactory military service. The resident permit is valid for 10 years and is renewable. At the end of the initial enlistment, the Legionnaire can extend his career by signing successive contracts of 6 months, 1 year, 2 years, or 3 years, until he reaches 15 years of service. This depends on rank and conduct. After 15 years of service, Legionnaires are entitled to a retirement pension payable even in foreign countries.

Fully aware of the legend of the Legion—numerous movies, television series, and novels have been written about it—France stokes its reputation by maintaining the Legion as a distinct entity within the French army. Nowhere is this move more evident that in the Legionnaire's distinctive uniform.

Working down, the kepi (or headwear; white in summer, khaki the rest of the year) officially became part of the uniform on July 19, 1939. It was first worn in Africa as a head cover, with an added neck protection against the hot sun. The uniform epaulets use a red and green combination, the colors used by the Swiss Guard while serving the French kings.

The blue sash, originally worn under the clothes as a protection against intestinal disorders, is now part of the parade uniform, also known as the Sappers or *pionniers* uniform. If a Legionnaire were in pionniers uniform and marching in a parade, he would be holding a leather apron and an axe. In combat, of course, body armor replaces the sash, and a rifle replaces the axe. All Legionnaire uniforms have as their insignia the Legion Grenade, a grenade with a hollow center bearing seven flames, two of them directed downward.

The Legion maintains it own band, known as the Principal Band, with about 100 musicians. Having achieved worldwide fame through its exhibitions, the band differs from other French military bands because of its fifes, its Chinese pavilion, and the way it carries its drums, with the lower ring at knee level.

When Legionnaires actually march in parade, their pace is 88 steps per minute, almost the same as that of the former kings' soldiers. The Foreign Legion has been marching to the time of the "Boudin" since 1870, when it became its official march. The name *Boudin*, or "sausage," probably derives from the rolled blanket worn across the chest.

When all the business trappings are taken away, what remains inviolate and unchanged is the Legionnaire code of honor.

THE LEGIONNAIRE'S CODE OF HONOR

1. Legionnaire, you are a volunteer serving France faithfully and with honor.

2. Every Legionnaire is your brother-at-arms, irrespective of his nationality, race, or creed. You will demonstrate this by an unwavering and straightforward solidarity, which must always bind together members of the same family.

3. Respectful of the Legion's traditions, honoring your superiors, discipline and comradeship are your strength, courage and loyalty your virtues.

4. Proud of your status as a Legionnaire, you will display this pride, by your turnout, always impeccable, your behavior, ever worthy, though modest, your living quarters, always tidy.

5. An elite soldier, you will train vigorously, you will maintain your weapons as if they were your most precious possessions; you will keep your body in the peak of condition, always fit.

6. A mission once given to you becomes sacred to you; you will accomplish it to the end and at all costs.

7. In combat you will act without relish of your tasks, or hatred. You will respect the vanquished enemy and will never abandon either your wounded or your dead, neither will you *under any circumstances* surrender your arms.

CHAPTER 8

PMCs IN IRAQ [2004]

Bob Denard and Mad Mike Hoare are the mercenary icons of the recent past. Their day, where the guy with the most guns always won, is long over. Today, being a mercenary is more complicated, just like everything else.

The modern PMC has offices in more than one country, with contacts all over the world. They market their services to private companies and governments. Their slick websites (see Appendix A) promise to mitigate risk in global trouble spots and maximize profits. Whatever these companies' real successes—and they operate under such secrecy that this is hard to assess—they have become an integral part of the new world order.

Just like any field, there are minor players and major players. Among the latter is a select group of PMCs that have been chosen for large security contracts for work in Iraq, contracts awarded by the U.S. government. What follows is by no means an exhaustive list of PMCs (see Appendix A) but rather a more specific look at some of those that have greatly benefited from the Iraq War.

CUSTER BATTLES

Clearly building upon the modern PMC concept as established by Tim Spicer, Custer Battles is named not after the general of infamy, but after the soldiers/entrepreneurs who head up their management team.

Scott Custer is a former U.S. Army officer who served with both the 101st Airborne Division and the 3rd Infantry Division. During his decade of military service, Custer worked clandestine operations in the Persian Gulf, Latin America, and Africa. Afterward, he furthered his military experiences by studying and earning a Master's degree in security studies from Georgetown and Oxford Universities. He worked several years as a defense consultant concentrating on counterterrorism and peace-operations initiatives.

Over the past three years, Custer has instructed hundreds of security managers and operational staff across the globe in risk assessment, emergency planning, and crisis response. According to the company, Custer has developed "methodologies for security planning, management, and operations to reduce risk while ensuring success in any activity."

On March 22, 2003, Fox News announced that Custer, who had recently appeared on Fox News as a military analyst, had done so well as such that he had been asked to appear on Fox News throughout the war with Iraq to discuss various aspects of the conflict. As part of his prior military training, Custer had spent time as an infantry officer in the Gulf.

What Fox News failed to note was that they were employing as an analyst someone who had a very real financial stake in what happened in postwar Iraq. Apparently that made no difference. Sure enough, on June 17, Custer Battles publicly announced that it had opened a representative office in Baghdad's Mansour District.

"In all my years of experience operating and investing in emerging and transitioning markets, I've rarely seen such opportunities," Mike Battles, Custer Battles co-founder and managing director of the Baghdad office, said. "The Iraqi workforce is well educated, eager, and anxious to continue their proud history of cultural and commercial success."

Mike Battles, the other principal in Custer Battles, has more than 10 years of experience in the U.S. military and intelligence community as well as the private sector. A West Point graduate with a Bachelor of Science degree in geopolitics, he served more than seven years in the U.S. Army as an infantry officer in airborne and special operations assignments, with extensive service throughout Eastern Europe and the Balkans.

After leaving the military, Battles served as an operations officer with the CIA. Between his intelligence, military, and business contacts—he was also a candidate for the U.S. House of Representatives from Rhode Island—he was in a prime position to start his own PMC.

Along with Custer, they began Custer Battles in 2001. Following the Sandline template, Custer Battles looks at a situation in its totality. Following is the copy from one of their in-house brochures that are con-fidentially distributed to potential clients:

> Every organization has some exposure to risk. Understanding this exposure is just half the battle. The other half is designing solutions to limit this exposure, while at the same time allowing an organization to continue to operate successfully. Restrictive control measures may reduce exposure to risk, but they also reduce an organization's ability to succeed. Unlike traditional risk management companies, our services are designed to enhance flexibility. Our solutions are tailored to every individual circumstance—no template or "canned" solution is ever used by the Custer Battles team.
>
> Iraq is a nation and marketplace wrought with challenges, obstacles, and malevolent actors. However, Iraq offers contractors, traders, entrepreneurs as well as multinational enterprises an unprecedented market opportunity. The ability to identify, quantify, and mitigate this myriad of risks allows successful organizations to transform risk into opportunity. Terrorist, sophisticated criminal enterprises, political and tribal turmoil, and a lack of modern infrastructure present formidable challenges to companies operating in all areas of Iraq.

This brilliant analysis of the situation in Iraq explains exactly what a modern PMC should be doing: identifying and quantifying the risk, offering a solution to a client, and implementing it with a clear goal in mind. Although no PMC would want to admit it, it was Spicer at Sandline who developed these concepts.

> Organizations who have a comprehensive understanding of the threats facing their efforts, combined with a flexible strategy for

overcoming these obstacles, will have a far greater chance of success. Risk management is not just about identifying hazards and implementing control measures to keep people safe. The Custer Battles approach to risk is about seeking opportunities, and designing solutions to enable these opportunities to be exploited. The greatest threat to success is failure to manage risk. Custer Battles focuses on delivering relevant, timely, and value-added information and recommendations to decision makers to give them a more complete understanding of a given situation.

In Iraq, that means Custer Battles maintains an intelligence network to help it assess and quantify the danger in any given assignment.

Ventures are more successful with the use of a detailed roadmap. While organizations often develop their "roadmap" based on their own industry expertise, failure to identify obstacles to success and establish alternative solutions can negatively impact the success of a venture. In the nebulous and hazardous Iraqi business climate, this roadmap must not only be comprehensive it must also provide the flexibility to maneuver rapidly and decisively. Custer Battles provides planning, proactive advocacy, and support designed to provide both an avenue for success as well as the flexibility to maneuver should the risk environment change.

Failing to plan is planning to fail.

Again, notice the reference to a roadmap, the template, despite the company's claim to the contrary, that Spicer developed at Sandline. As Spicer recognized, implementation was the most important thing. And as Hannibal realized, failure will result if your supply lines are broken. Not surprisingly, considering Battles is not only a West Point graduate but an expert in military history who lectures there, his company has learned from Hannibal's mistakes.

The reconstruction effort in Iraq is a major operational undertaking for our clients, and a key component of their success hinges on the development of a sound and secure logistics plan and execution schedule. Logistics in Iraq are routinely challenged by security threats (terrorist attacks and violent thievery), poor transportation infrastructure, and limited logistical resources. To facilitate customer success Custer Battles has developed an affiliate, Secure Global Distribution (SGD). SGD has created a managed logistical service, in which SGD integrates its experienced logistical personnel with the client to tailor, manage, and implement a concerted logistical effort with the flow, storage, and delivery of materials, goods, and personnel into and throughout Iraq.

This was the kind of move that Hannibal, Sir John Hawkwood, the San Patricios, and mercenaries throughout history would appreciate. Custer Battles had deliberately set up a subsidiary to specialize in logistical support, making certain that it supplies its security contractors in the field through a well-planned supply line. Then to make the most money possible, Custer Battles marketed itself in Iraq to companies that needed logistical support alone.

SGD

"Customers for SGD include private contractors, government entities, and nonprofit organizations. SGD is firmly established in Iraq, and provides secure transport for hundreds of millions of dollars worth of a wide variety of cargo including medical equipment, engineering equipment, generators, vehicles, prefabricated buildings, construction material, military equipment, and other high-value goods with zero loss or theft to date," the company acknowledges in its in-house brochure.

The beauty of SGD is the suite of services it offers to clients, as follows:

- **Air cargo service**. SGD provides air cargo services throughout the world to Baghdad and other airports in Iraq. SGD has established a network of scheduled and ad hoc charter air cargo service throughout the region from Middle East centers including Amman, Beirut, Bahrain, Dubai, and Kuwait. SGD uses both large and small aircraft for passengers and cargo to best suit client needs.

- **Sea freight.** SGD provides freight-forwarding ocean services from North America, Europe, and Asia to Iraq, through the regional ports of Umm Quasar (Iraq), Aqaba (Jordan), Beirut (Lebanon), and Kuwait.

- **Trucking/distribution.** SGD provides both inter- and intra-Iraq truck transportation. Inter-Iraq SGD trucks deliver from every border of Iraq to Baghdad and other distribution points. Intra-Iraq SGD delivers long or short haul to distribution points or field sites. The SGD fleet includes a wide variety of trucking and other transportation equipment.

- **Equipment leasing.** SGD offers long-term leasing of a variety of equipment to include tractor trailers, flatbeds, heavy haul and trailers, medium to small-ton trucks, refrigerated trailers, cranes, buses, personal vehicles, and other specialized equipment.

- **Receiving services.** SGD provides a variety of administrative and physical services to handle cargo: cargo acceptance, customs clearance for storage and re-export, offloading, expediting services, and implementation of inventory systems.

- **Warehouse/distribution centers.** SGD provides full warehouse distribution services in Iraq and in regional centers. Services include unloading, sorting, segregating, storing, consolidating, loading, and shipping of merchandise. Inventory controls are designed to client requirements. SGD constructs refurbished or lease-secure or -unsecured warehouse space as needed.

- **Secure cargo escort.** SGD provides armed security services for cargo in transit. SGD tailors escorts to match the threat and uses armed security personnel, weapons, communications equipment, out-rider vehicles, and other related equipment to perform all the security aspects of safe cargo transit.

With this kind of logistical support, it's no wonder that Custer Battles was awarded the airport security contract in Baghdad by the U.S. government. Security does not mean standing by x-ray machines as passengers board planes; instead, it is more proactive. Former special forces soldiers and Ghurkas are employed to defend the airport from mortar, rocket, and sniper attacks.

This isn't security in the traditional sense, but military work best left to trained soldiers.

GLOBAL-GUARDS

Based in Uruguay, Global-Guards is a security consulting company that got the contract to recruit indigenous pilots and mechanics for an American company. The latter had gotten the contract to transport civilians—mainly U.S. and British businessmen—to Iraqi territory from neighboring countries. The contract called for 32 pilots and 40 mechanics for UH-1H helicopters needed to do the job. The company recruited heavily from Chile.

Each pilot would receive a monthly wage of $12,000, or $3,000 per week. Mechanics would also do well, earning between $4,000 and $4,500 per week. With the Chilean minimum wage corresponding to approximately $180 per month, it was an offer that couldn't be refused. Recruitment was not a problem, even though the average wage of the pilots and mechanics was considerably less than the average of $1,500 to $2,000 a day that the average merc on the ground would get. Gurkhas—a British term for Nepalese soldiers serving the British crown—always tend to be paid considerably less than their Caucasian counterparts. Flying a copter in a war zone is no less dangerous than being a foot soldier in the same situation.

The transportation contract began in November 2004. The pilots and mechanics transported foreign executives from Jordan and Kuwait to the principle Iraqi cities, where they could do their business quickly and get out. Essentially, the mercs were functioning as "air taxis." One of the essential prerequisites for the job was a basic knowledge of English, because the mercs were actually working for an American of undisclosed identity.

During the recruitment process, Global-Guards only posted its e-mail address and post office box number on the job notice. When the *Santiago Times* attempted to contact the company at that address for an interview, there was no response.

Uruguay has become a central location in South American from which to recruit mercenaries. Blackwater International subsequently set up hiring operations there, and recruited 120 Chilean mercenaries for service in Iraq.

KELLOGG BROWN AND ROOT, A.K.A. KBR ENGINEERING & CONSTRUCTION

KBR is a unit of the Halliburton Company and provides "military support services." Its former CEO, Dick Cheney, became vice president of the United States under President George W. Bush. Halliburton subsequently got the contract from the U.S. government for much of the rebuilding of the Iraqi infrastructure after formal hostilities ended. KBR won a $28.2 million contract to build enemy prisoner-of-war (POW) camps, and $40.8 million to protect the Iraqi Survey Group, charged with searching for weapons of mass destruction (WMDs).

Since 1995, KBR has had the Balkan Support Contract, the largest contract for service support to U.S. Forces, amounting to more than $2 billion. KBR's philosophy as a company is based on a 1992 study the company did for the Defense Department. That study formed the template for the privatization of logistics for a downsized U.S. military. At its heart was a call to save the Pentagon hundred of billions of dollars by privatizing some of the military's functions. A short while after submitting the classified study, KBR won its first logistics contract during a competitive bid process.

Vice President Cheney was secretary of defense when KBR did its first study. Later he became chief executive of Halliburton, KBR's parent company, subsequently retiring before being selected as George W. Bush's running mate.

ARMOR HOLDINGS GROUP

Armor Holdings Group is a south Florida-based PMC and was on Fortune's 100 fastest-growing companies list in 1999. In Iraq, security contractors working for the company's subsidiary, ArmorGroup, protect the Baghdad headquarters and transport depots for Bechtel and the Halliburton subsidiary KBR, which have contracts to rebuild the Iraq infrastructure. The company also has a contract to provide convoy protection.

ArmorGroup describes itself as a global risk-management services business with more than 7,500 employees and offices in more than

38 countries. In business for more than 20 years, ArmorGroup has been providing risk-management services to corporate, government, and humanitarian organizations, particularly those that need to operate in hazardous or chaotic environments that put their people, physical, financial, and intellectual assets at risk.

"Risk management" is how PMCs primarily describe their services. It is code speak for providing military intelligence and armed personnel to protect businessmen doing business in a war zone of one sort or another.

ArmorGroup is headquartered in London, with operations across Europe, North and South America, Russia/CIS, Africa, the Middle East, and the Asia Pacific. The company claims that from 2002 to 2004, "ArmorGroup personnel have assisted clients in over 160 countries." Even allowing for exaggeration, this is big business.

In its mission statement, ArmorGroup says that its "mission is to enable its clients to operate in difficult and hostile environments at substantially reduced risk to their employees, intellectual property, and assets."

"Difficult and hostile" means "bad guys" with guns.

ArmorGroup's services cover a wide range of risk-management capabilities, broadly grouped into three areas:

- Global security risk management
- Security training and services
- Mine action

ArmorGroup is owned by ArmorGroup Management and Granville Baird Capital Partners (part of the U.S. Baird Group) with financial support from Barclays Bank PLC, a major international banking group. Interestingly enough, ArmorGroup subscribes to the following codes and legislation drawn up by sovereign governments and international agencies: the Voluntary Principles on Security and Human Rights; Code of Conduct of the International Red Cross and Red Crescent; Foreign and Corrupt Practices Act; Anti-terrorism, Crime and Security Act 2001; and the United Nations Mine Action Standards.

GLOBAL RISK STRATEGIES

Global Risk Strategies (GRS) is using a much cheaper source of manpower than these other companies. They hired more than 500 Fijian soldiers and 500 Nepalese, who had served in the British army's Gurkha regiments. Once hired, GRS flew them into Iraq to assist with GRS's $28 million contract to organize the changeover of Iraq's currency from "Saddam money" to free Iraqi money.

On December 1, 2003, GRS's Fijian contractors fired indiscriminately after a convoy carrying the new currency that they were guarding came under attack. In the end, 10 Iraqi civilians were killed and many others wounded. It didn't take long before other GRS contractors ran into deep trouble, too.

The bodies of two British GRS contractors working for the UN, were discovered on May 5, 2004, in the Mandol District of the Nuristan region of Afghanistan, 125 miles (200 kilometers) east of the capital, Kabul. The contractors were providing security to the UN workers who were there to help with free elections.

"Events such as these will not discourage either Global Risk Strategies or our client, the United Nations, from continuing to carry out the worthwhile reconstruction projects being undertaken throughout Afghanistan," the company said in its statement released after the bodies were found. Afghan President Hamid Karzai said the killings were a "cowardly act aimed at terrorizing. The people of Afghanistan will continue relentlessly on the path that the people of the country have chosen: the path of peace, prosperity, and reconstruction."

The UN Assistance Mission in Afghanistan issued a statement in Kabul also condemning the killings "in the strongest terms" and expressing sympathy with the families of the victims. These are the first foreign fatalities linked to the Afghanistan voter registration program. GRS maintains an "ethics code" for its employees. While laudatory, the CRG's ethics code seems simplistic in a complex world, especially Iraq:

- The management and employees of Control Risks Group are to exercise honesty, objectivity and diligence in performing their duties and undertaking their responsibilities.

- They should be loyal at all times both to the Group and those to whom they are rendering a service.

- They should not act in a manner which could discredit the Group.

- They should not enter into any activity which may result in a conflict of interest with the Group.

- They should not accept anything of value which could be described as an inducement or bribe which could impair their judgement [sic].

- They should not use confidential information for personal gain nor should any law or relevant regulation be contravened.

- Employees must report actual or potential infringements of this code to their head of office or divisional head who in turn must report it to the Ethics Committee.

DYNCORP

Based in Reston, Virginia, DynCorp is a subsidiary of Computer Sciences Corp. of San Diego. The DynCorp division has a $50 million State Department contract to provide 1,000 advisers to help organize Iraqi law enforcement and criminal justice systems.

On June 4, 2004, four DynCorp contractors were present during the Iraqi police raid on the home and offices of former exile leader Ahmed Chalabi in Baghdad.

A spokesman for the U.S.-run Coalition Provisional Authority said the DynCorp employees were "international police advisers." Military officials said the raid was an Iraqi police action with backup from U.S. soldiers. However, they neglected to add that the DynCorp contractors had joined in the action.

Then on May 31, 2004, Bruce Tow, a 54-year-old former cop who had gone to Iraq as a contractor working for DynCorp, to help train and rebuild the civilian police force, was killed in an ambush. Traveling with a group heading to Baghdad Airport, someone opened fire from a bridge overpass, and Tow was killed.

Tow had been working in Iraq since February 2004. A Denver police officer for 29 years, he spent his entire career in the SWAT unit, and had left the force about 5 years previous. He also worked as a bodyguard for Denver Broncos team owner Pat Bowlen. DynCorp did not release any information indicating that Tow had an extensive military background.

CONTROL RISKS GROUP

Control Risks Group, based in the United Kingdom, provides close protection security for civilians working with the Coalition who are employed by or seconded to the British Foreign Office.

Founded in 1975, Control Risks has since worked with more than 5,300 clients (including 86 of the Fortune 100 companies) in more than 130 countries. A rather sophisticated company, Control Risks offers a full range of value-added services to companies, governments, and private clients worldwide, including political and security risk analysis, confidential investigations, pre-employment screening, security consultancy, crisis management and response, and information security and investigations.

But it is, of course, in Iraq where the company grabs headlines. Mark Carmen, a contractor working for CRG, was killed on May 25, 2004, by a rocket-propelled grenade. The attack occurred about 50 yards from the entrance to the U.S. Coalition HQ in Baghdad. Carmen and three others were in a bulletproof 4x4 vehicle when the insurgents blasted it with the grenade. The company then issued this statement:

> Control Risks Group is deeply saddened to report that a colleague, Mark Carman, was killed in Baghdad yesterday at approximately 10.45 A.M. (UK local time). Mark, 38, was a British national and a former member of the British army. He was part of a team providing security to the Foreign and Commonwealth Office (FCO). Another civilian, Bob Morgan, working for the British government, was also killed in the attack. Our thoughts and sympathies are with the family and friends of both Mark and Bob.

ERINYS INTERNATIONAL

Based in South Africa and with offices in the United Arab Emirates and Iraq, Erinys International is a prime contractor to the Gulf Regional

Division of the U.S. Army Corp of Engineers, tasked with providing nationwide personal security details and protective services in Iraq.

The company is contracted to the Iraqi Ministry of Oil to recruit, train, equip, and manage 14,000 Iraqi security guards to protect the national oil infrastructure of Iraq. These services encompass access control, theft prevention, loss control, and emergency response services. Erinys is supported by 450 patrol vehicles throughout the country and also maintain air surveillance of the pipeline. It is a contract worth $100 million annually.

Erinys Iraq operates throughout the country under a north, center, south regional structure, each with its own independent headquarters, and a further 14 subsidiary sectors each with its own headquarters. The groups' operations and business are managed from a national headquarters in the Mansour District of Baghdad. Each sector and regional headquarters, along with the national HQ, maintains a 24-hour operations center. Overlaying this is a management and communications infrastructure that enables nationwide VHF, HF, and satellite voice/data communications.

Aside from national security programs, the company provides managed security guard forces and expatriate security services to many of the leading international companies and organizations involved in the reconstruction of Iraq. The company's services encompass site security and mobile security teams, convoy protection, diplomatic protection, and key point and personal protective services. The company divides its services into seven parts:

- **Security services and consultancy.** The Erinys security division is directed by former senior members of the UK armed forces with extensive private-sector experience providing specialist security advice and services to clients that include the United Nations, U.S. and UK governments, the international petrochemical industry, commerce, and the private sector.

- **Emergency action planning and crisis management.** Assisting the client to assess potentially damaging scenarios, analysis of the risks and exposure, and recommendation of appropriate countermeasures.

- **Specialist manpower.** Provision of qualified and experienced personnel for all levels of security, and for specialist training and project management.

- **Site security.** Security consultancy, security audits, and the provision of security management, training, personnel, and equipment.

- **Guard force management.** Selection, training, deployment, and management of local guard forces for key installations, including embassies in high-risk areas.

- **Transportation and logistics security.** Extensive experience of airline, airport, and port security; security of rail, sea, and overland routes, including cash and high-value goods in transit.

- **Human resources.** The provision of specialist, managed manpower for support operations in remote sites.

VINELL CORPORATION

The Vinell Corporation is currently a subsidiary of Northrop Grumman. They have the contract to train the Iraqi military and the Saudi National Guard, which protects Saudi Arabia's monarchy. For a PMC, the company has a rather long history.

Founded in 1931 by Allan S. Vinnell as a general contracting company, in 1946 the company began transition from general contractor to government services contractor. It has since gotten contracts from the U.S. government for every major war since World War II. In 1975, the company entered into a contract for the first time with the Saudis to train their national guard. Since then, it has gone on to become a "recognized leader in facilities operation and maintenance, military training, educational and vocational training, and logistics support in the United States and overseas."

The company claims to have "successfully completed projects on 5 continents and in more than 50 countries for a variety of government and commercial customers." The company asserts that "our technical expertise, experience, and outstanding record of achievement assure our clients that we will respond effectively and efficiently to meet their needs." The company breaks down its services as follows:

- **Military training.** Combat training, combat service support training, command and control training, live-fire exercises, after-action reports, field medical training, training support

- **Logistics services.** Supply and procurement, transportation, equipment operation and maintenance, international freight forwarding
- **Personnel support.** Housing and lodging management, food service, passenger travel, medical services, recreation management
- **Facilities operation and maintenance.** Building maintenance and repair, utilities operation and maintenance, environmental compliance, grounds and pavements maintenance, predictive testing and inspection, fingerprinting and biometrics
- **Vocational and education training.** High school and GED training, reading, mathematics, vocational training, English as a second language

In 1997, Vinnell was acquired by Thompson Raymos Woolrich (TRW). Ownership changed hands yet again in 2002 when Northrop Grumman bought the company. On June 8, 2004, Northrop Grumman's president posted this message on their website:

June 8, 2004

Message from Don Winter—Vinnell Employee Killed in Riyadh, Saudi Arabia

Today we learned that a Vinnell Arabia employee, Robert C. Jacobs of Murphysboro, Illinois, was shot and killed at his home in Riyadh, Saudi Arabia. The circumstances of the attack are still unclear and an investigation by Saudi authorities is now underway. While we are still gathering information about this tragedy, news agencies are reporting varied accounts of the event.

As you know, Northrop Grumman provides training services to the Saudi Arabian National Guard through Vinnell Arabia under a contract to the U.S. Army. Please remember the family of this employee and all of our employees in Saudi Arabia in your thoughts and prayers.

Don Winter
President
Northrop Grumman Mission Systems

CHAPTER 9

SOLDIERS OF FORTUNE

Contractors do not exist in some sort of existential middle ground between fact and fiction. They are real people, 99.9 percent of them male, with some sort of military background.

The popular assumption has been that mercenaries are usually ex-Green Berets or other types of special operations soldiers. Although many are, many are not. In this latter group are men who have not experienced combat—those who received their training in paramilitary organizations, usually police academies. As for standardized qualifications, if PMCs administer extensive psychological tests to weed out the psychopaths, it is not a well-known fact.

PMC recruiters do not work with a certain set of requirements accepted throughout the industry. Whereas one PMC will only use special operations soldiers as contractors, for example, another might recruit ex-cops. Some firms prefer "gurkhas," the term applied to non-Caucasian mercs, who are paid much less than their Caucasian counterparts. The mercenary business is the same then, as others, with people of color deliberately kept lower on the economic scale. That, of course, is building into the mercenary culture a significant racial gap in wages. Whether that's because the mercenary bureaucracy is simply a reflection of the society from whence it comes or simply the "haves" once again trying to keep it from the "have nots," is hard to say. Probably elements of both.

Getting lost in the racial gap, though, belies the paradigm that PMCs have created. No longer are mercenaries expected to be experts at specific types of soldiering as they have been throughout history. PMCs did not maintain industry wide, standard requirements. It is therefore next to impossible for contracting governments or companies to ascertain the particular credentials of every working contractor. It is just assumed that whoever is hired can do the job because they have been trained by someone to do it. That plus the natural secretiveness of these companies makes it particularly hard to get accurate information about their inner workings.

As for the mercs themselves, their lives are more affected by world events than the average person. Tim Spicer writes in his autobiography, "Wars attract mercenaries like honey attracts bees." Although that is true, world events in the 1980s were actually conspiring to put mercenaries out of business.

Probably the easiest way to understand exactly what contractors in Iraq do is to think of a Hollywood Western. A wagon train filled with settlers is headed west from St. Louis to Oregon. To make sure they get there in one piece, and the archetypal marauding Indians don't harm them, the Army sends along a cavalry unit to protect them.

Iraq is Oregon. To PMCs, it is the promised land of great riches beyond anything ever dreamed because of the lucrative contracts to rebuild the place. Bechtel and Halliburton are the settlers, bringing in their technicians to rebuild Iraq's infrastructure. The marauding Indians are the Iraqi insurgents. Now, when the U.S. Army was in control, the mercs played a supporting role; the cavalry really was at least trying to ride to the rescue. But with the country back in the hands of the Iraqis, and the US troops there now for support, the role of the cavalry has been privatized into the hands of the PMCs.

As world events began to build and demand outstripped supply, PMCs have recruited men who were not the experienced, trained, and, most important, disciplined mercenaries that Spicer favored. Instead, these PMCs began hiring thugs, the kind of men with limited military experience and even less discipline and self-control. Most important, where Sandline had set the standard of providing a military service in package form tailored to the goals of the client, many more PMCs were just interested in taking the money and running.

War profiteers, they had no interest in whether their participation made a war better or worse. For them, it was a question of making money as fast as they could and not asking questions. It was a perfect situation for the mercenaries' final ascendance to the world stage. In Iraq, the United States had figured out what Hannibal of Carthage had: It's cheaper and easier to employ mercenaries to help fight your battles than your own soldiers.

With the rise of the Internet, mercenary recruitment is only one click away. For example, Control Risks Group, a British PMC, makes it easy to find work with it. At its website, www.crg.com, it lists the following:

EMPLOYMENT OPPORTUNITIES

At the moment the following employment opportunities exist within the Group. If you would like to apply to join us, please use the link from the appropriate advertisement, specify in a covering note how you feel you meet our requirements, and attach your career history/resumé, stating your current salary.

We receive many unsolicited applications, and maintain an active database of potential candidates for employment. Many applicants are of a very high calibre and competition for positions is often intense. If your skills or experience do not match any of the following vacancies but you would like to submit your details to be included on our database, please email your CV/resumé to recruitment@control-risks.com specifying your areas of interest. All applications are treated in the strictest confidence.

Following those instructions is the list of jobs the company is currently interested in filling. For example, during the week of June 14, 2004, Control Risks was recruiting on its website for two ex-military officers to serve to fill a liaison task in the Middle East. "Will require a good understanding of Arabic. Attractive salary," the ad said.

Like any modern PMC, for Control Risks Group it wasn't just a matter of selling protection. Intelligence counted just as much for revenue. PMCs sell information about world security and make a pretty penny doing it. Consequently, Control Risks had positions open such as the following:

Travel Security Program Consultant, CR24

(London, UK)

A vacancy has arisen for a Travel Security Program Consultant within our CR24 department. The main responsibilities will be to promote and sell the Travel Security Program product and to provide customer support and account management to clients. Applicants should have 2+ years experience as well as good communication, presentation, and account management skills. Knowledge/experience in the travel industry is advantageous.

Regardless of the job chosen, all the applicant has to do is click the URL embedded in the ad. Up comes a pre-addressed e-mail to the PMC's in-house recruiter. Just attach your resumé, click Send, and you have just applied for a job at a modern PMC.

When the recruiter gets the resumé, he or she will evaluate it and make a decision whether to conduct a phone interview with the applicant. That may lead to interviews with line managers—that is, the people the applicant would be working with in the field, including superior officers. The applicant's credentials will be checked out very carefully and various competency tests may be administered. In the end, of course, it all comes down to money for risk: Can the applicant make the ultimate sacrifice of his life if he has to for a client and not his country? For this reason, many in the media and public alike view contractors as one step above a carnival geek.

The kinds of individuals who are attracted to the PMC business vary. Their public personas are burly, mustachioed, fierce-looking men wielding automatic weapons as they protect one individual or another in Iraq. Many are veterans of our nation's elite special operations forces, including the SEALs, Green Berets, and Rangers. Others are former cops. Their motivations to take what is obviously a very dangerous job in Iraq are varied.

(AP /Wideworld/Rob Cooper)

From left, U.S. nationals Gary George Blanchard, Joseph Pettyjohn, and John Lamonte Dixon, sit in leg irons in 1999 at the Harare Magistrate's Court where they were charged with mercenary activities including espionage, terrorism, and sabotage.

Some are like the soldiers of fortune of old, looking for adventure and big money at risk to life and limb. This group tends to be men in their 20s and 30s, like Gary George Blanchard, Joseph Pettyjohn, and John Lamonte Dixon. They were mercenaries arrested in Zimbabwe in 1999 for engaging in mercenary activities in the Congo, Tanzania, and Zimbabwe.

Then there are the retired service veterans in their 40s, who are looking to cash in on their military experience. Some are married with children, others divorced. Finally, there are the entrepreneurs like Spicer. These are the soldier/businessman/entrepreneurs that are the guiding forces behind most PMCs.

During the past decade, billions of dollars have been spent on private military contractors. Here's a quick look at the biggest contracts during that time period.

THE MERCENARY TOP TEN

1. **1998—$831 million for five years.** The Vinnell Corporation got the contract to supply and train the Saudi National Guard. The latter are the highly trained men who protect the Saudi monarchy from harm, enabling their employers to maintain stability.

2. **2004—$293 million for three years.** The redoubtable Colonel Spicer finds himself in second position with the contract he obtained for his company, Aegis Defence Services, from the Coalition Authority and the U.S. Defense Department. Aegis/Spicer is in charge of coordinating all the security contractors in Iraq; providing specific security for Program Management Office, which is monitoring Iraqi reconstruction; and up to 75 two-man security teams trained in "mobile vehicle warfare" [firing from a moving car] and "counter-sniping" [returning fire].

3. **1998—$100 million—offered but denied.** Gen. Sami Abacha controlled the Nigerian government. Some people wanted him overthrown. They contacted Executive Outcome about doing the job. EO declined the one-time $100 million offer. That turned out to be a very smart move when Abacha died from natural causes that same year.

4. **2003—$52 million.** DynCorp was the beneficiary on this one, the contract to provide security to President Hamid Karzai of Afghanistan.

5. **2003—$50 million.** DynCorp did it again. This time it was the contract to create the new Iraqi police force. Coupled with the previous $52 million, the company already had yearly billables in excess of $100 million.

6. **2003—$48 million.** The Vinnell Corporation again, this time getting the contract to train nine battalions of the Iraqi army. Sidenote: More than half of the first completed battalion chose to subsequently leave the army.

7. **2003–2004—$39.2 million.** Erinys International got the hazardous duty of protecting the Iraqi oil pipeline. Requiring 14,500 security

contractors, their job is to protect against Iraqi insurgents instituting pipeline attacks.

8. **1995–1997—Executive Outcome.** The first was still the best. EO got the contract to defend Sierra Leone's capital from an invading rebel army. Later, EO mercenaries stormed the rebel stronghold. When the war was over, EO had wound up defeating two coup attempts by the rebel army. In a brilliant move, EO allowed a third party to stage an internal coup that succeeded. The new government was sympathetic to EO's business interests in the country.

9. **2003–2004—19.9 million.** CACI Systems provided "interrogation services" to the U.S. military. One CACI contractor has been implicated in the Abu Ghraib prison scandal.

10. **2000—$220,000.** Onix International provided a team of former New Zealand special operations soldiers to rescue a businessman being held hostage in East Timor. Two hundred grand split many ways might not seem like much for putting your life on the line, but for many men with military and paramilitary backgrounds, it is sometimes more than enough.

Perhaps because of the high startup costs and other reasons, PMC investment seems to attract the rich sons of millionaires, like Blackwater's Erik D. Prince or Executive Outcome's Simon Mann. A friend of Tim Spicer's, Mann was one of 70 mercenaries who were arrested in Zimbabwe in 2004 for attempting to overthrow the government of Equatorial Guinea. The Mail and Guardian Online describes him as "an establishment deviant."

That is as good a description of a mercenary as anyone will ever get.

Simon Mann is the son of an English cricket captain who made millions from the Watney's brewing empire. Educated at Eton and Sandhurst, Mann joined the elite Scots Guards, where he made Tim Spicer's acquaintance. Following Spicer, he passed the rigid selection process for the SAS on his first try. He became a trooper commander in 22 SAS. While serving with the SAS, Mann became an intelligence and counterterrorism expert.

Canada, Central America, Northern Cyprus, Germany, Norway, Northern Ireland, he served in all those places. When he left the army in 1981, "I think he wanted a new challenge. After a while some people find army life a little bit mundane," said a former associate.

During the early days of his post-army life, Mann sold secure computer software. What made him move into the private military company business is unclear. But it is not inconceivable to believe that a wealthy young man who craved action might find more mundane jobs boring, as his associate observed.

By the late 1980s, Mann was providing bodyguards to billionaire Arab sheiks, not to protect them in their home countries but their Scottish estates that were being victimized by poachers. During the Gulf War in 1991, Mann put his army uniform back on and served on the staff of British Gulf War commander Sir Peter de la Billiere.

After the war ended, Mann went back into business. In 1993, he helped finance Executive Outcome and became a partner with Eeben Barlow. By 1995, when EO had become too high profile, he sold out; his cut was $10 million. Using part of it, he helped set up Sandline International with Tim Spicer.

In 1997, the same year of the Sandline scandal, Mann bought an English estate called Inchmery. During 1944, it was the training ground for Polish paratroopers preparing for D day. It had also been a residence of the Rothschild family. Mann didn't own it; he bought it in the name of Myers Developments, a company registered in an offshore tax haven called Guernsey. He rented it out and moved back to South Africa with his family.

Mann had not lived the archetypal mercenary's life. Although he liked women, he didn't love 'em and leave 'em; he married them and had kids with them and seemed to love his family. He had three children from two prior marriages, and three more with his then-wife Amanda. They moved into a multimillion dollar Dutch cape home. It was a beautiful gabled house in Constantia, a tony suburb favored by British expatriates. Mann enjoyed his leisure, becoming an avid fisherman. He patronized sculptors, collected art, and had dinner parties for a small group of exclusive friends. Respected and admired by all his friends, none of the latter knew where Mann got his money; he was very secretive about his business enterprises.

In another of many life-imitating-art events in his life, Mann became an actor. He played the role of Col. Derek Wilford, commander of the paratroopers who fired on marchers in Derry, in a British docudrama called Bloody Sunday. In a published interview, Mann claimed that he had taken the role partly to defend the army and partly to aid the Northern Ireland peace process. Director Paul Greengrass said of Mann: "He is a humane man, but an adventurer. He is very English, a romantic, tremendously good company."

He certainly got good reviews for the role. Mann might have continued in acting. Once again, something took hold of him. Maybe it was the old wanderlust and yearning for action. Maybe he just needed the money because his high lifestyle had eroded his $10 million poke. Whatever his reason, what happened next was just plain stupid: He decided to pull a Denard and invade an African nation with a core group of mercenaries and stage a military coup.

A group of alleged mercenaries are led to a hall at Chikurubi maximum prison, in Zimbabwe, for plotting a coup against Equatorial Guinea.

The attempted mercenary takeover of Equatorial Guinea will probably go down in American journalism as one of its darkest hours. News outlet after news outlet chose to ignore it. Like much of what happens on the African continent, the American press once again showed its true colors. It happens that they missed not only one of the most politically significant stories of the year, it was probably the most exciting.

It starts with a poor West African country. Small in size, Equatorial Guinea lies between Gabon and Cameroon. It is a former Spanish colony with an overabundant mosquito population; malaria is rampant. There was no reason to suspect that the country's fortunes would change. And then, they found oil.

The discovery of vast offshore oil reserves and gas fields in the early 1990s made Equatorial Guinea's economy the world's fastest growing. Suddenly this poor West African country that had been spit on by everybody was suddenly in a position where it could meet a significant part of the world's energy demands. This was not something that would run out in the foreseeable future, like diamond or gold mines. This was oil and gas, and if the geologists were correct, an inexhaustible supply.

Osama bin Laden has proved what a madman with a billion dollars can do. How about the ruler of a whole nation? For the past 30 years, through poverty and now vast wealth, Equatorial Guinea has been run by one man: Teodoro Obiang Nguema Mbasogo, 62-years old in 2004.

Mbasogo calls himself president. He's actually a dictator and, some say, a cannibal with peculiar tastes in human flesh. He has been widely accused in his own country of eating the testicles of the men who opposed him, reportedly partaking after having them executed. And it should be emphasized, Mbasogo has none of Hannibal Lecter's wit or panache.

Still, the dictator/president/testicle aficionado is smart enough to get his cut from the offshore oil drilling. That makes him one of the wealthier dictator/president/testicle aficionado's extant. Nguema has maintained power through the post-oil era by keeping the oil production steady. With a production high of 350,000 barrels a day, that translates into enriching Equatorial Guinea by £500 million a month. It has become the Kuwait of Africa.

The oil industry, and its very powerful corporate and political allies in the West, is far more demanding than Nguema's oppressed populace has ever been. Dallas-based Triton Energy, which has close ties to President George W. Bush, Exxon Mobil, and Chevron Texaco have together invested more than $5 billion in Equatorial Guinea's nascent oil production. Some oil industry analysts predict the country's oil can soon provide the United States with 5 percent of its annual needs.

But the riches were undermining the solidarity of Obiang Nguema's ruling Mongomo clan. It dominates the armed forces and the presidential entourage. Money can be divisive in the best of families, but in the Mongomo clan it has become a fratricidal struggle for succession.

Obiang wanted his favorite son, Teodorin to take his place when his time was up. The problem was, Teodorin, an international playboy, was not a favorite of his powerful relatives who opposed the "coronation." The opposition party also felt threatened by the succession.

Obiang subsequently accused Ely Calil, a Chelsea-based tycoon, of plotting a coup to put his buddy, Severo Moto Nsa, into the presidency. The quid pro quo was oil concessions. This is why Obiang Nguema is so paranoid about being the victim of a coup. His biggest fear comes from his extended family. He himself staged a coup against his own family in 1979.

Obiang overthrew his equally unsavory uncle, Macias Nguema, with the help of his own mercenaries, his Moroccan security guards. These Moroccan elite have been known to execute by firing squad up to 150 dissidents at a time in the national soccer stadium while a military band plays "Those Were the Days, My Friends."

After oil company lobbying, the U.S. embassy in Malabo, Nguema's capital, was reopened in 2002 after being closed in the early 1990s when the ambassador received death threats. It is into this maelstrom of greed, power, and violence that British soldier of fortune Simon Mann and his collaborators in the plot to overthrow the country's presidential dictator deliberately walked.

Western intelligence agencies may well have endorsed the plot—in a plausibly deniable manner—to secure stability for Equatorial Guinea's oil production and to rid the former Spanish colony of a notably brutal and avaricious ruling clan. At this point, details get murky, but what has become clear was evidence to show a multifaceted attempt to overthrow Obiang. The Mail and Guardian Online reported:

> Since last year, Nick du Toit, a former South African mercenary, has forged ties with one faction of the ruling clan involving fishing rights and customs control. It is rumored that his real task was to somehow hobble the military, especially the president's Moroccan bodyguards, to clear the way for a small invasion force.

Du Toit had previously worked for Executive Outcome and brought in his old boss Mann. Allegedly, Mann was promised $5 million, with Calil as a go-between, to enable an armed overthrow of Obiang's regime. Mann recruited "66 veterans of apartheid South Africa's bush wars, many of them black mercenaries from Angola and Namibia."

Setting up a training base at a farm outside Johannesburg, Mann trained his soldiers. The alleged plan was to gather crates of AK-47 rifles, mortars, and 30,000 rounds of ammunition. It would all be put on a plane with the Mann-led mercs; they'd land in Equatorial Guinea, open the crates, arm themselves, depose Obiang, and take over.

At 7:30 P.M. on March 7, 2004, a Boeing 727-100 owned by Logo Logistics, Mann's company, was impounded after arriving at Harare, Zimbabwe. The crew and passengers were arrested. So was Mann, who had been in Harare already for several days, awaiting the men and the arms shipments. A short while later, Du Toit and 14 other mercenaries were also arrested.

The governments of Equatorial Guinea and Zimbabwe crowed. They announced to the world that they had foiled a military coup. Mann's written confession, dated March 9, was leaked to a South African newspaper. Then the governments began fighting for possession of the mercs.

South Africa jockeyed to extradite the South African mercs on its anti-mercenary law. Of course, the other reason South Africa was doing that was because Zimbabwe had threatened to use the death penalty, even though it was not its own government that had been endangered. As for Equatorial Guinea, it was pushing for extradiction; they wanted the mercs in *their* custody. Zimbabwe threatened a dank cell and a hangman's noose for what the African media dubbed "the Zimbabwe 70."

It is hard to believe a man of Simon Mann's expertise and street smarts would believe that you could still pull a "Denard" and take over a country with force of arms. Certainly, as one of EO's founders, he knew better. Even the personnel Mann selected did not seem the best for the job. Some were men in their 60s, overweight, out of shape. How to explain such a debacle that might cost these mercenaries their lives?

"Amateur hour. It was doomed to fail because they had absolutely no respect for operational security. Everybody knew it was happening. Good lord, what idiots, the whole thing seems inept. Are they just ignorant about what goes on in these places?" said one Mann acquaintance.

Simon Mann did what any smart defendant would do, mercenary or not—he got a good "mouthpiece." Mann hired Zimbabwe attorneys Jonathan Samkange, of Byron, Venturas and Partners, one of Equatorial Guinea's best defense attorneys. Samkange analyzed the situation and decided to deal. Mann agreed, and they cut a deal with the government of Equatorial Guinea.

In return for pleading guilty to contravening the Zimbabwe Firearms Act by conspiring to purchase dangerous weapons without end-user certificates, and pleading guilty to contravening the Public Order and Security Act (POSA) for attempting to possess dangerous weapons, the government offered to drop the rest of the charges. It was a fascinating denouement in the biggest mercenary crisis of the millennium.

While most of the world stayed focused on the Abu Ghraib brutalities, and a finding by an army court that two Titan contractors were involved in the Abu Ghraib tortures, in Equatorial Guinea a government had decided to take what at first glance appeared to be a principled stance against mercenary activity on its terrain.

From official government rhetoric that the mercs should be tried and hanged, the government of the country, which had had a reputation as being "dodgy," had decided in the end that conducting a kangaroo court and then executing the 70 was not exactly a good public relations move. Obiang had struck international gold by tempering his passion with common sense.

For Mann, it was an opportunity to save not only his life but the lives of the men who were serving under him. As their commander it was his job to spare them as much of the heat as he could. Although it is not clear that part of Mann's plea involved drastically reducing the charges against his men, that is exactly what happened.

On Friday, August 27, 2004, Simon Mann walked into a Zimbabwe court and appeared before Magistrate Mishrod Guvamombe. He pled guilty to the charges. At the same time, 2 of the 70, Jacobus Horne and Jacobus Herminus Carlse, were simultaneously exonerated of all charges. Horne and Carlse, who had come to Harare as an advance party, were set free after presiding Magistrate Guvamombe acquitted the 66 other accused mercs on charges of contravening Section 13 of POSA (conspiracy to possess dangerous weapons). As part of the plea deal, the 66 defendants pleaded guilty to contravening the Immigration Act and the Civil Aviation Act. Violating the government's Immigration Act carries a maximum penalty of a $1.5 million fine or not more than two years in prison. Violating the Civil Aviation Act entails a fine of $200 or one month's imprisonment.

From out of the long-ago American past, in the government forged after Washington's decisive victory over the Hessians, came the universally respected American concept of convicting a defendant only when reasonable doubt has been overcome. And so, in acquitting the 66 on the POSA charge, Magistrate Guvamombe said the state had failed to prove its case beyond reasonable doubt. Defense attorney Jonathan Samkange then addressed the court.

Samkange knew that the maximum fine for contravening the Firearms Act was $1 million, whereas that for violating POSA the penalty was $250,000. More important, there was the distinct possibility of jail time. He reminded the judge that Mann was 54 years old, married with six children, and that his expectant wife was due to give birth to their seventh child next month. He said that Mann had pleaded guilty to the charges and the court should take that into consideration because he had not wasted its time.

"If he had challenged everything that the state had said, I believe this case could have taken five years," said Samkange, reminding the court that

Mann had been in custody for almost six months and had been treated worse, the attorney claimed, than any serving prisoner. Samkange then urged the court to impose a fine instead of a prison term.

"In all statutory offences where the legislature has stated a fine is to be imposed and alternatively given a custodial sentence, it is improper for the court to ignore the legislature and impose a custodial sentence," Samkange told the magistrate.

When it was his turn, State Prosecutor Stephen Musona said that the court should impose a jail term because Mann was the leader of the group and the one who purchased the weapons.

"This court has the discretion to impose a fine or a prison sentence and it (the state) is asking the court to impose a five-year sentence for contravening the Firearms Act and 10 years for attempting to possess dangerous weapons," Musona said.

Musona reminded the court that Mann's plane, a Boeing 727-100, and the $200,000 Mann was carrying when arrested, were supposed to be used for the purchase of firearms to overthrow the government of Equatorial Guinea. He urged the court to, in its decision, give both to the state. Musona not only wanted the mercenary in prison, he wanted to really hurt him in the pocketbook, too.

Samkange contested the state's case. He said a person should not be punished harshly for thoughts and attempts to do something as had happened in his client Mann's case. Samkange told the magistrate that the plane was valued at about $3 million and stated that to confiscate it as a penalty for such an offence would be extremely unfair. In turn, Magistrate Guvamombe said he needed time to consider the submissions from both parties, and delayed sentencing until September 10.

Afterward, outside the courtroom in Zimbabwe, it was the same as it would be in the United States—reporters with notebooks and cameras crowding around the principals in the case. Samkange said that the sentencing of the 67 mercs who had pleaded guilty to contravening the Immigration Act, should take into consideration that the mercs had already spent a long time in prison, without even being convicted of a crime. However, he stated, "I am very pleased; I have always had confidence in the judiciary. I am pleased the system works."

Samkange said the trial's fairness demonstrated to the world that Zimbabwe's justice system was fair and independent. And so, it looked like the case would be over on September 10, when the mercs were sentenced. South Africa had some surprises in the interim, when they decided to charge the South Africans Horn and Carlse, the recently freed mercs, under the country's anti-mercenary law.

Harry Carlse and Lourens Horn had just returned home from Zimbabwe, where the pair claimed they were stripped, beaten, and threatened with electric shocks in a top-security facility. "They have been charged under the Regulation of Foreign Military Assistance Act. They will receive a summons to appear in court, most probably next week," lawyer Alwyn Griebenow said after meeting police in Pretoria with Carlse and Horn.

If convicted under the anti-mercenary law, Carlse and Horn could face up to 15 years in prison. But although the law is meant to curb mercenary activities in South Africa's "neighborhood," rarely is it enforced with teeth. Previous convictions under the anti-mercenary legislation have not resulted in jail terms.

"We believe they have contravened the Regulation of Foreign Military Assistance Act. The act prohibits people from taking part in any military activity outside the borders of the republic without the permission of the authorities. They had no permission," Nkosi said.

Asked whether a plea bargain was possible, he said, "The door is open. If they would give us information that we would not otherwise have, that would make their situation better." That, of course, would impact on the remaining 68 South African mercenaries, including Mann, awaiting sentencing in Zimbabwe. Even if they got off there, they would probably be charged on their return. It was the last kind of publicity South Africa could want.

It was bad for business that South Africa's own former cops had become mercs and hired themselves out for a military coup in another country. Whether South Africa made an example of them or not, all their activities did were besmirch the progressive reforms the government had been trying to institute since Nelson Mandela was freed from prison and became

CHAPTER 9: SOLDIERS OF FORTUNE

the country's first black president. Then Mark Thatcher stepped into the picture.

The South African cops arrested Mark Thatcher, son of former British Prime Minister Margaret Thatcher, and accused him of financing the March coup attempt in oil-rich Equatorial Guinea. It turned out that Mark Thatcher was Simon Mann's neighbor in Cape Town. It also turned out that he was arrested by a crack South African police unit, the Scorpions, because he was planning to leave his luxury Cape Town home and relocate to Texas by late August 2004.

When the cops showed up at Thatcher's luxury home on the slopes of Table Mountain, he had already sold his four vehicles, including two top-of-the-line off-road vehicles. Placed under house arrest until he put up £2 million, Thatcher's name catapulted the case into the headlines in even the blasé American media.

There were also reports in what emerged was a lengthy investigation into Thatcher's activities, that a key witness in the investigation has disappeared. Sam Daniels, a computer expert, was alleged to be the coup paymaster. He had gone missing, carrying, the government said, the "wonga list"—the names and contact details of wealthy and powerful individuals who contributed funds to finance the failed coup.

South Africa revealed that Thatcher had been under surveillance for more than a week before officers in plain clothes came out of the early-morning dawn and stopped in at Thatcher's home on Dawn Street early on Wednesday, August 25. Thatcher, 51, was charged with co-financing the coup attempt against Equatorial Guinea's dictator/president/testicle aficionado, Teodoro Obiang Nguema, in the amount of £300,000.

The Scorpions had stuck to him like their namesakes. When they discovered that Thatcher, who had lived with his wife and two children in Cape Town since 1995, was planning to leave for Texas quickly, they were forced into action. The cops were afraid that if he left South Africa, it would take years to extradite him.

During the search of Thatcher's Cape Town home, the Scorpions confiscated the air tickets on which Thatcher, his wife (Diane Burgdof, a Texan heiress), and their two children, (Michael, 15, and Amanda, 11) were to fly to the United States. Ever the thoughtful father, Thatcher had enrolled Michael and Amanda in American schools for the start of the new academic year beginning in September 2004.

Thatcher family spokesman, Lord Bell, denied that Thatcher had been planning to flee. He said that Baroness Thatcher, a.k.a. former Prime Minister Margaret Thatcher, was "obviously distressed" over the arrest of her son. She was also "very confident" that when the case came to trial, her son would be cleared, and with good reason. The British aristocracy has a long tradition of taking care of its own. Rarely, if ever, are the children of prime ministers convicted of major crimes.

Questions about the attempted coup in Equatorial Guinea remain. The only bigwig charged was Thatcher. Who really financed Mann and his operatives? No one's talking.

Then there's the matter of what the western intelligence services knew. The U.S. CIA, the French Direction Générale de la Sécurité Extérieure (DGSE), and the British MI6, did they know in advance that Mann was going in and a coup in Equatorial Guinea could be imminent? Zimbabwe and Equatorial Guinea think so. Both countries claimed that the governments of the United States and Great Britain were behind the coup.

"The mercenaries were aided by the British secret service—that is MI6—American Central Intelligence Agency, and the Spanish secret service," claimed the Zimbabwean home affairs minister Kembo Mohadi. Zimbabwe's foreign minister, Stan Mudenge, went even further, stating that the coup plot was more than just an attempt to overthrow a country's dictator.

"Apparently, this was not one mission … after the diversion in Equatorial Guinea, they were going to the DRC [Democratic Republic of Congo]." Mudenge offered no substantiation of his charges.

It was left for the Glasgow *Sunday Herald* to do the best reporting on what really happened in Equatorial Guinea. Investigations editor Neal McKay claimed the following in his article of August 28, 2004:

> The gossip and rumour within British and American intelligence circles points towards the UK and US certainly knowing that the coup was in the offing—even if there was no direct participation.

However, some intelligence figures in African countries have claimed that agents of MI6 and the CIA had been telling senior figures in Equatorial Guinea's military and intelligence services that if a coup did take place that they should sit tight, hold still and not defend Obiang ... that in return for their inaction they would be well looked after by any post-coup government.

That would seem to imply that the United States would allow Mann to succeed in his endeavor in order to put in a more compliant ruler, less of a wildcard than Obiang. McKay continues, saying that there is a South African intelligence report detailing that government's fear of an attempted coup in Equatorial Guinea. In fact, it turned out to be one of the worst-planned coups in history. The reporter claims that at an academic meeting in London, U.S. and Foreign Office personnel were in attendance and discussed rumors that a coup was imminent. This happened well before the actual event. Considering the leaks, the Western intelligence services' claims that they were not aware of what was happening are hard to believe.

It was South African intelligence that tipped off Zimbabwe and Equatorial Guinea that someone was going to try to replace Obiang with Severo Moto, the self-styled president-in-exile, who lives in Spain. That's how the coup plot was busted and Mann arrested immediately when he touched down in Zimbabwe.

One of Moto's friends is Spain's former Prime Minister Jose Maria Aznar. Some in the international community believe that Spain, America's staunch antiterrorist ally and Equatorial Guinea's former ruler, was trying to get its fingers on its former colony's oil by helping to install a new ruler, more subservient to the West. To date, no documentation has emerged to substantiate this charge.

Back in Equatorial Guinea, another one of the mercenary leaders, Nick Du Toit, said that unnamed "higher-up politicians" in the United States had encouraged the coup. He also claimed that Simon Mann told him that Spain had promised to recognize the post-coup government. Du Toit's wife, Belinda, then claimed that Equatorial Guinea prison guards had stamped on Du Toit's feet until his toenails fell off during "interrogation" sessions in the capital city of Malabo.

For his part, the dictator Obiang made the charge that the last stage of the attempted coup "consisted of the military support which was meant to come from Spain through the warships which, at that very moment, were already stationed in the territorial waters of Equatorial Guinea under the pretext of defending the legitimate government of Equatorial Guinea."

A special adviser to Obiang, Miguel Mifuno, said the Spanish warship contained 500 soldiers. "Our intelligence sources say that the warship was going to arrive on the same day that the coup attempt was going to take place, March 8," Mifuno said. "It was already in our territorial waters with 500 soldiers aboard. Meanwhile there was a team of foreign mercenaries already in Equatorial Guinea who knew where we lived. They had plans to kill 50 people and to arrest others. Spain was providing all the facilities for the coup. [The boat] was there to provide resources for the mercenaries."

Spain completely denied the charges, saying it had absolutely no complicity whatsoever in the attempted coup and the hiring of the mercenaries.

"I believe that because the attempt was organized in Spain by opposition members, the intelligence services in Spain were aware of it," said Obiang. He added that mercenaries were "a trade that international economic powers and the multinationals are using ... the petroleum wealth of Africa is the new honey that attracts the foreign bees to our home ...."

Equatorial Guinea was trying a separate group of 19 men, mostly foreigners, accused of being involved in the coup plot. The man accused of leading the group, South African Nick du Toit, has admitted taking part, and prosecutors are pressing for the death penalty.

"In the course of questioning, we have found they were financed by enemy powers, by multinational companies, by countries that do not love us. There are other countries that knew about this attempt and did not contribute information. We will have to qualify them as enemies. Multinational firms operating here and outside who contributed to this operation are also enemy companies."

It was a U.S.-registered plane that flew the mercenaries into Zimbabwe. The Glasgow *Sunday Herald* pointed out in its article that a company linked to Mark Thatcher was supposed to fly Moto from Spain to Mali on the night before the coup attempt. If that were true, the idea would be to have Moto arrive in triumph in Equatorial Guinea. Mann testified in a Zimbabwean court, "I was told he would land in an aircraft 30 minutes after the main force had landed."

In the wake of the attempted coup, the United States has frozen bank accounts worth hundreds of millions of dollars belonging to Obiang and his family. The funds were discovered in American bank accounts. Spain, meanwhile, was trying to mend its diplomatic bridges.

In the wake of the coup's failure, Spain reaffirmed that it recognizes only Obiang's as the "legal government" of Equatorial Guinea, and said it would "examine the political exile status" of Moto. Back in the United States, Secretary of State Colin Powell said he didn't know anything about any coup plans. Back across the Atlantic in Blighty, the British Foreign Office denied vociferously any claims of MI6 involvement in the coup.

"Utter rubbish," said the Foreign Office spokesperson with characteristic British understatement.

The conviction of Simon Mann by the Zimbabwean court came at the worst possible time for Tim Spicer, his old Scots Guards and Sandline buddy. Suddenly, mercenary activity, which usually goes under the radar, made it onto the front pages, even in America. Spicer had to face severe criticism when his company, Aegis, was awarded the $293 million Iraqi contract. People out of his past stepped forward to claim what a monster he was in Northern Ireland when he served there. Then, just when the criticism was dying down, Mann's alleged coup plot in Equatorial Guinea drew the international media spotlight to the international mercenary trade.

Democratic presidential candidate John Kerry demanded that the Pentagon investigate the deal. He joined with his Senate colleagues Hillary Rodham Clinton, Ted Kennedy, Chris Dodd, and Charles Schumer in responding not only to Spicer's company getting the contract without what appeared to be a competitive bidding process, but also the old allegations about his conduct in Northern Ireland.

The five senators sent a letter to Secretary of Defense Donald Rumsfeld. In it, they mention a number of serious concerns regarding Aegis's contract and Spicer himself:

The United States Government requires all contractors to be "responsible bidders." Contractors have to "have a satisfactory record of integrity and business ethics." We would like to know whether the government considered human rights abuses—or an individual who vigorously defends them—as part of this record.

This, of course, refers to Spicer's alleged breaking of a UN arms embargo in Sierra Leone.

Additionally, the United States government requires consideration of the contractor's "past performance." We would like to know whether the contracting team adequately reviewed the contractor's record, identified past human rights abuses or defense of abuses, and whether the contractor received a poor past performance rating on that basis.

We would also like to know the extent to which these factors were evaluated in awarding this contract to Aegis. If they were evaluated, we would like to know the rationale for awarding the contract.

A reasonable request. The letter continues:

In light of the recent revelations of abuses of detainees in Iraq, it is important that U.S. actions, whether by military personnel or contractors, have respect for the law. It is troubling that the government would award a contract to an individual with a history of supporting excessive use of force against a civilian population.

The senators' intentions notwithstanding, this appeared to be more of a politically based paragraph than anything else, because Spicer has never even been charged with human rights abuse.

"Certainly we understand the urgent need to establish a secure environment, but the United States government is also working to create a democracy in Iraq in which respect for fundamental human rights is guaranteed," the senators' letter continued.

Ironically, the two British soldiers under his command who Spicer allegedly helped get a reduced sentence for killing 18-year-old Peter McBride in Northern Ireland, not only were released, they were allowed to rejoin their regiment and served in Iraq during the 2003 invasion and subsequent occupation.

The Washington-based lobbying group the Irish National Caucus (INC) thanked the five senators for their support. Support for the campaign to wrest the contract out of Spicer's hands continued to build. Powerful Massachusetts Congressman Marty Meehan was also recruited to the INC's cause.

"I am very grateful to these five Senators," INC President Father Sean McManus said. "They are showing sensitivity to the family of Peter McBride, and a concern for basic human rights and decency. President Bush must do likewise. He must cancel this contract. President Bush must decide if he wants the respect of Irish-Americans or the gratitude of Timothy Spicer for the fat contract. He cannot have both."

Peter McBride's mother Jean also welcomed the senators' support.

Peter's anniversary is this coming Saturday and it is comforting to see such high profile support from the U.S.," she said. "We are awaiting judgment from the courts in the battle to have [the two soldiers] kicked out of the British Army and its great to see that our family is not alone. Surely someday soon justice will be done."

Clearly, Aegis is not without its resources. Aegis' advisory board includes two "formers": the former British ambassador to the United Nations, and the former chief of the United Kingdom General. Of course, Spicer also has his personal contacts. In addition, some in the media have floated the idea that Aegis's Iraq contract is American payback for British participation in the Iraq conflict (because U.S. taxpayers are footing much of the bill).

With George W. Bush elected to a second term, and with his public statement that he will not reinstitute a draft taken at face value, the future looks ever brighter for mercenary employment in Iraq.

EPILOGUE

In the time leading up to his sentencing, Simon Mann had managed to smuggle a letter out of his prison cell. Making its torturous way back to England, it wound up being quoted in several British newspapers.

In the letter, Mann writes that only "major clout" can save him. Of course, he's referring to a prison sentence; he was not facing anything greater. Mann also wrote that he feared conviction if subjected to "a real trial scenario."

On September 10, 2004, in the morning, a grizzled Simon Mann shuffled into the makeshift courthouse inside the Chikurubi maximum security prison near Harare, where the mercs had been held since their capture. The trial and sentencing were held at the prison because prison authorities had only one truck to transport all the mercenaries almost 10 miles (15 kilometers) from Chikurubi prison to the Harare magistrate's court in Harare. They were worried that the lone truck or the escort vehicles might break down, making it possible for the mercs to overwhelm their guards and escape.

Chains bound Mann at his hands and feet. He wore prison khaki and shorts and colorless wire-rimmed glasses, and had a gray-streaked beard. He looked more like a disheveled, confused academic than a crack mercenary leader. Looking down from the bench, Magistrate Mishrod Guvamombe referred back to the facts of the case.

"The accused was the author of the whole transaction. He was caught while trying to take the firearms out of the country," said Magistrate Guvamombe. The offenses "were well planned and well executed and that must be reflected in the penalty."

Judge Guvamombe sentenced Simon Mann to seven years in jail. Clearly, no one had interceded; the fix was not in. Simon Mann was not going to be rescued. Like any mercenary in the ancient world, he would have to pay for hiring out his services to the losing side.

The court also hit Mann in the pocketbook, stripping him of the jet he had ridden in on. Mann was led away in shackles to begin his sentence.

But the magistrate wasn't finished. He brought the other 65 mercenaries in. For the immigration offenses they had pled to, Judge Guvamombe sentenced them to a year behind bars.

The reaction was immediate. Inside the courtroom, relatives of the mercenaries broke down and wept as the verdict was read. "I am devastated. I can't believe it. They have already done six months and with this sentence it is now 18 months," said Jean Rogers, whose husband was one of the mercenaries.

Back in Britain, the *Guardian* newspaper, reporting on the so-called "wonga list" of alleged millionaire backers of the failed coup. The paper said that it [the list] had been given to South African police by two of Mann's former colleagues. The list, which the *Guardian* reported seeing, said that Mann contributed $500,000 toward the coup. A London-based Lebanese oil millionaire also allegedly came up with $750,000.

It didn't take long after the verdict for Mann's friends in parliament to rush to get him out. Conservative legislator Henry Bellingham, who knows Mann, said, "I find it very difficult to believe the allegations made against him. The (British) government should seek his return to the UK for the matters to be investigated here. Here is a British citizen who had a distinguished army career, and the government should be trying to help him."

He added, "Any sentence from a court in Zimbabwe, where the whole legal system has been discredited, is something the British government must take a close interest in," which it did.

The British Foreign Office said that Mann, who possesses both British and South African passports, "At his request, and with the approval of the Zimbabwean authorities, consular staff in Harare have visited him [Mann] in prison, and will continue to do so. Our embassy staff has also regularly attended his court appearances."

EPILOGUE

The day of the mercenary army that could conquer an African nation is over. If there's any doubt about that, consider this, just one more story lost in the Equatorial Guinea mercenary scandal shuffle.

President Obiang Nguema might be a doctor and testicle eater, but he is also one smart dude. He had his lawyers walk into a Pretoria, South Africa, courtroom on August 8, 2004, for the purpose of applying for access to bank documents of Simon Mann and three others allegedly involved in financing the failed coup.

Obiang's attorneys then asked the Royal Bank of Scotland to disclose the bank details of two companies Mann managed. They also wanted the contents of certain private safes in the bank, which might contain key contracts, to be made available for their investigation.

Obiang was turning the mercenaries' methods against them without even firing a shot.

THE TWENTY-FIRST-CENTURY AMERICAN MERCENARY

BY W. THOMAS SMITH JR.

They know no country, own no lord. Their home the camp, their law the sword.

—Silvio Pellico, 1788–1854, Enfernio de Messina

The four men—cramped two to a bench—sat in a dark, wooden booth in a corner of the barroom and sipped brown whiskeys. They were bearded and sported haircuts a bit longer than regulation. All were dressed in sweatshirts and jeans. One was wearing a leather bomber jacket and mountain boots. The others were wearing denim jackets and tennis shoes. They were dangerous-looking men—a decade or so older than most of us in the room—heavily muscled, with dark complexions, thick necks, and powerful hands that looked as if they could crack the whiskey glasses in their palms.

But they were "in our bar"—a seedy, smoke-filled watering hole connected by a set of double doors to one of the most popular houses of ill-repute in the port city of Pohang, South Korea.

Most of the bar's and the whorehouse's patrons were my fellow Marines—members of the vaunted 1st Battalion, 5th Marine Regiment—and an equal number of prostitutes literally bussed in from other South Korean cities because the Marines had landed and there was money to be made.

We had all had too much to drink, had run off most of the sailors (the exception being the Navy medical corpsmen attached to our unit; we considered them to be more leatherneck than bluejacket), and we were mustering a few of our best brawlers to go over to the booth and invite the four men to leave "our" establishment. Like young bucks challenging the older, dominant males, we wanted all the does to ourselves, even if we had to pay for them.

Just as we were about to dispatch our goon squad toward the booth, a half-drunk, half-overseeing Marine gunnery sergeant swayed over to where we were sitting and smacked his hand down hard on the wooden tabletop. "Stay the fuck away from those men," the gunny slurred. "You boys don't have any idea who those men are. I'm telling you, they equal nothing but trouble for you guys. They're mercs."

We looked at each other. "Mercs?" Indeed, "merc" was a somewhat mythical moniker in those days for mercenaries, professional soldiers, soldiers of fortune, hired guns, or contract warriors. "But what could they possibly be doing in Korea in the mid-1980s?" I wondered.

Sure, gunfire was occasional exchanged up along the frictional demilitarized zone (DMZ) separating the democratic south from the Communist north, and occasionally Communists did infiltrate along the coastline. In fact, there had been a recent attempted infiltration by Communist commandos not far from our base, Marine Corps Expeditionary Camp Muchuk. But that wouldn't explain the purpose of these four men so far south of the DMZ.

Of course, we would never know why the men were in Pohang, and we would never see them again after that night. Nevertheless, we were all somewhat fascinated by their presence. We had never seen "a real-life mercenary" up close, and we assumed that no matter what they were doing, they surely were up to some sort of mischief.

Our perception was, of course, colored by the American military's traditional aversion toward contract soldiers: It was a negative perception that had been passed to us by our nation's founders.

In his general order to the Continental Army (July 2, 1776), Gen. George Washington stated, "A freeman contending for liberty on his own ground is superior to any slavish mercenary on Earth."

Ironically, American Commodore John Paul Jones, the great Naval hero—who upon being asked to surrender during a sea battle in 1779, shouted to his British foes, "I have not yet begun to fight"—was also a merc in the sense that he hired out his services to the Russian Navy after the American Revolution.

Throughout American history, contract warriors generally have been viewed as seedy characters, not worthy of the same respect accorded either professional uniformed soldiers or sailors of national armies and navies, or conscripts of those same armies and navies. After all, professional soldiers and sailors served for duty, honor, and country. Conscripts served because they were drafted. Mercs served because they loved war and money.

Two centuries after Washington issued his general order, America's official distaste for mercenaries again resurfaced.

After World War II, the United States government rejected the pen and refused to become a signatory nation to proposed protocols additional to the Geneva Conventions (awkwardly entitled "the Protocol Additional to the Geneva Conventions (GC) of 12 August 1949 and relating to the Protection of Victims of International Armed Conflicts (Protocol I), 8 June 1977").

Following the U.S. lead, many other nations also refused to become signatories to the Protocol Additional to the Geneva Conventions. Therefore, article 47 of the protocol (known as "the mercenary article") became, at best, an attempt to internationalize the definition of *mercenary*.

According to the article, a mercenary is any person who ...

- Is specially recruited locally or abroad in order to fight in an armed conflict;
- Does, in fact, take a direct part in the hostilities;

- Is motivated to take part in the hostilities essentially by the desire for private gain and, in fact, is promised, by or on behalf of a Party to the conflict, material compensation substantially in excess of that promised or paid to combatants of similar ranks and functions in the armed forces of that Party;
- Is neither a national of a Party to the conflict nor a resident of territory controlled by a Party to the conflict;
- Is not a member of the armed forces of a Party to the conflict; and
- Has not been sent by a State which is not a Party to the conflict on official duty as a member of its armed forces.

"You don't get a good disciplined force when you've grabbed people off the streets to form a military," said John Stockwell, the former head of the Central Intelligence Agency's Angola task force, in an interview for CNN Interactive's Cold War episode, "Soldiers of Misfortune."

Stockwell was describing to CNN writer Bruce Kennedy just how poor the selection process was for contract warriors in Angola during the 1970s. "Two of the mercenaries," he added, "were literally street sweepers in London who were recruited off the street."

Mercenaries in the second half of the twentieth century were not simply retired or former soldiers looking for action and a quick buck. Contract warriors were in fact recruited from among those employed in a variety of occupations and avocations. And many of those were lured into the trade from rather unsavory backgrounds.

In the wake of the Watergate break-in and ensuing scandal in the early 1970s, allegations—some true, some false—began emerging in both congressional circles and in the proverbial court of public opinion regarding misdeeds on the part of a few members of the U.S. intelligence community and a few of the characters the U.S. government had contracted for special work.

The ill-fated Bay of Pigs operation (aimed at overthrowing the regime of Fidel Castro in Cuba) and the politically botched war in Vietnam had prompted some U.S. Senate leaders, particularly Sen. Frank Church (D-Idaho), to refer to the intelligence community as a "rogue elephant on a rampage." The American government was in many ways out of control, at least that's what many Americans believed.

On January 27, 1975, a Senate fact-finding panel chaired by Senator Church was established and tasked with conducting investigations and hearings in an attempt to shed light on alleged abuses of power by the CIA, the FBI, and other agencies.

Officially titled "The Select Committee to Study Governmental Operations with Respect to Intelligence Activities," the Church Committee conducted numerous interviews and held 60 days of open hearings into CIA activities worldwide, including possible agency-sponsored assassination plots against foreign leaders, foreign coups d'etat, unauthorized spying on American citizens, and a lack of governmental oversight.

According to findings, the CIA was allegedly involved in no fewer than eight government-authorized plots to assassinate Castro from 1960 to 1965. And most of those plans included the use of contractors—mercenaries. Apparently, however, none of the plots moved far enough beyond the planning stages that an actual attempt was ever made to kill the Cuban president. However, the plans were every bit as colorful as the mercs hired to carry them out.

One of the alleged plots to kill Castro included lacing a box of the Cuban president's favorite cigars with a deadly form of botulism so potent that it would kill him as soon as he put one in his mouth, or injecting him with the same from a hypodermic needle concealed in a ballpoint pen. The cigars were given to one of the CIA's Cuban agents who claimed he could get them to Castro. The pen was presented to another who requested something "more sophisticated." Neither attempt materialized.

A CIA-Mafia plot was also hatched and progressed beyond the planning stages, but with no results.

Unlike the Soviet Union's First Chief Directorate of the KGB, the CIA had no internal corps of trained assassins. Consequently, the agency's so-called wet work had to be subcontracted.

In all cases, mercs were considered to be the best men for the job.

Despite the findings of the Church Committee and other congressional bodies tying the hands of the intelligence community, and severely limiting the U.S. government's ability to contract private warriors, merc work continued to flourish over the next several decades. And contract warriors became the stuff of legends in places such as the African bush and alleyways at 2 A.M. in Eastern European cities.

Critics continued to voice displeasure over the employment of contract warriors; and magazines, books, and movies produced throughout the 1980s and 1990s served to fuel that criticism as well as the mystique of the mercenary and the lure of the soldier-of-fortune wannabe.

"Mercenaries are already of concern because some have been involved in massacres, executions, looting, and rapes in a number of recent conflicts," wrote David Isenberg, a senior research analyst with the Center for Defense Information, in a 1997 monograph titled "Soldiers of Fortune, Ltd.—A Profile of Today's Private Sector Corporate Mercenary Firms."

"Because mercenaries are frequently not part of the command structure of regular military forces, lack ethnic or cultural connections to the civilian population, and often have been discharged from prior military service because of disciplinary problems, they may be more likely than regular soldiers to engage in systematic human rights abuses and violations of the laws of war. Although some mercenary firms have not been accused of such abuses, it is an open question as to whether they will manage to remain above such abuses in the future."

Isenberg added, "Will mercenary firms have a positive or negative impact on international security and stability? Some human rights groups believe that, under current domestic and international law, mercenaries lack accountability. Increasing accusations against mercenary personnel of egregious human rights violations fuel the debate."

Isenberg further described individual mercs or contract soldiers as "non-nationals" traditionally hired by other individuals, companies, or governments for the purpose of participating directly in armed conflict. The primary motivation, according to Isenberg and others "is monetary gain rather than loyalty to a nation-state. Contrary to generally misleading references in popular culture, mercenary groups do not impose themselves; they are sought after and hired as a means of conducting military operations, both externally and internally, just like regular military forces."

A British House of Commons "green paper" titled "Private Military Companies: Options for Regulation " (published in February 2002) alludes to the fear and lack of trust legitimate governments continue to harbor toward mercenaries.

"In the 1960s and 70s mercenaries were a real threat to legitimacy and self-determination," the paper reads. "They were often associated with attempts to preserve quasi-colonial structures; and they took part in a number of attempted coups. Neither of these has been the case with PMCs in the 1990s. There remains however a theoretical risk that they could become a threat to the governments that employ them. Although this danger cannot be completely discounted, it is difficult to see what a modern PMC would have to gain from trying to take over control of a country. A PMC which attempted anything of the sort would damage its reputation and reduce its prospects of obtaining business elsewhere."

The green paper adds, "Since PMCs are paid to deal with conflict situations some argue that they have no interest in bringing conflict to an end (unlike national armies who are paid in peacetime). For example, Nana Busia writes: 'the raison d'etre and modus vivendi of mercenaries is instability and it is in their interest that a perpetual state of instability is maintained.' (*Campaign Against Mercenarism in Africa, Africa World Report*). This problem is surely a matter for those hiring PMCs—if they write performance clauses into the contracts they should be able to give the PMCs a clear incentive to complete whatever tasks they have been employed for. In practice it is often the parties to the conflict who have reasons for prolonging it—for example in order to exploit mineral resources illegally.

"An extension of this view is the argument that PMCs are prone to switch sides, selling their services to a higher bidder if one emerges. This is always possible but it is the kind of behavior that would in the long run ruin a PMC's reputation and its business prospects. More of a problem is the tendency of employees of PMCs to offer their services to rivals. There have for example been reports of former EO employees working for the RUF in Sierra Leone or for the government in Kinshasa."

Nevertheless, critics have been unable to deny that both the terrorist attacks of September 11, 2001, and the subsequent war on terror have redefined the role, the necessity, and in many ways the respect of America's contract warriors.

Modern mercs are as much a part of the war on terror as conventional soldiers or special operations commandos. In fact, the vast majority of contract warriors have previous experience humping a pack and a rifle on Uncle Sam's payroll. And like American GIs in the twenty-first century, mercs are working throughout the world: The vast majority of them are concentrated in those countries where American soldiers, sailors, airmen, and Marines are currently conducting operations—Afghanistan and Iraq.

Like their traditional military counterparts, contract warriors work long hours. In Iraq, for instance, mercs on patrol or conducting other combat operations routinely work 13-hour days, 6 days per week. Some pull the day shift. Others are operating at night.

In most cases, mercs are highly skilled operators. However, despite that skill level, their often-extensive military background, and their increasing prevalence around the world since 9/11, the general public continues to have reservations about contract warriors, and not all members of the American military have a favorable opinion of them.

Maj. Francis Piccoli, a Marine officer based in Iraq, says he has never worked with mercs, but adds he would "be wary of any individuals working in that capacity with the military who were not subject to the Uniform Code of Military Justice": This is arguably a reasonable wariness considering the history of mercenary soldiers. As previously stated, mercs often have been known to operate outside of the law, and conversely the laws of their own state often do not protect them.

Still, companies and governments are contracting mercenaries in increasing numbers post 9/11, and mercs are offering their services to organizations and individuals they know desperately need them.

Some merc hopefuls today approach private military companies (PMCs) with a resumé and an updated physical. Others—prior to pitching themselves to the PMCs—pay war-fighting experts such as retired U.S. Navy SEAL Commander Richard "Demo Dick" Marcinko to train them in an abbreviated boot camp environment. Such training, the potential mercs hope, will make them more attractive to the PMCs.

INTERVIEW WITH RICHARD MARCINKO—"THE SHARK MAN OF THE DELTA"

A mythical figure in special operations circles, Marcinko—affectionately referred to as "the Sharkman of the Delta" (a throwback moniker to his days as a SEAL in Vietnam)—is the founder and first commanding officer of two of the U.S. Navy's premier special operations units: SEAL Team Six (arguably the world's best-trained counterterrorist force, which has been reconstituted as Naval Special Warfare Development Group, or DEVGRU) and RED CELL (a SEAL unit tasked with testing Navy and Marine Corps security forces throughout the world).

Marcinko, author of 13 best-selling books, including *Rogue Warrior,* has been involved with contract warriors in various capacities. Asked if he had ever worked as a contract warrior, Marcinko hesitated, and then laughingly replied, "I can't answer that." But he readily admitted having trained mercenaries, and his grasp of the evolution of the modern merc—at all levels of pay and purpose—is unmatched.

In his own words, "When considering a merc in the past, you have fixations on Rhodesia and those kinds of places. There, the personalities involved were basically soldiers/adventure seekers who were just not satisfied with a normal job. Some of them just got lost in the challenge of going overseas, and some had a fixation of being a hero, or in charge, or they were just some sort of control freak."

W. Thomas Smith Jr: So being a mercenary is not all about money?

Richard Marcinko: It is and it isn't. The twenty-first-century merc is more money focused because the opportunity to make big money is so much greater today than it was 10, 15, 25 years ago. If you go back 15 years, the pay was somewhere in the neighborhood of $2,000 per month plus subsistence. Sometimes more.

[The accuracy of Marcinko's figures are reinforced by Isenberg's merc profile, which states that fees paid to Executive Outcome's hires in the late 1990s ranged "anywhere from $2,000 to $13,000 per month depending on the worker's experience and area of expertise." In addition, military instructors contracted by EO received approximately $2,500 per month, whereas pilots were paid a monthly fee of about $7,000.]

WTS: You mention subsistence.

Marcinko: Well, yes, subsistence was included, but you would be living in a remote site, so you'd really not be subsisting all that well. Certainly there was not the communications like we have today. There was not the sophistication of money drops. The craft was rudimentary, so people would be paid an advance and collect the balance later, and sometimes the money went to offshore accounts. The [merc] would come out of the bush, go someplace for a month, spend his money and go broke, and then go back in.

Again, the work was a combination of adventure, challenge of being in a war, and also you have to consider that the merc might be someone who might be getting in trouble living in normal society, but not in all cases.

WTS: What about today?

Marcinko: In the post-Afghanistan-invasion world, the mercenary now becomes more of a contract worker of honor—a skilled craftsman. He's a knuckle-dragging bush person who is armed with sophisticated technologies, bringing in weapons systems on the target utilizing satellite communications, digital scanners, laser target markers, and all of the above and then some.

WTS: So it's accurate to say that the modern mercenary is equipped with many of the same weapons systems employed by Navy SEALs, Army Delta Force types, and other special operators?

Marcinko: Yes.

WTS: Then why is there not total or near-total reliance on U.S. military special operators? Why contract out that kind of work when it costs so much more to do so?

Marcinko: One of the biggest problems we are having today in terms of the U.S. military is the scream for increasing the number of special operations forces in all of the services: The SEALs, the green beanies [Army Special Forces], the air force techies and combat control teams, and the Marines. They are all in demand. There's been an increase in authorized strength within the armed services. And I would say that's fine, but to be a true spec ops operator, you have to have time-in and maturity and some skills before you can move into the advanced training. And you don't just get those numbers from the street.

Now, considering that, we are getting noncommissioned officers and chief petty officers who after 20 years are going to begin collecting 50 percent of their base pay for retirement. If they put in another 10 years, they're still going to be in Afghanistan, Iraq, Iran, Syria, the Philippines, those kinds of places, and they're only going to pick up an additional 25 percent of that same base pay. Their pay will incrementally increase each year somewhere in the neighborhood of 2 to 3 percent.

WTS: So, you're not talking about a lot of money when compared to the income generated by a contract soldier.

Marcinko: That's right. A contract person or merc today is going to make $18,000 to 20,000 a month. That's a big damn difference. They contract in at three-month or six-month packages, go out, and take a blow. The last I checked—of course this always changes with legislation—the first $112,000 is tax free. So an E-7 in any of those special branches can get out, get contract work, gross $200,000 a year, and be tax free on anywhere from $89,000 to $112,000. And they're saving that money or sending it elsewhere because there is no frigging place to spend it where they are living.

Blackwater [North Carolina-based Blackwater USA, a global security company] has been scarfing up deputy sheriffs, basically from the South, because they've simply run out of spec ops guys for the number of contracts they have. A deputy dawg sheriff somewhere down South is grossing $24,000 to $26,000 if he's lucky. He'll make that in one month overseas. So, he goes over there for six months, comes home, pays for his house, and then goes fishing, hunting, or trapping for the rest of his life.

That's what's happening in Iraq, and it will continue as we go through the reconstruction over there. You're going to need security, and the contractors are going to have to provide their own. Now they won't get the $1,000+ per day: They'll get maybe $600 per day. But that's almost more in one month than he's been making all year.

Having said that: We have homeland defense to consider. These guys are leaving positions that are part of our homeland defense package just like our National Guard and Reservists. So you see, there is a talent drain.

WTS: So contract or merc work is certainly an attractive option for former military guys eager to get into the fight or underpaid cops looking for adventure and a means of making ends meet, financially.

Marcinko: It is certainly an attraction today from a financial standpoint, and it's no longer frowned upon in the sense of whether or not it is considered to be legitimate, honorable work. It's not like a merc is a sickie who can't cope with society today. Merc work is now an honorable and attractive profession.

For instance, we have SEAL teams that are in Afghanistan sitting along a runway outside of Kabul, and they have to have haircuts, be clean-shaven, and wear uniforms. If they are not on patrol, the conventional commander might say, "Okay, go out on the runway and pick up trash." So now you have this young tiger who went through all this kick-ass training and he wants to go out there and kill the enemy. Instead, he's got to go mess cooking or picking up trash on the runway. Now, while that's going on, here comes a bunch of crusty, scruffy-looking, over-the-hill-gang former SEALs he knows driving up in a Landrover; and they're pulling down $20,000 per month and going out and shooting bad guys. So morale for the active-duty guys goes out the window.

So that really is the evolutionary process from being a merc on the ground helping a guerilla fight against the government, or take out a government, or sustain the survival of some ethnic group *to* a guy who is today making big bucks functioning in an environment that is a lot less nasty than the bush. They might be in an encampment, or in the Green Zone, or with an ethnic chief and helping him with support. They're also doing things such as meeting airplanes and picking up multimillion-dollar payrolls.

WTS: Describe a day in the life of one of these contractors.

Marcinko: Well, let's take a basic guy—not a SEAL or a spec ops guy—but a truck driver who was snapped up out of Texas or Louisiana: As a contractor, overseas, he is going to be paid anywhere from $800 to $1,000 a day to make his run [similar to the duties of a military driver in a supply unit]. Now he's not going to be making that run every day. But he knows that every day he *does* make that run, he's going to be shot at.

Once he starts that run from Kuwait and floors that big machine up the highway, he's going to come up on villages where the road is no wider than a sidewalk and he's going to have to keep on rolling. He can't stop, because he knows if he does, an IED [improvised explosive device] or a B-40 round [rocket-propelled grenade] is going to get him. So he knows he's going to run the gauntlet every time he puts his foot on the pedal.

WTS: How old are these contract warriors?

Marcinko: The young bucks are in their late 20s and 30s. The older guys are banging in there at around 50 or 55.

WTS: 50 and 55? Isn't that a bit old to be doing this kind of work?

Marcinko: Hey, be careful (laughing). No, seriously, the older guys are really good. They know what to look for. They're seasoned. They pace themselves. They know when to engage. They don't jump out and say, "Hey, I'm going to get some blood today." They say, "I might get some blood today, but it's not going to be my blood." So 30s to mid-50s is a good range. It's certainly not the 19 and 20-year-olds.

WTS: What motivates the older guys to do this kind of work?

Marcinko: Money. Look, I get calls every day from guys who just need a quick fix, financially. They're over 40. They're in a mid-life crisis. They still don't have a pot to piss in. So I train them.

WTS: How long does it take you train a merc?

Marcinko: Depends on what they are going to do. You can wrap them up in about three weeks, but again, it depends on what their job is. They're certainly not going to be doing work like the guys in Task Force 121 [a U.S. special operations target-hunting unit comprised of Navy SEALs, Army Delta Force operators, CIA operations officers, and a handful of British Special Air Service commandos] who are out hunting bin Laden or searching for weapons of mass destruction. We're talking about guys who are going to do things like provide security.

The categorical breakdowns are the contractors who are working as bodyguards. They are going to provide security for high-risk personnel like government officials. The next category is security for logistical convoys and payroll delivery. Then you have stationary security—or stationary patrols—where they guard a compound, a building, or a construction. The pay scale fluctuates between those three categories. But even the guy simply watching a gate, but in a supervisory role, is going to be making at least $500 per day.

WTS: What does it take to be a merc? What does one need to understand about the work and about himself on an individual level.

Marcinko: Well, you have to have the balls to be there in the first place. It's dangerous work. There is no way around that. Also you can't mind living in remote places and under austere conditions. In Iraq, for instance, it's going to be 125 degrees during the day, cooling down to around 112 at night. No beer. No TV. No women. That said, in the Green Zone, the Iraqi women are now realizing that prostitution is a worthwhile deal (laughing).

WTS: How do contractors keep fit? Do they work out?

Marcinko: No. For one thing, it is so frigging hot. Plus with the frequency of activity, working out is not really an issue or an option. The biggest problem is boredom and dehydration.

WTS: What is the length of a stint pulled by a merc?

Marcinko: Short stints are only three months. The average is a six-month stint, followed by a one-month blow [liberty], then back in-country for another six months.

WTS: Are most contractors married or single?

Marcinko: It's a mix. In fact, many are married and just can't make ends meet. Some are doing the work to pay for their kids' college education.

WTS: Who's hiring? Is it just the private companies who need security or deliveries?

Marcinko: A lot of these guys [mercs] are going back and forth on government contracts that—like the privately owned companies—are paying big bucks. So it's not just a DynaCorps or some big corporation. And the ones on government contracts are quasi-official and government-cleared because they come out of the teams [SEAL teams and other special operations units].

WTS: What are the basic requirements for a merc?

Marcinko: The companies or agencies that contract the workers require a doctor-administered physical. There are also physical-fitness standards one has to meet. The company will check with the local sheriff to see what kind of trouble one might have been in. Then they do an FBI background investigation. Then they'll take a look at your shooting skills and they'll train you. Once you are packaged up, they contract you.

WTS: Why would a merc hopeful contact you for mercenary training, if they are going to be trained by the company contracting them?

Marcinko: Because the hopeful has either been turned down or they know they can't successfully complete the company course. They also know that the company training won't be as tough as mine, so they figure they can get trained by me, go to the company, and say, "Hey, I'm Dick Marcinko-trained." Then the company will say, "Well, if you are Rogue-Warrior-trained, you must be okay."

WTS: So, the money's good. Living conditions are spartan and isolated. We understand the dangers, and accept the risks. What are some of the downsides facing an American merc in the twenty-first century?

Marcinko: The big thing is that in places like Afghanistan and Iraq, the U.S. government is not providing real-world intelligence to the contract people on the ground. In Iraq, we have an embassy, but even when [Ambassador L. Paul] Bremer was over there, there was a notice that came out daily about the activity in-country, but it didn't tell you who the real players were, what the danger was, and not everybody had access to it because you had to have a compound with communications equipment where you could go in and see what was coming in officially.

As a result, some of the contractors in Iraq have since established their own intelligence cells and they provide intelligence to the contractors only. Still, John Q. Public, the truck drivers who run the gauntlet up and down the highway, get their intelligence by word of mouth.

WTS: Did a lack of intelligence result in the ambush-killings of the four contractors in Fallujah back in the spring of 2004?

Marcinko: First off, they were bored. They went out in a "soft car," in other words, a car that had not been hardened with ceramic armor. They were sort of doing a pre-reconnaissance to see what they wanted to do.

Now it's easy to sit back here safe and do a little Monday-morning quarter-backing and say "their hearts were in the right place, but they didn't understand the enemy well enough." The reality is, they should have had a hard car, and floored it. When the ambush hit, they needed to blow-and-go. Instead they had a soft car and got nailed.

A THRIVING BUSINESS

Just how prolific is the merc industry? It has grown from "nothing to huge in just two years because of Iraq," said Charles Heyman of Jane's Consultancy during a 2004 interview conducted by Jeremy Lovell of Reuters News Service.

"I estimate that there are at least 20,000 private security contractors operating in Iraq. It is an industry that has done very well in 2004." Jane's Consultancy is a subsidiary of Jane's Information Group, a British-based firm known for its accurate analysis of military, aerospace, naval, and global security information.

According to Lovell in "Iraq: Boom Time for Ex-Dogs of War" (Reuters, September 22, 2004), "Estimates of the numbers of private security contractors in Iraq range up to 30,000 or more because there is no central register and as private armies they write their own rules. It makes them the second largest group in the country after the 130,000-strong U.S. Army contingent."

He adds, "It is a far cry from the mercenary bands who rampaged across post-colonial Africa under the leadership of the likes of 'Mad Mike' Hoare, 'Black Jacques' Schramme, and Bob Denard."

Contract warriors have quickly become major players in the ongoing war on terror. That won't change. The war—combined with a near-exponential increase in the globalization of free markets and the subsequent demand for security—will keep the PMCs in business, and the PMCs will continue producing risk takers hoping for the adventure of a lifetime and some fast money to boot.

A former U.S. Marine Corps infantry leader and paratrooper, W. Thomas Smith Jr. is an author-journalist who has written for a variety of publications, including USA Today, George, National Review Online, U.S. News & World Report, BusinessWeek, *and* The New York Post. *His books include* Encyclopedia of the Central Intelligence Agency *and the* Alpha Bravo Delta Guides to Decisive 20th-Century American Battles, American Airborne Forces, *and* The Korean Conflict.

A lecturer to Fortune 500 companies and the U.S. Armed Forces, Smith serves on the adjunct faculty at the University of South Carolina's School of Journalism and Mass Communications.

APPENDIX A

PMCs: ONE CLICK AWAY

The following private military companies are available on the web at the addresses shown. Many of these companies offer direct ways to contact them for more information about their products and services.

A

AD Consultancy
www.adconsultancy.com

AirScan, Inc.
www.airsca.com

AKE Limited
www.akegroup.com

AMA Associates Limited
www.worldsecurity-index.com/details.php?id=755

ArmorGroup
www.armorgroup.com

ATCO Frontec Corporation
www.atcofrontecsecurity.com

Atlantic Intelligence
www.atlantic-intelligence.fr/fr/accueil.php

Avient (Pvt) Ltd.
www.azfreight.com/azworld/az28505.htm

B

Beni Tal
www.beni-tal.co.il

Blackwater USA
www.blackwaterusa.com/

Booz Allen Hamilton, nc.
www.boozallen.com

C

COFRAS
www.groupedci.com/pages_fr/branches/cofras_frame.html

Control Risks Group, Ltd.
www.crg.com

Cubic Corporation
www.cubic.com

Custer Battles
www.custerbattles.com

D

Defence Systems Limited
www.mineaction.org/unmik_org/departments/ops/mco/dsl.htm

Defense Security Training Service Corporation
www.defensecurity.com

DynCorp, Inc.
www.dyncorp.com

E

Erinys Iraq Limited
www.erinysinternationa.com

Executive Outcome, Inc.
http://members.tripod.com/~PasqualeD/ExecOutcome-
PROTECTION.html

G

Genric
www.genric.co.uk

Global Impact
www.closeprotection.ws

Global Marine Security Systems
www.gmssco.com

Global Risk Management (UK) Ltd.
www.grmukltd.com

Global Risk Strategies
www.globalrsl.com

Global Studies Group, Inc.
www.gsgi.org

GlobalOptions, LLC
www.globaloptions.com

Globe Risk Holdings, Inc.
www.infomine.com/index/suppliers/Globe_Risk_Holdings,_Inc..html

The Golan Group
www.grupogolan.com

Gormly International
www.gormlyintl.com

Ground Systems
www.groundsystems-index.com/index.php

Group 4 Falck A/S
www.group4falck.com

H

Hart Group, Ltd.
www.hartgrouplimited.com

Hill and Associates, Ltd.
www.hill-assoc.com

I

ICP Group Ltd
www.icpgroup.ltd.uk

International Charter Incorporated of Oregon
www.icioregon.com

International Peace Operations Association
www.ipoaonline.org

ISEC Corporate Security
www.privatemilitarycompany.com

ISE Intelligence & Security Executive (The Intelligence & Security Services Broker)
www.intel-sec.demon.co.uk/

K

Kellogg Brown & Root, Inc.
www.halliburton.com

M

Maritime Index
www.maritime-index.com/index.php

Meyer & Associates
www.meyerglobalforce.com

Military Professional Resources Incorporated
www.mpri.com

MRCInvestigations
www.mrcinvestigations.com

N

Northbridge Services Group, Ltd.
www.northbridgeservices.com

P

Pistris, Inc.
www.pistris.com

Presidium International Corporation
www.presidium.net

O

Olive Security (UK) Limited
www.olivesecurity.com

R

RamOPS Risk Management Group
www.ramops.com

Richmond Group Intl
www.richmondgroupintl.com

Rubicon International Services, Ltd.
www.rubicon-international.com

S

Sandline International
www.sandline.com

Sayeret Group, Inc.
www.sayeretgroup.com

Southern Cross Security
www.southerncross-security.com

Special Ops Associates
www.specialopsassociates.com

Strategic Consulting International
www.sci2000.ws

Sumer International Security
www.thesandigroup.com

The Surveillance Group
www.thesurveillancegroup.co.uk

T

TASK International, Ltd.
www.task-int.com

THULE Global Security International
www.brainstemdowry.com/work/thule

Trident Maritime
www.trident3.com

TripleCanopy
www.triplecanopy.com

Trojan Securities International
www.trojansecurities.com

V

Vinnell Corporation
www.vinnell.com

W

Wackenhut Corporation
www.wackenhut.com

Westminster Group Plc
www.wg-plc.com

World Security
www.worldsecurity-index.com/index.php

SOUTH AFRICA'S ANTI-MERCENARY LAW

South Africa's controversial anti-mercenary law is constantly in the news for the simple reason that more contemporary mercenaries have come from South Africa than anywhere else. They are the Thracians of the time. But unlike the Thracians, after they are captured in a foreign country doing mercenary work, they can be prosecuted under the South African law.

The South African law has also been used as a model by other countries to create similar laws to curb mercenary activities. Here, then, is the South African anti-mercenary law, as passed by the South African government.

Republic of South Africa, 20 May 1998

[d] No. 15 of 1998: Regulation of Foreign Military Assistance Act, 1998

ACT

To regulate the rendering of foreign military assistance by South African juristic persons, citizens, persons permanently resident within the Republic and foreign citizens rendering such assistance from within the borders of the Republic; and to provide for matters connected therewith.

PREAMBLE

The Constitution of the Republic of South Africa, 1996, provides in section 198(b) that the resolve to live in peace and harmony precludes any South African citizen from participating in armed conflict, nationally or internationally, except as provided for in the Constitution or national legislation. In order to implement aspects of this provision and in the interest of promoting and protecting human rights and fundamental freedoms, universally, it is necessary to regulate the rendering of foreign military assistance by South African juristic persons, citizens, persons permanently resident in the Republic and foreign citizens who render such assistance from within the borders of the Republic.

Be it enacted by the Parliament of the Republic of South Africa, as follows:

DEFINITIONS

1. In this Act, unless the context indicates otherwise "armed conflict" includes any armed conflict between a) the armed forces of foreign states; (b) the armed forces of a foreign state and dissident armed forces or other armed groups; or (c) armed groups;

(ii) "Committee" means the National Conventional Arms Control Committee as constituted by the National Executive by the decision of 18 August 1995;

(iii) "foreign military assistance" means military services or military-related services, or any attempt, encouragement, incitement or solicitation to render such services, in the form of military assistance to a party to the armed conflict by means of advice or training; personnel, financial, logistical, intelligence or operational support; personnel recruitment; medical or paramedical services; or procurement of equipment; security services for the protection of individuals involved in armed conflict or their property; any action aimed at overthrowing a government or undermining the constitutional order, sovereignty or territorial integrity of a state; any other action that has the result of furthering the military interests of a party to the armed conflict, but not humanitarian or civilian activities aimed at relieving the plight of civilians in an area of armed conflict.

(iv) "mercenary activity" means direct participation as a combatant in armed conflict for private gain;

(v) "Minister" means the Minister of Defence;

(vi) "person" means a natural person who is a citizen of or is permanently resident in the Republic, a juristic person registered or incorporated in the Republic, and any foreign citizen who contravenes any provision of this Act within the borders of the Republic;

(vii) "Republic" means the Republic of South Africa;

(viii) "register" means the register of authorisations and approvals maintained in terms of section 6.

PROHIBITION ON MERCENARY ACTIVITY

2. No person may within the Republic or elsewhere recruit, use or train persons for or finance or engage in mercenary activity.

Rendering of foreign military assistance prohibited

3. No person may within the Republic or elsewhere—

(a) offer to render any foreign military assistance to any state or organ of state, group of persons or other entity or person unless he or she has been granted authorisation to offer such assistance in terms of section 4;

(b) render any foreign military assistance to any state or organ of state, group of persons or other entity or person unless such assistance is rendered in accordance with an agreement approved in terms of section

4. (1) Any person who wishes to obtain the authorisation referred to in section 3(a) shall submit to the Committee an application for authorisation in the prescribed form and manner.

(2) The Committee must consider any application for authorisation submitted in terms of subsection (1) and must make a recommendation to the Minister that such application be granted or refused.

(3) The Minister, in consultation with the Committee, may refuse an application for authorisation referred to in subsection (2), or may grant the application subject to such conditions as they may determine, and may at any time withdraw or amend an authorisation so granted.

(4) Any authorisation granted in terms of this section shall not be transferable.

(5) The prescribed fees must be paid in respect of an application for authorisation granted in terms of subsection (3).

Approval of agreement for rendering of foreign military assistance

5. (1) A person who wishes to obtain the approval of an agreement or arrangement for the rendering of foreign military assistance, by virtue of an authorisation referred to in section 3(b) to render the relevant military assistance, shall submit an application to the Committee in the prescribed form and manner.

(2) The Committee must consider an application for approval submitted to it in terms of subsection (1) and must make a recommendation to the Minister that the application be granted or be refused.

(3) The Minister, in consultation with the Committee, may refuse an application for approval referred to in subsection (2), or grant the application subject to such conditions as they may determine, and may at any time withdraw or amend an approval so granted.

(4) Any approval granted in terms of this section shall not be transferable.

(5) The prescribed fees must be paid in respect of an application for approval granted in terms of subsection (3).

Register of authorisations and approvals

6. (1) The Committee shall maintain a register of authorisations and approvals issued by the Minister in terms of sections 4 and 5.

(2) The Committee must each quarter submit reports to the National Executive, Parliament and the Parliamentary Committees on Defence with regard to the register.

CRITERIA FOR GRANTING OR REFUSAL OF AUTHORISATIONS AND APPROVALS

7. (1) An authorisation or approval in terms of sections 4 and 5 may not be granted if it would—

(a) be in conflict with the Republic's obligations in terms of international law;

(b) result in the infringement of human rights and fundamental freedoms in the territory in which the foreign military assistance is to be rendered;

(c) endanger the peace by introducing destabilising military capabilities into the region where the assistance is to be, or is likely to be, rendered or would otherwise contribute to regional instability and would negatively influence the balance of power in such region;

(d) support or encourage terrorism in any manner;

(e) contribute to the escalation of regional conflicts;

(f) prejudice the Republic's national or international interests;

(g) be unacceptable for any other reason.

(2) A person whose application for an authorisation or approval in terms of section 4 or 5 has not been granted by the Minister may request the Minister to furnish written reasons for his or her decision.

(3) The Minister shall furnish the reasons referred to in subsection (2) within a reasonable time.

OFFENCES AND PENALTIES

8. (1) Any person who contravenes any provision of section 2 or 3, or fails to comply with a condition with regard to any authorisation or approval granted in terms of section 4 or 5, shall be guilty of an offence and liable on conviction to a fine or to imprisonment or to both such fine and imprisonment.

(2) The court convicting any person of an offence under this Act may declare any armament, weapon, vehicle, uniform, equipment or other property or object in respect of which the offence was committed or which was used for, in or in connection with the commission of the offence, to be forfeited to the State.

EXTRATERRITORIAL APPLICATION OF ACT

9. Any court of law in the Republic may try a person for an offence referred to in section 8 notwithstanding the fact that the act or omission to which the charge relates, was committed outside the Republic, except in the instance where a foreign citizen commits any offence in terms of section 8 wholly outside the borders of the Republic.

REGULATIONS

10. The Minister, in consultation with the Committee, may make regulations relating to—

(a) any matter which is required or permitted in terms of this Act to be prescribed;

(b) the criteria to be taken into account in the consideration of an application for an authorisation or approval in terms of section 4 or 5;

(c) the maintenance of the register; and

(d) any other matter which may be necessary for the application of this Act.

EXEMPTIONS

11. The Minister, in consultation with the Committee, may exempt any person from the provisions of sections 4 and 5 in respect of a particular event or situation, and subject to such conditions as he or she may determine.

[SHORT TITLE]

12. This Act shall be called the Regulation of Foreign Military Assistance Act, 1998, and shall come into operation on a date fixed by the President by proclamation in the Gazette.

APPENDIX C

ANCIENT ROME AND MERCENARIES

In the introduction to his histories, Polybius wrote the following:

Can any one be so indifferent or idle as not to care to know by what means, and under what kind of polity, almost the whole inhabited world was conquered and brought under the dominion of the single city of Rome, and that too within a period of not quite fifty-three years? Or who again can be so completely absorbed in other subjects of contemplation or study, as to think any of them superior in importance to the accurate understanding of an event for which the past afford no precedent.

It is evident; therefore, that no one need think it his duty to repeat what has been said by many, and said well. Least of all I: for the surprising nature of the events which I have undertaken to relate is in itself sufficient to challenge and stimulate the attention of every one, old or young, to the study of my work.

Had the praise of History been passed over by former Chroniclers it would perhaps have been incumbent upon me to urge the choice and special study of records of this sort, as the readiest means men can have of correcting their knowledge of the past. But my predecessors have not been sparing in this respect.

The most instructive, or rather the only, method of learning to bear with dignity the vicissitudes of fortune is to recall the catastrophes of others.

HOW MERCENARIES LED TO CARTHAGE'S DOWNFALL

Probably the best analysis ever done of why no mercenary army, until Hannibal's, could defeat Rome was Polybius's comparison between the Carthaginian and Roman civilizations. A key element for his claim of Roman superiority is the Carthaginian need to rely on mercenaries, which he sees as a weakness rather than a strength. Polybius writes:

> The government of Carthage seems also to have been originally well contrived with regard to those general forms that have been mentioned. For there were kings in this government, together with a senate, which was vested with aristocratic authority. The people likewise enjoy the exercise of certain powers that were appropriated to them. In a word, the entire frame of the republic very much resembled those of Rome and Sparta. But at the time of the war of Hannibal the Carthaginian constitution was worse in its condition than the Roman. For as nature has assigned to every body, every government, and every action, three successive periods; the first, of growth; the second, of perfection; and that which follows, of decay; and as the period of perfection is the time in which they severally display their greatest strength; from hence arose the difference that was then found between the two republics.

> For the government of Carthage, having reached the highest point of vigor and perfection much sooner than that of Rome, had now declined from it in the same proportion: whereas the Romans, at this very time, had just raised their constitution to the most flourishing and perfect state. The effect of this difference was that among the Carthaginians the people possessed the greatest sway in all deliberations, but the senate among the Romans. And as, in the one republic, all measures were determined by the multitude; and, in the other, by the most eminent citizens; of so great force was this advantage in the conduct of affairs, that the Romans, though brought by repeated losses into the greatest danger, became,

through the wisdom of their counsels, superior to the Carthaginians in the war.

If we descend to a more particular comparison, we shall find that with respect to military science, for example, the Carthaginians, in the management and conduct of a naval war, are more skillful than the Romans. For the Carthaginians have derived this knowledge from their ancestors through a long course of ages; and are more exercised in maritime affairs than any other people. But the Romans, on the other hand, are far superior in all things that belong to the establishment and discipline of armies.

For this discipline, which is regarded by them as the chief and constant object of their care, is utterly neglected by the Carthaginians; except only that they bestow some little attention upon their cavalry. The reason of this difference is, that the Carthaginians employ foreign mercenaries; and that on the contrary the Roman armies are composed of citizens, and of the people of the country. Now in this respect the government of Rome is greatly preferable to that of Carthage. For while the Carthaginians entrust the preservation of their liberty to the care of venal troops; the Romans place all their confidence in their own bravery, and in the assistance of their allies. From hence it happens, that the Romans, though at first defeated, are always able to renew the war; and that the Carthaginian armies never are repaired without great difficulty. Add to this, that the Romans, fighting for their country and their children, never suffer their ardor to be slackened; but persist with the same steady spirit till they become superior to their enemies. From hence it happens, likewise, that even in actions upon the sea, the Romans, though inferior to the Carthaginians, as we have already observed, in naval knowledge and experience, very frequently obtain success through the mere bravery of their forces.

For though in all such contests a skill in maritime affairs must be allowed to be of the greatest use; yet, on the other hand, the valor of the troops that are engaged is no less effectual to draw the victory to their side. Now the people of Italy are by nature superior to the Carthaginians and the Africans, both in bodily strength, and in courage. Add to this, that they have among them certain institutions by which the young men are greatly animated to perform acts of bravery. It will be sufficient to mention one of these, as a proof of the attention that is shown by the Roman government, to infuse such a spirit into the citizens as shall lead them to encounter every kind of danger for the sake of obtaining reputation in their country.

When any illustrious person dies, he is carried in procession with the rest of the funeral pomp, to the *rostra* in the forum; sometimes placed conspicuous in an upright posture; and sometimes, though less frequently, reclined. And while the people are all standing round, his son, if he has left one of sufficient age, and who is then at Rome, or, if otherwise, some person of his kindred, ascends the rostra, and extols the virtues of the deceased, and the great deeds that were performed by him in his life. By this discourse, which recalls his past actions to remembrance, and places them in open view before all the multitude, not those alone who were sharers in his victories, but even the rest who bore no part in his exploits, are moved to such sympathy of sorrow, that the accident seems rather to be a public misfortune, than a private loss. He is then buried with the usual rites; and afterwards an image, which both in features and complexion expresses an exact resemblance of his face, is set up in the most conspicuous part of the house, inclosed [sic] in a shrine of wood. Upon solemn festivals, these images are uncovered, and adorned with the greatest care.

And when any other person of the same family dies, they are carried also in the funeral procession, with a body added to the bust, that the representation may be just, even with regard to size. They are dressed likewise in the habits that belong to the ranks which they severally filled when they were alive.

If they were consuls or praetors, in a gown bordered with purple: if censors, in a purple robe: and if they triumphed, or obtained any similar honor, in a vest embroidered with gold. Thus appeared, they are drawn along in chariots preceded by the rods and axes, and other ensigns of their former dignity. And when they arrive at the forum, they are all seated upon chairs of ivory; and there exhibit the noblest objects that can be offered to youthful mind, warmed with the love of virtue and of glory.

For who can behold without emotion the forms of so many illustrious men, thus living, as it were, and breathing together in his presence? Or what spectacle can be conceived more great and striking? The person also that is appointed to harangue, when he has exhausted all the praises of the deceased, turns his discourse to the rest, whose images are before him; and, beginning with the most ancient of them, recounts the fortunes and the exploits of every one in turn. By this method, which renews continually the remembrance of men celebrated for their virtue, the fame of every great and noble action become immortal. And the glory of those, by whose services their country has been benefited, is rendered familiar to the people, and delivered down to future times.

But the chief advantage is that by the hope of obtaining this honorable fame, which is reserved for virtue, the young men are animated to sustain all danger, in the cause of the common safety. For from hence it has happened that many among the Romans have voluntarily engaged in single combat, in order to decide the fortune of an entire war. Many also have devoted themselves to inevitable death; some of them in battle, to save the lives of other citizens; and some in time of peace to rescue the whole state from destruction. Others again, who have been invested with the highest dignities have, in defiance of all law and customs, condemned their own sons to die; showing greater regard to the advantage of their country, than to the bonds of nature, and the closest ties of kindred.

APPENDIX D

MERCENARY MISCELLANEOUS

THE MERCENARY HISTORIAN— THE ANCIENT WORLD

Xenophon began his life as a mercenary and ended it as one of history's greatest historians.

After his travels and battles, Xenophon settled down in Sparta and Athens, and then became a historian. The reason for the detailed account of the Battle of Cuxana is that Xenophon took it all down and later published his account in the *Anabasis* (Up Country March). Eight years writing it, the *Anabasis* was published in 371 B.C.E. and survives to the present.

Xenophon died some time around 357 B.C.E. He was approximately 87 years old, proving that the life of a historian in the ancient world was exceedingly longer than the life of a soldier.

WHAT WAR WAS REALLY LIKE—THE MIDDLE AGES

Unlike the spectacles of testosterone-driven armies clashing amid flying swords, limbs, blood spurting everywhere, and an overwhelming wall of sound, battles in the Middle Ages could actually be rather timid affairs, at least at the beginning.

Soldiers at arms may have been stupid men; mercenaries were not. They did not charge headlong into a mob with sword slashing away like some movie hero. What actually happened was that with both sides advancing on each other, they would grind to a halt when they got close. No one was charging into a line of knights with raised spears. No one was anxious to impale themselves. Rather, they wanted to wait, like a normal person would, to size up the enemy. Unfortunately, when a miles-long column stops, there's an inertia that sets in, a ripple effect that pushes the lead group forward, whether they like it or not, into harm's way.

Spears would clash with spears, with swords, even daggers, and the end result was two armies at a complete standstill, pushing against one another like it was a rugby match. Shields would block any stray blows and, if not, most sword strikes would glance off well-made armor. Only a wayward piece of metal like a dagger or a well-placed sword thrust through one of the armor's seams could actually do any damage. In such an environment, the "match" would go on for hours until one side or the other tired. The intervention of cavalry and archers would hasten any debacle to follow.

THE DESPICABLE HESSIANS— THE EIGHTEENTH CENTURY

During the Revolutionary War, European liberals despised the German princes' greed. Mirabeau, then a fugitive in Holland, and later to play a key part in the French Revolution, published a pamphlet called "To the Hessians and Other Nations of Germany, Sold by Their Princes to England." In it, he took the German princes to task for their greed while extolling the virtues of the Americans.

But the most insightful pamphlet published during this period was produced by the other side.

In the public library at Cassel is a pamphlet published in 1782. Attributed to Schlieffen, the minister of Landgrave Frederick II, the author reminds the reader that "men had in all ages slaughtered each other, that the Swiss had long been in the habit of fighting as mercenaries, that the ten thousand Greeks under Xenophon did the same, and it is unjust to blame my contemporaries for what seems to be a natural instinct of mankind. The present letting-out of troops by Hesse is perhaps the tenth occasion of the sort since the beginning of the century."

A MERCENARY LOVE STORY—IVORY COAST, 2004

Sam Bockarie was a notorious womanizing mercenary from Sierra Leone by the time he met Awa Michel in the late 1990s. It was a match made in mercenary heaven: The bride was better with a gun than the groom and just as deadly with a knife.

Described in a South African wire service report as a "short, dark, robust woman in her mid-thirties," Awa Michel hails from the Mandingo tribe of northern Liberia. In the early 1990s, she joined ULIMO-K, a rebel group that later allied itself with Charles Taylor's National Patriotic Front of Liberia (NPFL). After Taylor came to power in the 1997 presidential election, Michel got into President Taylor's Anti-Terrorist Unit (ATU), where she was given 21 months of special operations forces training.

At the end of 2002, Michel and other members of the ATU were reportedly told by Taylor personally that they were to go on a secret mission to the Ivory Coast. After infiltrating this neighboring country, they were to attack Ivory Coast government forces.

When Michel and the others got across the border, the man who met them was Bockarie, former military commander of Sierra Leone's Revolutionary United Front (RUF) rebel group. He was working as a soldier of fortune for Taylor.

With Bockarie commanding, the ATU soldiers attacked Ivory Coast towns near the Liberian border. Then they went east to help Ivorian rebels recapture Man, a large city that went back and forth during the fighting. The ATU headed south, the goal being to capture San Pedro, the country's second largest port. Meeting heavy resistance, the ATU was beaten back. During this battle, Awa Michel took a bullet in the back that came out through her left breast.

Seriously wounded, she turned on the man who had shot her. "I killed the white man who shot me," she gloated later to a reporter. "I didn't let him escape. Imagine shooting me and then going scot-free. No way, I deal with that man, I finish him off."

But Michel was still seriously wounded and not fit to travel. When a mercenary is wounded in battle, there may not always be a medic nearby, and so it was with Michel. Bockarie decided to leave Michel behind with an Ivorian warlord named Adams. Bockarie told Adams, "Look after my wife and treat her well. If she dies, you die."

Michel claimed that she had a celibate relationship with Bockarie. Bockarie did not live long enough to refute the claim. Taylor would later report that the merc from Sierra Leone was killed by Liberian government forces while trying to infiltrate back across the border from the Ivory Coast with a band of Sierra Leone mercenaries. Other reports from diplomats in Monrovia, Liberia's capital city, said that Bockarie was killed secretly in Monrovia on Taylor's orders after they had an argument.

Michel was nursed back to health by Adams, whose real name was Adama Coulibaly. He was the rebel warlord who controlled the Korhoga region of the Ivory Coast. In gratitude, Michel became one of Adams' Liberian mercenaries. Eventually, he put this trusted warrior in command of his 42-member mercenary bodyguard.

In early May 2003, Master Sergeant Ousmane Cherif was sent to control "the volatile situation in Man and Danane and the rest of the 'Wild West' of Cote d'Ivoire and deal with the Liberian and Sierra Leonean mercenaries there who were making trouble." The Liberian and Sierra Leonean mercs had been accused of "widespread atrocities against civilians."

Cherif went in shooting. Michel later told a reporter than Cherif killed many of her Liberian colleagues. "He has to die, too, you just can't kill Liberians like that," she later said.

As of May 2004, Awa Michel was living in a Liberian refugee camp near the town of N'zerekore in southeastern Guinea. She still works for Adams, but makes little or no money. However, she may soon be out of work. Under the terms of the agreement formally ending the Ivory Coast civil war, the government and rebels have both agreed to rid themselves of any mercenaries in their employ. If and when that happens, Michel would probably find that her skills are very much in demand.

But perhaps it was Daniel L. Cowan, writing in the *Winston-Salem Journal* on April 23, 2004, who said it best: "The Roman Empire used mercenaries and increased the use, right before the collapse and fall of the empire. Mercenaries, despite their prowess as professional soldiers, have never been very successful when pitted against fighters who think that they are defending their homeland."

MERCENARIES IN BURMA

Burma has been ruled by a military junta of one sort or another since World War II. Like any totalitarian government, ethnic minorities are to be eliminated or assimilated rather than tolerated. So it is with the Karen of Burma.

The Karen are an ethnic minority who live in Burma's southeastern jungles. They have been fighting a losing 40-year battle for an independent homeland. The whole Karen culture, including language, religion, and method of writing, are totally different from the Burmese.

These differences led to a Karen rebel insurgency against the military government in Burma that began in 1985 and continues until 2004 and perhaps beyond. The principal military phase of the Karen resistance occurred from the late 1980s into the early 1990s.

Realizing they did not have the training to mount a guerilla resistance movement, the Karen hired Western mercenaries to train them. Mercenaries from the United States were hired to teach such basic military skills as map making, intelligence gathering, military organization, drills in ambushes, and escapes, plus training with AK-47s and mortars. It was the very fact of their superior training that made the mercs more valuable as trainers rather than fighters, a trend that would develop more and more during the coming decade.

During the Karen fighting in 1989, it was reported that a Burmese army sniper killed a French mercenary, and an Australian merc allegedly died from wounds he received in a government-ordered mortar attack. Their bodies, however, were recovered by the Karens, thus avoiding the embarrassing spectacle of seeing those bodies paraded on national TV by the government to show that the rebels can't even fight their own battles.

The mercenary training the Karen rebels received helped to sustain their rebellion through the 1990s and into the next millennium. Although they were never able to mount a serious military threat, neither were they overwhelmed by government forces. The "delaying actions" taught to the guerillas by their mercenary teachers bought the Karen rebels 15 years to develop a political wing within their organization.

The Russian-made AK-47 was the standard assault rifle the Western mercenaries used to train the Karen rebels. The mercenaries taught the rebels how to fire the weapon semi-automatically and in automatic bursts.

The "A" in the name is for *Avtomat*, the "K" for *Kalashnikova*. The translation in English is "Kalishnikov Automatic Rifle." Kalishnikov is a company as well known in Russia for producing firearms as Colt is in the United States. AK-47s or Kalishnikovs as they are known in the trade, are a popular weapon, and are in the arsenals of 50 different nations. The AK-47 was introduced in 1947, thus the "47" in its name.

Kalishnakov himself, the inventor of the rifle, gave a recent interview in which he revealed that he's now licensing his name for Vodka, which is what he says he wants to be remembered for.

As of 2004, the Karen National Union and the Burmese government had entered into peace talks. The Burmese have had a change of heart: Not only would a Karen peace pact be a major publicity coup for the government, it would also bring to an end civil war that has wracked Burma since the end of World War II. Regardless of whatever peace is ultimately achieved, it is doubtful the Karen could have survived as long as they have without mercenary intervention.

TURKISH MERCENARIES IN CHECHNYA—2004

The Russians have never been known as a people who tolerated resistance from those they were oppressing. Like many rebel movements through the centuries, the Chechen fighters realized that if they were going to be successful in breaking free of Russian influence, they needed more firepower on their side, more than they could supply with their own people. The Chechens therefore imported mercenaries to fight against the Russians.

Taking careful note of their enemy, Russia's Itar-Tass news agency reported in February 2004 that "mercenaries from about 10 foreign countries" were operating in Chechnya. The majority were Turkish citizens.

On the basis of just one Turkish mercenary who had entered Chechnya from Georgia, Russia's government decided that the issue of strengthening Russia's borders with the Caucasus countries was "very acute and a state priority."

Later in the year, Chechnyan terrorists, including mercenaries, attacked a Russian school and killed children. John Hawkwood must have been turning over in his grave.

CUSTER BATTLES LOSES ONE IN IRAQ

No matter how professional the field officers of a PMC may be, they will occasionally lose their lives pursuing their profession. That is the name of the game. Nations have to decide whether they would rather lose paid mercenaries/contractors in battle or army troops. For the families of the dead, it is never easy.

The family of the contractor killed in the line of duty suffers the same pain and anguish as the one whose child is killed in service to their country. Take the case of Michael Bloss. Bloss, 38 years old, was a contractor who was gunned down while guarding electrical workers near the town of Hit, west of Baghdad.

Bloss had been a British commando, formerly with the British army's elite Parachute Regiment. Serving in war zones, including Northern Island, Bloss eventually left the service. He then worked as a ski instructor at a Denver, Colorado, ski resort for eight years, before being lured back into the military life by Custer Battles, which recruited him and sent him to Iraq.

Prior to his death, Bloss sent his friends at the Denver ski resort a series of e-mails in which he described the dangers inherent in service in Iraq. According to one news report, Bloss wrote:

> We are expecting to be overrun tonight, and we may have to fight our way to a safe haven. Unfortunately, all the safe havens are already under attack.
>
> I don't wish to alarm you. We'll probably be OK. I'll e-mail when I'm safe.

He never did, because he wasn't. Bloss's job to provide security for electrical workers placed him in great danger. After being ambushed by Iraqi insurgents, Bloss was able to get the electrical workers to safety, unharmed, before dying in a hail of gunfire.

Describing the loss of his son as "devastating, especially after losing my wife and my brother, and now my son, in less than a year," Bloss's father, Michael, subsequently called Custer Battles to ask how many people the company had in Iraq. When the reply came back as 1,200, Michael Bloss asked how many had been killed.

The reply was just one. So far.

APPENDIX E

BIBLIOGRAPHY

BOOKS

Fawcett, Bill. *Mercs: True Stories of Mercenaries in Action.* New York: Avon Books, 1999.

McClintock, Michael. *Instruments of Statecraft: U.S. Guerilla Warfare, Counterinsurgency, and Counterterrorism, 1940–1990.* New York: Pantheon Books, 1992.

Mockler, Anthony. *The Mercenaries.* Texas: Free Companion Press, 1969.

Spicer, Tim, Lt. Colonel. *An Unorthodox Soldier: Peace and War and the Sandline Affair.* Edinburgh and London: Mainstream Publishing, 1999.

ONLINE SOURCES

ArmorGroup home page. London: ArmorGroup International Limited. www.armorgroup.com.

Blackwater USA home page. Virginia: Blackwater USA. www.blackwaterusa.com.

"Britons killed in Afghan attack." London: the BBC, 2004.
http://news.bbc.co.uk/1/hi/world/south_asia/3685865.stm.

"Carthage." St. Petersburg, FL: Wikipedia.
www.fact-index.com/ c/ca/carthage.html.

Chinaka, Cris. "Zimbabwe sets July 19 for trial of 70 'mercenaries.'"
Harare: Reuters, June 23, 2004.
www.alertnet.org/thenews/newsdesk/L2325374.htm.

Control Risks home page. London: Control Risks Group.
www.crg. com/html/index.php.

CSC home page. El Segundo, CA: CSC.
www.dyncorp.com.

"El Cid." Normal, IL: Illinois State University, 2004.
http://lilt.ilstu.edu/bekurtz/elcid.htm.

Gable, C.I. "Mercenaries from Mainland Capture Messina." Atlanta:
Boglewood Corp., 2001.
www.boglewood.com/sicily/messina.html.

"Home." McLean, VA: Custer Battles LLC, 2004
www.custerbattles.com/index2.html.

Hooker, Richard. "Rome: The Punic Wars." Pullman, WA: Washington
State University, 1996.
www.wsu.edu:8080/~dee/ROME/ PUNICWAR.HTM.

"Illustrated History of the Roman Empire." romanempire.net.
www.roman-empire.net/army/cannae.html.

"Industry." United Kingdom: British Battle.com, 2004.
www.britishbattles.com/long-island.htm.

Kennedy, Bruce. "Soldiers of Misfortune." Atlanta: CNN Interactive, 2004.
www.cnn.com/SPECIALS/cold.war/episodes/17/spotlight/.

"List of Military Service Provider Companies." HK94.com, 2004.
www.hk94.com/defense-contractor.php.

McManus, Barbara F. "Spartacus: Historical Background." New Rochelle:
VRoma.org, 1999.
www.vroma.org/~bmcmanus/spartacus. html.

Porter, John R. "The Punic Wars." Saskatchewan: University of
Saskatchewan, 2004.
http://duke.usask.ca/~porterj/CourseNotes/punicwars.html.

Rossi, J.R. "The Flying Tigers." Flying Tigers Association, 1998
www.flyingtigersavg.com/tiger1.htmFlyingTigers.com.

Sandline home page. South Africa: Sandline International.
www. sandline.com/site/index.html.

Scott, Leader, tr. "Sir John Hawkwood: Story of a Condottiere."
London: T. Fisher Unwin, 1998.
www.deremilitari.org/RESOURCES/ARTICLES/hawkwood.htm.

Smith, Michael. "Iraq Security Contract Won." London: News Telegraph,
May 29. 2004.
www.telegraph.co.uk/news/main.jhtml?xml=/news/2004/05/29/
wirq129.xml&sSheet=/news/2004/05/29/ixnewstop.html.

"The Baghdad Boom." *The Economist*, March 25, 2004.
http://sandline.com/hotlinks/Economist-Baghdad.html.

"The Battle of Crecy." St. Petersburg, FL: Eckerd Community College,
2004
http://acasun.eckerd.edu/~oberhot/crecy.htm.

"The Hessians." Riverside, CA: americanrevolution.org, 2004.
www.americanrevolution.org/hess6.html.

Ueda-Sarson, Luke. "The Battle of Gela, 405 BC." Christchurch, NZ, March 12, 2001. www.ritsumei.ac.jp/se/~luv20009/Gela.html.

Webb, Gary. "The Contras, Cocaine, and Covert Operations." San Jose: *San Jose Mercury News*, 1996. www.gwu.edu/~nsarchiv/NSAEBB/NSAEBB2/nsaebb2.htm.

INDEX

C

W-X-Y-Z